LERNA

VOLUME I

THE FAUNA

LERNA

A PRECLASSICAL SITE IN THE ARGOLID

RESULTS OF EXCAVATIONS
CONDUCTED BY
THE AMERICAN SCHOOL OF CLASSICAL STUDIES AT ATHENS

VOLUME I

THE FAUNA

BY

NILS-GUSTAF GEJVALL

WITH A FOREWORD BY
JOHN L. CASKEY

AMERICAN SCHOOL OF CLASSICAL STUDIES AT ATHENS
PRINCETON, NEW JERSEY
1969

ALL RIGHTS RESERVED

PRINTED IN GERMANY *at* J. J. AUGUSTIN, GLÜCKSTADT

To
HIS MAJESTY THE KING OF SWEDEN

FOREWORD

Dr. Gejvall's study of the ancient fauna is presented as the first volume in a series of definitive reports on the results of excavations at Lerna, which were conducted by the American School of Classical Studies in the years 1952 through 1958.

Preliminary reports of the archaeological investigation have appeared in *Hesperia* and other journals. It had been our intention to issue more detailed accounts of the stratigraphy, architecture, and objects found, with the evidence for relative dating, before now. Since 1958, however, other academic obligations have intervened and the publication has been temporarily postponed. This delay is regrettable, since analysis of the successive layers must provide a chronological framework for studies of all classes of objects recovered in the course of the excavations. Nevertheless, we felt no doubt that it was better to issue single volumes of the present sort, which could usefully stand alone, as soon as they were ready for the press, than to hold them for what might have seemed a more logical place in the sequence. Dr. Gejvall's is now ready, and we are grateful to him for taking the lead.

A brief review of the whole enterprise may here be appropriate.

The existence of an ancient site beside the Lernaean springs and marshes, at the modern village of Myloi in the Argolid, has been known for sixty years or more. C. W. Blegen first pointed it out to me some twenty years ago and observed that the place would be well worth excavating. In 1952, when the occasion arose, the American School undertook to explore it through preliminary soundings. The need of another excavation at a small preclassical site of this kind seemed clear: none had been carried out in the region for a score of years, during which many problems of the Bronze Age were being reexamined; and whereas work had proceeded fruitfully at the great Mycenaean centers, remains of the underlying prehistoric settlements at those sites were generally found to have been obliterated or made inaccessible by walls and floors of the palatial buildings.

The first tests at Lerna gave promising results, revealing deep deposits of debris from successive habitations, and it was decided to continue the excavation until all the layers could be examined in areas large enough to give representative samples of the architecture, in horizontal planes, as well as the essential vertical sequences. Obviously this would require expenditure of considerable resources over several seasons, and on behalf of all my colleagues in the work I gratefully acknowledge the support given us by the Managing Committee of the American School at a time when other much larger obligations were making heavy demands upon the institution. From the start we also received hearty cooperation and encouragement from the Greek Archaeological Service, which in those years was organized as the Directorate of Antiquities under the Ministry of Education.

Annual campaigns of digging were carried on, normally for periods of six to eight weeks, in the summers of the years 1953 through 1957. The staff comprised four or five supervisors, each in charge of one sector, an architect and surveyor, usually several other specialists and assistants, and an experienced foreman, the late Evangelos Lekkas of Corinth. Fifteen to twenty local workmen were employed. In 1958, as in 1952, there was only a short period of excavation.

Starting from three of the first soundings, we moved outward and extended the areas until they covered about 2400 square meters in all and most of them had coalesced into two big sectors, which were joined together by a broad trench (see the plan in *Hesperia*, XXVI, 1957, p. 144). These and the small subsidiary soundings were all on the southern side of the mound, the northern part being covered by an orchard and therefore not available to us. Estimating that the total inhabited area at its greatest extent was somewhat more than 16,000 square meters, one sees that we broke the surface of only about one-seventh of it; and since we reached virgin soil, some seven meters below the highest remaining part of the mound, in only a few small places, one may calculate roughly that we excavated no more than one-twentieth of the total volume. Yet ours was a large excavation as compared with most others at sites of this kind, and we believe that a reliable sampling was obtained of remains from all the periods represented, except perhaps the very earliest.

Of the earth and debris which we removed in the course of the digging one may estimate approximately that 1% by volume is assignable to the first settlement and 3% to the second, whereas about 18% came from remains of the third, 32% from those of the fourth, and 38% from those of the fifth; near the eroded surface of the mound the quantities were relatively smaller, only 2% representing the sixth settlement, 4% the seventh, and 2% the post-Mycenaean accumulations. Characteristics of these successive habitations are summarized briefly below.

The digging was slow, much of it being done with knives and small picks, and the process was closely observed at all times by supervisors who took notes and saw that each significant feature was described and recorded in photographs and measured drawings. At the end of each season we were permitted to take all the movable objects to the museum at Old Corinth, where we enjoyed many facilities, among which were two of exceptional value: first, adequate space for work tables and temporary storage, and second, the year-round services of a remarkable vase-mender, George Kachros. Thanks to his patient persistence, extraordinary visual memory, and sharp eye for joins, to say nothing of his wise and humorous ways with his fellow workers, a very great number of pots and objects were made whole that might otherwise have remained in fragments. And thus each excavator, throughout the year that followed each campaign, was able to observe the material as it took shape and to revise his reports accordingly.

Through this process we were able by 1957 to distinguish characteristic features of the chief periods in chronological sequence. These *periods*, designated by roman numerals, are represented by debris of corresponding *layers*. Each layer generally comprises several *strata*, which mark the *phases* of the period. These we designate by capital letters. For the multitude of smaller subdivisions and variations there can be no rigidly consistent terminology.

The periods, briefly, are as follows.

I. Early Neolithic. A layer one to two meters thick, with numerous successive habitation-levels but few house walls, was found on virgin soil in all the areas tested to that depth. The pottery, not plentiful, includes characteristic "Rainbow" and spongy wares; domestic implements are of chipped and polished stone, obsidian, and bone. The dead were buried in pit graves on the site.

II. Middle Neolithic. The layer is fully two meters thick in some places, with as many as eight building levels. Fine glazed ("urfirnis") and patterned wares are typical of this period. The tools are of stone, bone, and terracotta, and there are terracotta female figurines. Intramural burial continued to be practised.

FOREWORD

At the top of this layer were found traces of occupation in a late Neolithic stage of culture, with dark burnished and dull-painted ceramic wares and a few pit graves. Presumably there had been houses on the site at this time, but their remains had been cut away by the settlers of Period III.

The site appears to have been abandoned at the end of the Neolithic Age and left unoccupied throughout the first stage of the Early Bronze Age, Early Helladic I, which is represented elsewhere in the Argolid and is best known at Eutresis in Boeotia. None of the characteristic red and brown burnished pottery of that stage has been found at Lerna.

III. Early Helladic II. This was a long period with many stages of building and rebuilding, which may be divided into four principal phases. The town was fortified with a circuit wall and towers, and some of the houses were big. Of these the latest and most elaborate was the House of the Tiles, which was burnt in a great conflagration. C–14 dates indicate that the destruction occurred late in the third millennium B.C. The pottery throughout is typical of Early Helladic II, comprising sauceboats, askoi, and saucers, with very little patterned ware; a few pieces show connections with the Early Cycladic culture. Implements were of copper or bronze and terracotta, less frequently of stone and bone. Clay sealings, showing a great range of rectilinear and curvilinear designs, were used to secure containers of valuable goods. Graves have not been discovered.

IV. Early Helladic III. A settlement of quite different character followed the destruction of the House of the Tiles. A low circular tumulus of debris was shaped over the ruins of the great building and new houses, usually apsidal with a porch at the open end, were built outside its border. At least four architectural phases can be distinguished. As the strata accumulated, the tumulus was gradually covered and built over. C–14 dates are around the close of the third millennium and the transition to the second. The pottery is of new types, including two-handled tankards and jars with painted patterns, two-handled bowls in an early version of gray Minyan ware, plain wares, slipped and burnished wares, and a lumpy coarse ware. A Trojan jar was found, imported probably from Troy IV. Among the miscellaneous objects are numerous implements of copper or bronze and of bone and several small anchor-shaped double hooks of terracotta. A few infant burials were found among the houses.

V. Middle Helladic. This was another long period made up of many phases. The transition from Lerna IV was gradual, not marked by any sharp break in continuity. The character of the closing phases of Period V is not known with certainty since the topmost strata have been lost in parts of the mound through erosion of the surface. Apsidal and rectangular houses are found in this period. In Phase V A, which is dated within the twentieth century B.C. by C–14 analyses, pots in the style of Middle Minoan I A were imported from Crete, Cycladic wares from the islands, and small handmade jars from an unknown source, possibly central Europe. Characteristic of the whole period are gray Minyan, dark Argive Minyan, and Matt-painted wares, and a hard brittle fabric with patterns in lustrous paint. Minoan and Cycladic imports continue throughout in moderate quantities. Notable among the miscellaneous implements are bronze tools of new types, bored stone hammer-axes, and many bone pins of very fine quality. The dead were buried between or under the houses in pit graves and stone cists, infants sometimes in jars; some 235 of these graves were excavated.

VI. Late Helladic I. Two large shaft graves comparable to the royal graves at Mycenae were found at Lerna. They had been emptied and refilled in ancient times. The vast quantities of pottery from the filling are of late Middle Helladic and the earliest Mycenaean styles, with many pieces of corresponding Cycladic types. A few smaller graves and deposits of contemporary date occur on the site but any buildings that stood here have been lost through erosion. Graves and scattered potsherds show that some activity continued in Late Helladic II.

VII. Late Helladic III. On the eastern side of the mound there were houses and a street of Mycenaean times, in which pottery of III A and III B styles was found; here too was a cist grave of a child with III B pots. Part of a skeleton of a horse was discovered south of the hill in association with sherds of the same date.

Remains of post-Mycenaean settlements are scanty: a sprinkling of sherds of all major periods from Protogeometric to Late Roman; late Geometric graves on the mound and in a cemetery on the lower slopes of Mount Pontinos; well shafts of classical Greek times, and part of a late Roman kiln.

Much of the chronological information that has been obtained from this excavation is based on the types of pottery recovered from layers of debris in their stratified sequence. But although plentiful and of fundamental importance, pottery is by no means the only class of materials that shed light on the date, the foreign relations, and the ecology of the local culture here illustrated. Apart from the multitude of artifacts that were numbered individually in the Lerna inventory, samples of organic and inorganic matter of many kinds were collected and preserved for analysis. Some have already been studied, others await the attention of specialists.

Two of the largest collections were those of the animal bones and shells, which form the subject of the present monograph, and of the human skeletons, which will be dealt with by Dr. J. Lawrence Angel in the second volume of the series. Dr. Gejvall, a scientist of distinction whose special field is vertebrate zoology and who has taken part in archaeological excavations for many years, is singularly well qualified to undertake a study of this kind. At Troy (where he and I met as young members of Professor Blegen's staff in 1937) he examined the animal bones found in that excavation; his preliminary reports were published and a definitive analysis of the Trojan material is to be presented shortly. Since the second World War he has pursued osteological researches in northern Europe and Mediterranean lands. In 1958 he generously took time from his many other duties to travel to Greece and to make a record of the bones from Lerna, which had been kept in stratigraphical order and at that time filled some 2300 bags and larger containers in the museum at Corinth. After identifying all bones, whole and fragmentary, of animals of the common species he selected the pieces which called for further examination and these were sent to Stockholm, where the study has continued with the facilities and support of the Museum of Natural History, the University of Stockholm, and its newly established Laboratory for Osteological Research. A substantial part of the expense was met by a grant (No. GS–49) from the National Science Foundation of the United States. For administrative purposes this grant was awarded to J. L. Caskey at the University of Cincinnati but the funds were applied wholly to Dr. Gejvall's work in Sweden. As will become apparent in the following pages, he has enjoyed the collaboration of many colleagues, and by employing advanced analytical and statistical methods has been able to carry the research further than archaeologists have usually attempted to do in the past. To the best of our knowledge, no comparable study has been made up to now of material from the Peloponnese.

Since the heroic days of excavation in Aegean lands when great achievements were brought about largely by the insight and energy of individuals, archaeological research has come to depend more and more on the cooperation of many. In the process, contributions by specialists are duly recorded, but the equally important — in some ways still more important — work of others can never be fully estimated or acknowledged. At Lerna more than a score of people,

FOREWORD

apart from the foremen and skilled laborers, were engaged in the field and later in the workrooms and museums. Their accomplishments will be made known insofar as possible at appropriate places in this series of reports. Here, in addition to an inadequate general acknowledgement, I would express very special appreciation of the part played by the late Serapheim Charitonides, then Epimelete of Antiquities in the Argolid, who supervised major sectors of the digging with rare skill and devotion throughout the first four seasons, and of the contributions of Elizabeth Gwyn Caskey, who supervised excavation each year in the field, kept and coordinated many of the records, and later revised a number of the reports, verifying among others the hundreds of references to excavation data that occur in the present study by Dr. Gejvall.

Support and friendly assistance were given to us generously by many members of the Greek Archaeological Service under its successive directors, Professors A. K. Orlandos and S. Marinatos. We think with special gratitude of the late Dr. J. Papademetriou, who as Ephor of the Argolid in 1952 oversaw the beginning of the enterprise and thereafter gave it his continuing attention, and of his successor as Ephor, the late Dr. N. Verdelis. It was under their authority in 1959 that the collection of antiquities from Lerna was transferred from the workrooms at Corinth to the archaeological museum at Argos. There it is now housed in two rooms, one a gallery for public display of the most interesting pieces, the other a storeroom containing material of importance for the stratigraphical record.

At the conclusion of the campaigns of excavation pits and trenches were refilled in order that much of the land might be returned to cultivation. The largest of the areas investigated and a long strip of land providing a pathway to it from the main highway were bought from the owners, George and Panayiotis Kotsiopoulos, who had generously and patiently allowed us to dig on their properties for seven years. This chief area was walled and terraced to show the position of various buildings that illustrate the successive levels of habitation, and a few trees, vines, and flowering plants were set out. Thanks to the fertile soil of the region and the abundant supply of water, but most particularly to the devoted care of the place by a former workman, Manolis Mavrias of Myloi, these plants have flourished over the past ten years. They surround the large open-sided building that now covers and protects the crude-brick remains of the House of the Tiles.

Much further excavation could be done at Lerna with interesting results, and a time may well come when it will appear profitable for another expedition to resume the investigation in other parts of the site. For the moment, our task is to complete the study of the large body of materials already collected and to issue an account of them in the series of publications which Dr. Gejvall inaugurates with the present volume.

The American School of Classical Studies at Athens acknowledges with gratitude a generous contribution toward the publication of this volume from the University of Cincinnati.

UNIVERSITY OF CINCINNATI

JOHN L. CASKEY

PREFACE

A series of important contributions to archaeology and social history has been made possible by the scientific evaluation of animal remains, i.e. bones, teeth, shells etc., the debris from meals, which have been obtained in the course of excavations. This is also of value to the natural sciences within anthropology, paleodemography, zoology (viz. paleoanatomy), and genetics, to mention a few.

The most telling term for this branch of science would be archaeo-osteology or osteo-archaeology. The choice between these two names may well depend upon whether the person using it is an archaeologist or a scientist. Unfortunately archaeo-osteologists are very few and the disproportion between stored and accessible but uninvestigated material and such specialists seems to be general. In many countries, especially in Europe, vast collections of bone material are stored, excavated at the cost of many millions of dollars with the help of many archaeological and geological specialists. The material in some of these collections has been washed, restored, carefully labelled and made ready for scientific investigation, while in others it is still in the condition in which it came from the excavation perhaps a century ago.

There are many reasons for this situation, but one of the most obvious and deplorable is the fact that during the "atomic era" it is not "modern" to be occupied with such antiquated and "old-fashioned" studies as anatomy and morphology. Science is dominated by other ideas which make a greater claim on government support even in countries where one might expect fairer distribution of research assistance.

All over the world the winds are fair for the social sciences, and this is true for archaeology too. But all the care that is put into the handling of the excavation material is less valuable than it should be due to the fact that the field archaeologist, when interpreting his finds in the laboratory and at his desk, must deliver a truncated or abortive report, if he has not had his bone material thoroughly evaluated by a specialist. The human bones represent the man behind the archaeological finds, the animal bones tell the story of game and fishing, domestication and farming, agriculture, and the preparation of food; we can even trace changes in the biotope through them and get information about paleoclimatology.

Human and animal osteology as service sciences for archaeology and social history offer the most promising fields for breaking down the conservative artificial limits between humanistic and natural sciences. American archaeologists who have always tried to be forerunners in teamwork ought to be able to accomplish this breakdown. The greatest difficulty is, however, the lack of field osteologists.

From the areas of excavations in Greece and Italy large quantities of both human and animal skeletal remains have been saved during the last decades. This collection from Lerna in the Argolid was made during the excavation conducted by the American School of Classical Studies in Athens from 1952–1958. Professor John L. Caskey, Director of the excavations, has kindly entrusted the following study to me.

The archaeological reports of these campaigns are published in the following issues of *Hesperia*: XXIII, 1954, pp. 3–30; XXIV, 1955, pp. 25–49; XXV, 1956, pp. 147–173; XXVI, 1957, pp. 142–162; XXVII, 1958, pp. 125–144; XXVIII, 1959, pp. 202–207.

OSTEOLOGICAL RESEARCH LABORATORY N-G. GEJVALL

UNIVERSITY OF STOCKHOLM

TABLE OF CONTENTS

FOREWORD BY JOHN L. CASKEY	i
PREFACE	vii
ACKNOWLEDGEMENTS	xi
BIBLIOGRAPHY	xiii
ABBREVIATIONS	xvi
MATERIAL AND METHODS	1
DESCRIPTIONS OF SPECIES WITH OSTEOLOGICAL AND CULTURAL INTERPRETATIONS	14
DOMESTIC DOG	14
WOLF	18
WILD BOAR AND DOMESTIC PIG	19
SHEEP AND GOAT	24
WILD OX AND DOMESTIC CATTLE	29
ASS AND HORSE	34
VOLE	37
HEDGEHOG	37
RED FOX	38
BROWN BEAR	39
BADGER	40
COMMON OTTER	41
BEECH MARTEN	41
WEASEL	42
LYNX	42
EUROPEAN HARE	42
RED DEER	44
ROE DEER	46
BIRDS	47
AMPHIBIANS	49
REPTILES	49
FISH	49
MOLLUSCS	50
THE IMPORTANCE OF THE FAUNA	51
FAUNA AND BIOTOPE	55
SUMMARY	58
MEASUREMENTS	60
APPENDIX. THE PROGRAMMING BY ULF BJÄLKEFORS	98
LIST OF PLATES	100
FIGURE	
FLOW SCHEDULES	
DIAGRAMS	
PLATES	

ACKNOWLEDGMENTS

This work has been financed by a National Science Foundation grant (No. GS–49, 1963). During 1964 our work also received financial support from the University of Stockholm (funds for research support No. 691.49). Both these funds have been administered by the University of Stockholm. The National Science Foundation grant was obtained through the initiative and support of Professor Caskey, now Head of the Department of Classics, University of Cincinnati. Valuable support was also given by Professor Carl W. Blegen.

This study had to be carried out during a period of reorganization when new plans were being made for work in Swedish human and animal osteology. Professor Greta Arwidsson of the University of Stockholm, chief of its Department of Nordic and Comparative Archaeology, who herself has great knowledge of and interest in archaeo-osteology, carried through the formation of our research group and its inclusion in the University, as well as the author's release from his regular work at the Academy of History and Antiquities; she has also done everything possible to lighten the burdens which would normally be put on his shoulders. The work was done in the Section of Vertebrate Zoology of the Museum of Natural History in Stockholm; the Director, Professor Alf Johnels, kindly gave our group working space in the museum and allowed us to use its collections of skeletal material.

The scientific evaluation of the bone fragments and the determination of species, which were done in a preliminary way in the museum in Ancient Corinth, have been somewhat revised since. Groups of fragments of sheep and goat, of wild and domestic cattle, of horse and ass were taken to Munich in May 1965. There comparisons were made of this material and the collections which were available in order to complete the determinations. This was made possible through the efforts of one of the most skilled experts on prehistoric European animal osteology, Professor Dr. Joachim Boessneck of the new Institute for Paleoanatomy, Domestication Research and History of Veterinary Medicine of the University of Munich, who kindly arranged for this comparative study. Professor Boessneck also took us to the Staatliche Zoologische Sammlungen in Nymphenburg Castle, where Dr. Th. Haltenorth kindly allowed us to use its large collection of comparative material.

The fragments of bird bones, relatively few but very important, were partly identified by us. These results were revised and corrected by the well known expert on avian osteology, Intendant Dr. Johannes Lepiksaar of the Museum of Natural History in Gothenburg. Dr. Lepiksaar made some additional determinations of the most difficult fragments of bird bones, as well as of the undetermined remains of reptiles and fish.

The 26 species of molluscs represented by shells and fragments were identified by the well known authority in this field, Professor Emeritus Nils Odhner of the Department of Invertebrates of the Museum of Natural History in Stockholm. Intendant Dr. Ulf Bergström of the Museum of Natural History in Stockholm has contributed valuable suggestions on taxonomical and faunistic problems. The programming for the IBM 1401 computer was done by Mr. Ulf Bjälkefors, also in Stockholm.

We are deeply grateful to the Trustees and Institutions which we have mentioned for financial support, and to all the people mentioned both for scientific assistance and for the help they gave in facilitating the work. It is for us an agreeable duty to express to each one of them our sincere indebtedness and gratitude.

All planning for the computer processing of this material, including the construction of all the codes, and all the coding, the making of tables, plates and statistics as well as the collaboration with our programmer was entrusted to my wife Anna-Britta.

BIBLIOGRAPHY

A.A.A.S.H.: *Acta Archaeologica Academiae Scientarum Hungaricae*, Budapest
Act. Bern.: *Acta Bernensia*, Bern
Act. Zool. Fenn.: *Acta Zoologica Fennica*, Helsinki
Anal. ştiinţ. Univ. Al. I. Cuza: *Analele ştiinţifice ale Universităţii "Al. I. Cuza" din Iaşi* (Serie Noua) Secţiunea II (Ştiinţe naturale), a) Biologie, Iaşi
Årbok. Mus. Bergen.: *Bergens Museums Årbok*, Naturvitenskapelige Rekke, Bergen
Archae. L.: *Archaeology of Lund.* Studies in the Lund Excavation Material, Lund, 1957
Arstr. Göteb. Nat. Hist. Mus.: *Göteborgs Naturhistoriska Museums Arstryck*, Göteborg
Handb. biol. ArbMeth.: *Handbuch der biologischen Arbeitsmethoden by Abderhalden*, Leipzig
Handl. K. Vitt-Akad.: *Kungl. Vitterhets Historie och Antikvitets Akademiens Handlingar*, Stockholm
Hesperia: Journal of the American School of Classical Studies at Athens
Jb. Röm. Germ. Zentr. Mus.: *Jahrbuch des römisch-germanischen Zentralmuseums Mainz*, Mainz
Kühn-Arch.: *Kühn-Archiv.* Arbeiten aus der landwirtschaftlichen Fakultät der Universität Halle-Wittenberg, Berlin
L.U.Å.: *Lunds Universitets Årsskrift* (Acta Universitatis lundensis), Lund
Luc. Stat. Zool. Mar. Univ. Al. I. Cuza: *Lucrările Sesiunii Ştiinţifice a Staţiunii Zoologice Marine "Prof. Ivan Borcea" Agigea, Universitatea "Al I. Cuza,"* Iaşi
Opus. Arch.: *Opuscula Romana*, Acta Instituti Romani Regni Sueciae, Lund
Säug. Mitt.: *Säugetierkundliche Mitteilungen*, Stuttgart
Schr. dt. Akad. d. Wiss.: *Schriften der deutschen Akademie der Wissenschaften zu Berlin*, Berlin
Skr. norske Vidensk-Akad.: *Skrifter utgitt av det Norske Videnskaps akademi i Oslo*, Oslo
Stud. Tierrest. Bay.: *Studien an vor- und frühgeschichtlichen Tierresten Bayerns*, München
Z. Tierzücht. ZüchtBiol.: *Zeitschrift für Tierzüchtung und Züchtungsbiologie*, Berlin and Hamburg
Z. Zücht.: *Zeitschrift für Züchtung*, Berlin, 1930–1938

Bergquist, H. and Lepiksaar, J.: "Animal Skeletal Remains from Medieval Lund," *Archae. L.*, 1957
Bökönyi, S., "Eine Pleistozän-Eselart im Neolithicum der Ungarischen Tiefebene," *A.A.A.S.H.*, IV, 1954
Bökönyi, S., "Die Entwicklung der mittelalterlichen Haustierfauna Ungarns. Ur- und frühgeschichtliche Haustiere in verschiedenen Gebieten." Teil III des Kieler Symposions 1961, *Z. Tierzücht. ZüchtBiol.*, LXXVII, 1, 1962
Bökönyi, S., Kalláí, L., Matolcsi, J., Tarján, R., "Vergleichende Untersuchungen am Metacarpus des Urs und des Hausrindes," *Ibid.*, LXXXI, 4, 1965
Boessneck, J., "Ein Beitrag zur Errechnung der Wiederristhöhe nach Metapodienmassen bei Rindern," *Ibid.*, LXVIII, 1, 1956a
Boessneck, J., "Tierknochen aus spätneolithischen Siedlungen Bayerns," *Stud. Tierrest. Bay.*, 1956b
Boessneck, J., "Zur Entwicklung vor- und frühgeschichtlicher Haus- und Wildtiere Bayerns im Rahmen der gleichzeitigen Tierwelt Mitteleuropas," *Stud. Tierrest. Bay.*, 1958
Boessneck, J., "Zu den Tierknochenfunden aus der präkeramischen Schicht der Argissa-Magula," *Germania*, XXXVIII, 3/4, Frankfurt am Main, 1960.
Boessneck, J., "Die Tierreste aus der Argissa-Magula vom präkeramischen Neolithicum bis zur mittleren Bronzezeit," *Die deutschen Ausgrabungen auf der Argissa-Magula in Thessalien*, I, Bonn, 1962
Boessneck, J., Jéquier, J.-P. and Stampfli, H. R., "Seeberg, Burgäschisee-Süd, Die Tierreste," *Act. Bern.*, II, 3, 1963
Boessneck, J., Müller, H.-H. and Teichert, H., "Osteologische Unterscheidungsmerkmale zwischen Schaf (Ovies aries Linné) und Ziege (Capra hircus Linné)," *Kühn-Arch.*, LXXVIII, 1–2, 1964
Brehm-Ekman, *Djurens liv*, Stockholm, 1938

Brentjes, B., "Der geschichtliche Tierweltwechsel in Vorderasien und Nordafrika in altertumkundlicher Sicht," *Säug. Mitt.*, XIII, 3, 1965
Brinkmann, A., "Canidenstudien V–VI," *Årbok. Mus. Bergen*, VII, 1924
Butzer, K. W., "Late Glacial and Postglacial Climatic Variation in the Near East," *Erdkunde*, XI, 1, Bonn, 1957
von Bülow, D.: *see* Hansen, P., von Bülow, D. and Lotze, K.

Caskey, J. L., "Excavations at Lerna, 1954," *Hesperia*, XXIV, 1, 1955
Caskey, J. L., "Excavations at Lerna, 1955," *Ibid.*, XXV, 2, 1956
Caskey, J. L., "Excavations at Lerna, 1956," *Ibid.*, XXVI, 2, 1957
Caskey, J. L., "Excavations at Lerna, 1957," *Ibid.*, XXVII, 2, 1958
Caskey, J. L., "Activities at Lerna, 1958–1959," *Ibid.*, XXVIII, 3, 1959
Caskey, J. L., "The Early Helladic Period in the Argolid," *Ibid.*, XXIX, 3, 1960

Dahr, E., "Studien über Hunde aus primitiven Steinzeitkulturen in Nord-Europa," *L.U.A.*, NF, Avd. 2, XXXII, 4, 1937
Duerst, J. U., "Vergleichende Untersuchungsmethoden am Skelett bei Säugern," *Handb. biol. ArbMeth.*, VII, 1. Teil, pp. 125–530, 1930

Ellenberger, W. und Baum, H., *Handbuch der vergleichenden Anatomie der Haustiere*, 18. Aufl. Springer, Berlin, 1943
Ellermen, J. P. and Morrison-Scott, T. C. S., *Checklist of Palaearctic and Indian Mammals 1758–1946*, London, 1951

Frank, K. G., "Neue Funde des Pferdes aus dem keltischen Oppidum von Manching," *Stud. Tierrest. Bay.*, XIII, 1962

Gejvall, N-G., *The Fauna of the Different Settlements of Troy, Part I: Dogs, Horses and Cattle* (Stencilled), 1946
Gejvall, N-G.: *see* Sahlström, K. E. and Gejvall, N.-G.
Gejvall, N-G., "Esame preliminare del materiale osseo reperito negli scavi effettuati a Luni (Provincia di Viterbo, Comune di Blera) a cura dell' Istituto Svedese di Studi Classici in Roma." Appendix in Östenberg, C.-E., "Luni sul Mignone e Problemi della Preistoria d'Italia," *Opus. Arch.*, XXV, 1967

Haimovici, S.: *see* Necrasov, O. and Haimovici, S.
Hansen, P., von Bülow, D., Lotze, K., *Das Ansprechen des Damschauflers*, Hannover, 1964
Herre, W., "Domestikation und Stammesgeschichte," in Heberer, G., *Die Evolution der Organismen*, G. Fischer, Stuttgart, 1959
Hilzheimer, M., *Natürliche Rassengeschichte der Haussäugetiere*, Berlin and Leipzig, 1926
Hopf, M., "Nutzpflanzen vom Lernäischen Golf," *Jb. Röm. Germ. Zentr. Mus.*, 1962
Huxley, J., *Evolution. The Modern Synthesis*, London, 1944

Jéquier: *see* Boessneck, Jéquier and Stampfli

Kállai: *see* Bökönyi, Kállai, Matolcsi, Tarján
Kelm, H., "Zur Systematik der Wildschweine," *Z. Tierzücht. ZüchtBiol.*, XLIII, 1939
Kurtén, B., "The Carnivora of the Palestine Caves," *Act. Zool. Fenn.*, CVII, 1965

Lambrecht, K., *Handbuch der Palaeornithologie*, Berlin, 1933
Lepiksaar, J.: *see* Bergquist and Lepiksaar
Lepiksaar, J., "Die vor- und frühgeschichtlichen Haustiere Südschwedens," *Z. Tierzücht. ZüchtBiol.*, LXXVII, 1962
Lepiksaar, J., "Djurrester från Gamla Lödöse (1100–1400–talet)," *Årstr. Göteb. Nat. Hist. Mus.*, 1965
Lotze, K., *Das Ansprechen des Hirsches*, Hannover, 1963
Lotze, K.: *see* Hansen, von Bülow, Lotze

Matolcsi, J.: *see* Bököyi, Kállai, Matolcsi, Tarján
Mertens, R.: *see* Wermuth, Mertens

Müller, H.-H.: *see* Boessneck, Müller, Teichert
Müller, H.-H. "Die Haustiere der mitteldeutschen Bandkeramiker," *Schr. dt. Akad. d. Wiss. Sektion für Vor- und Frühgeschichte*, 1964

Narr, K. J., "Kulturgeschichtliche Erwägungen zu frühen Haustiervorkommen," *Z. Tierzücht. ZüchtBiol.*, LXXVI, 1961
Necrasov, O., Haimovici, S., "Sur la présence d'une espéce pléistocène d'équides — Equus hydruntinus Reg. — dans le Néolithique Roumain," *Anal. ştiinţ. Univ. Al. I. Cuza*, V, 1959
Necrasov, O., Haimovici, S., "Sur la présence de la dorade (Aurata aurata L.) dans les eaux du littoral Roumain de la Mer Noire, pendant le Néolithique,", *Luc. Stat. Zool. Mar. Univ. Al. I. Cuza*, 1959
Necrasov, O., Haimovici, S., "Nouvelle contribution à l'étude de Equus (Asinus) hydruntinus Reg. (Note II)," *Anal. ştiinţ. Univ. Al. I. Cuza*. VI, 2, 1960
Nobis, G., "Zur Kenntnis der ur- und frühgeschichtlichen Rinder Nord- und Mitteldeutschlands," *Z. Tierzücht. ZüchtBiol.*, LXIII, 2, 1954

Oberdorfer, F., "Die Hunde des Latène-Oppidums Manching," *Stud. Tierrest. Bay.*, VII, 1959
Ondrias, J. C., "Die Säugetiere Griechenlands," *Säug. Mitt.*, XIII, 3, 1965
Opitz, G., "Die Schweine des Latène-Oppidums Manching," *Stud. Tierrest. Bay.*, III, 1958

Papadopoulo, D. O., "Das griechische brachyzere Rind," *Z. Zücht.*, XXX, 1934
Petri, W., "Neue Funde des Hundes aus dem keltischen Oppidum von Manching," *Stud. Tierrest. Bay.*, X, 1961

Reed, C. A., "Animal Domestication in the Prehistoric Near East," *Science*, CXXX, No. 3389, 11. Dec. 1959

Sahlström, K. E., Gejvall, N-G., "Gravfältet på Kyrkbacken i horns socken, Västergötland, II," *Handl. K. Vitt-Akad.*, LX, 2, 1948
Schneider, F., "Die Rinder des Latène-Oppidums Manching," *Stud. Tierrest. Bay.*, V, 1958
Schultze-Westrum, Th., "Die Wildziegen der ägäischen Inseln," *Säug. Mitt.*, XI, 4, 1963
Schweizer, W., "Zur Frühgeschichte des Haushuhns in Mitteleuropa," *Stud. Tierrest. Bay.*, IX, 1961
Silver, I. A., *The Ageing of Domestic Animals, Science in Archaeology*, London, 1963
Stampfli: *see* Boessneck, Jéquier, Stampfli

Tarján: *see* Bökönyi, Kállai, Matolcsi, Tarján
Teichert: *see* Boessneck, Müller, Teichert
Thiele, J., *Handbuch der Weichtierkunde*, Jena, 1935

Wagner, K., "Rezente Hunderassen. Eine osteologische Untersuchung," *Skr. norske Vidensk-Akad.*, Mat.-Naturvid., Kl. 3 Bd., No. 9, 1930
Wermuth, H., Mertens, R., *Schildkröten — Krokodile — Brückenechsen*, Jena, 1961

Zeuner, F. E., *A History of Domesticated Animals*, London, 1963

ABBREVIATIONS

ad	= adult	Mc	= metacarpus
An	= antler	meas	= measured, measurement
Ansh	= antler shed	MIND	= minimum number of individuals (calculated)
Arc	= Archaic		
At	= atlas	Mo	= molar
Ax	= axis	Mp	= metapodial
BIND	= coherent sample of fragments belonging to one individual	Mt	= metatarsus
		Mx	= maxilla
bronze	= traces of bronze or other metals	neo	= neonatal
burn	= with traces of burning	NRM	= Museum of Natural History, Stockholm
Ca	= calcaneus	Pa	= patella
Ce	= centrotarsale	path	= with pathological changes
Cl	= clavicula (coracoid in birds)	Pe	= pelvis
Class	= Classical	Ph	= phalanx
Co	= costa	PM	= premolar
Cp	= carpometacarpus	Ra	= radius
Cr	= cranium	Ro	= Roman
crtr	= crushed in transportation	Sa	= sacrum
ctm	= with cut marks	Sc	= scapula
dx	= right	sen	= senile
f	= fragment	Sh	= shell
Fe	= femur	sin	= left
Fi	= fibula	S & M	= surface and mixed (layer)
foe	= foetus, foetal	St	= sternum
fr	= front	subad	= subadult
Fu	= furcula	Ta	= talus (astragalus)
gn	= with traces of gnawing	Ti	= tibia
H	= Helladic	trans	= transitional
Hc	= Horn-core	Tita	= tibiotarsus
H of T	= House of the Tiles	Tu	= tusk (canine)
hi	= hind	Ul	= ulna
Hu	= humerus	unatt	= unattached or unassigned (layer)
iHG	= in Human Grave(s)	undet	= undeterminable
Inc	= incisor	Ve	= vertebra (other than At, Ax)
ind	= individual	wkd	= worked (as tool)
L	= Lerna	y	= young
La	= later	I:1 (etc.)	= Plate I, fig. 1 (etc.)
LH	= Late Helladic	♂	= male
Ma	= mandibula	♀	= female
ma	= mature	⚦	= castrate

MATERIAL AND METHODS

The scientific investigation of excavated animal bone fragments may follow any one of several different lines, but the method chosen always depends upon the size of the material and the archaeological or cultural problems involved. It is very important that the bones be delivered in well dated and convenient units as was the case with the present material.

When time and money permit it is of course advantageous for the worker to do the preparatory stages of his investigation at the earliest possible opportunity, that is at the site during the excavation, so that he may consult directly with the archaeologists when the finds occur and may be able to make notes on the physical properties and the position of the bone fragments in the different layers and strata.

The author made the preliminary study of the present material during six weeks of the spring of 1958 in the storerooms of the Museum in Ancient Corinth. The material was delivered in units of the number and kind seen in the following table, 1.

TABLE 1

LIST OF BONE SAMPLES

Dating L	Few fragments	%	Small bag	%	Medium bag	%	Large bag	%	Teneke	%
I			31	2.5	12	1.8	3	0.7		
II	3	11.5	202	16.4	243	36.5	22	5.3		
III	5	19.2	153	12.4	45	6.8	24	5.8	1	2.0
IV	8	30.8	311	25.2	168	25.3	156	37.6	18	36.8
V	10	38.5	439	35.5	147	22.1	181	43.6	20	40.8
VI			4	0.3	3	0.4	7	1.7	9	18.4
VII			19	1.5	21	3.2	4	1.0	1	2.0
Class			12	1.0	16	2.4	2	0.5		
Roman			2	0.2						
S&M			62	5.0	9	1.4	16	3.8		
Unatt					1	0.1				
Total	26		1235		665		415		49	

The preliminary registration of the material handed over in bags and containers of different sizes (cf. Table 1) was done in the following way: the contents of each unit were emptied onto a large table and spread over it, each fragment and splinter was subjected to a careful ocular inspection which permitted separation into species, and within each species the fragments were sorted according to bone type. The smallest splinters were grouped together into units; all measurable fragments were taken out for further investigation, as were also all bone fragments and shells which could not immediately be referred to a definite species. For each unit number (the excavation lot number) a card was made (larger units needed a series of cards), and on these cards all preliminary notes were written using a simple system of abbreviation, a mnemotechnical code, generally the same used in the introductory list of this book. These notes contain a variety of information beginning with the species of animal and continuing with the number of fragments of the species, giving for jaws and extremity bones the part and the side (except for fragments too small to be determined without much expenditure of time). Other characteristics registered were erupted teeth and stage of eruption, abrasion and abnormal number of teeth (cf. oligodonty in dogs), marks of cutting and gnawing, traces of burning, coloring by metal (bronze), pathological changes or sequelae of fractures, shed antlers etc. All the measurable fragments and other fragments and samples which were to be saved for later investigation were numbered in black ink.

When deciding about the subsequent procedure in view of the number of registrations we called upon our experience with a preliminary study of some 3200 bone fragments from the Etruscan site of Luni in the province of Viterbo (Gejvall 1967). This led us to think it would be worthwhile to process our data on a computer capable of handling a collection as big as that from Lerna, especially because of the scarcity of staff available for the project. In consideration of our experience as we worked with the animal bone remains from Lerna we now strongly recommend that both archaeologists and scientists try some form of computer technique for handling large materials of any kind. It is our intention hereafter to process in this way large quantities of human as well as animal bones, using a common method for computer handling of this kind of material.

Our next steps with the present collection were as follows: the preliminary notes were carefully transferred onto printed coding lists of special construction (Fig. 1) with the information in the same order as the 80 column punch cards that were used for the computer handling of the material (cf. Appendix, The Programming, pp. 98–99). A series of special codes was built up to cope with the different problems to be solved; thus we have one code for the archaeological layers and strata, split up into settlement, phase and subphase, another for the animal groups and species, one for the bones, one series of smaller codes for the items involved in closer determination, including specials for observed frequency, part of fragment, side, more specific codes for tooth eruption, abrasion and a subjective age determination. Then follows a series of other codes dealing with the physical properties which were observed in the material, that is the cuts and other marks we have mentioned, and finally a compact code of the measurements used. All registered codes except the measurements cover columns 1 to 28 of the punch card, the remaining 52 columns being reserved for the measurements. When constructing the measurement code we used the common osteometric technique described by Duerst (1926) in *Abderhaldens Handbuch der biologischen Arbeitsmethoden*, but with additions from the work of a series of more modern authors including J. Boessneck and his school in Munich.

In cases where the number of measurements of a fragment, for instance of a mandible, exceeds eight, it was necessary to extend the punching to a second card. In order to bring this to the attention of the key punch operator in time the two columns preceding the first measurements have been used to indicate the number of measurements to come. In addition every measurement is preceded by two columns indicating the order number of the measurement which follows; this was done in order to facilitate the sorting out of every kind of measurement of every species and bone for further statistical treatment.

As a direct result of building up the various codes, moving from the larger towards the smaller units, it was possible to reduce appreciably the number of columns and digits necessary to accommodate the number of measurements used today in osteology. Since the sorting according to animal species and bone was done before the sorting for measurements the latter could be adjusted so that all lengths, regardless of bone and animal species, could be given the same position of digits. The same thing is true for breadths, diameters, circumferences etc., and thus the code was held to a minimum space. In order to cope with fragments with a larger number of measurements (well preserved mandibles sometimes need 30 measurements) we have constructed a special code for such fragments on the basis of simple statistics showing the frequency of occurrence of the measurements. Our experiment showed that the total number of actual measurements is just under 160 but 19 of these are of extraordinarily high frequency, whereas the bulk of mandibular and maxillar measurements are of very low frequency. This, of course, applies only to a collection of fragmentary material such as the present one. These frequencies of the various measurements have been our guide in the construction of the measurement code and also in the programming.

We have tried to estimate age of the domestic animals from the eruptional schedule of the milk dentition and the permanent teeth, from the estimated abrasion of the bite or of single teeth, and finally on a subjective basis. These three approaches have been incorporated in three different codes: the eruption code of the teeth includes 32 different stages, the abrasion four stages, and the estimation seven stages (foetus, neonatal, young, subadult, adult, mature and senile). As for the interpretation of single cases or specimens, we began by using Ellenberger and Baum's (1943) list of age determination, but later we included also the more recent data given by Silver (1963). However, the author wants to emphasize that the results of age estimation are merely approximate since we are dealing with material from the distant past and a changing biotope as well as with racial uncertainties which cannot be estimated. Age estimation, however, along general lines has its importance from a cultural standpoint; we have therefore included it in our tables (cf. Table 9, p. 13).

The estimation of sex from single fragments of bone is a complex problem. We have attempted it for only a few groups of bones, namely horn-cores of cattle and sheep, for the principal purpose of identifying the castrates. Our determinations include some horn-cores for whose sexing we are indebted to Professor Boessneck in Munich.

Table 3 (p. 6) shows that in some cases lots of bones, usually found in pits or graves, were isolated in such a way that it is possible to assert that the whole lot belongs to one individual. It is the opinion of the author that these lots usually represent animals which died of a disease or were buried as part of a sacrifice. Otherwise why should their bones remain untouched? For the most part such fragments are very brittle, of young specimens, burned or for some other reason in such condition as to give very few measurements and little information. We have listed these as BIND in our tables. From a statistical point of view, in order not to increase the discrepancy between estimates based on single fragments and on these lots containing whole individuals, we have counted only the number of measurable fragments of BIND.

The total number of fragments, after we deducted 203 small splinters and a few intrusive human bones, mostly of newborn infants, amounts to 25,287 units, cf. Tables 3-6. There are 8,724 identified shells of land and sea molluscs, 3 fragments of a crab and 2 from a sea urchin. The distribution of shells saved from the various layers is seen in Table 4; not quite all shells were saved.

The fragments of vertebrates amount to 15,621 units. In all 78 bones and bone fragments of birds were found, and are listed in Table 3. There are 1,682 fragments of reptiles, mostly of the carapace of the Greek turtle. One fragment and also one BIND of an amphibian, a large toad, and two unidentifiable fragments are included in the material, as well as 16 fragments, mostly vertebrae, of fish. All BIND-lots are put in parentheses in Table 3. The total for the land vertebrates is 13,845 fragments and groups of splinters, and includes very few whole bones. The groups of small splinters registered are 936 or *ca.* 3.7% of the total number of fragments.

It is quite clear that for morphological reasons we could not in our preliminary registration separate the bones of the small caprovines (sheep and goat) except for some of the horn-cores and some skull fragments. The important work of Boessneck *et al.* (1964) was not accessible at that time. The absolute and percentual distribution of these species must therefore be viewed with some reservations. When lots containing many measurable fragments of one individual

(BIND) occur in settlements or layers which gave us few fragments altogether one must admit that this puts the picture out of focus for these periods; this is the case with the domestic dog in Classical and Roman layers. Before we have checked the number of mandible fragments or other fragments of high frequency it is impossible to tell anything definite about the number of individuals represented (MIND, see below). On the other hand one must remember that lots containing many fragments of one individual are registered as only one individual each, whereas one individual must also be implied by the presence of even one fragment of a rare species (e.g. of the wolf or the lynx). Such anomalies cannot be avoided in any investigation of this kind, and present a statistical problem of great interest and complexity. We have tried to use the present collection and others of a similar kind to discover how many fragments of the size normally found in debris are necessary as a foundation for the minimal number of individuals (MIND) calculated on fragments of high frequency (mandibles, maxillae, horn-cores etc.). Our conclusion is that we must count on at least 300 fragments, and we are not sure that when we are dealing with less than that number of fragments of domestic cattle, pig, sheep and goat that our estimate of MIND will be at all realistic (Diagram 1). For the methods of calculating MIND used by scientists for various collections see Boessneck (1960) and the bibliography he cites.

TABLE 2

KEY TO THE DATING OF BONE MATERIAL FROM THE SUCCESSIVE SETTLEMENTS AND COMBINED STRATA OF LERNA

	+ Lerna	+ later	Surface; S&M; Mixed	LH	HofT	Class	Unatt
L I	II						
L II	III		×				
L III	IV				×		×
L IV	V	×					×
L V	VI, VII	×	×			×	×
L VI		×					
L VII	V		×	×		×	
Class			×				
Roman							
S&M							
Unatt							
iHG							

TABLE 3
ANIMAL REMAINS ACCORDING TO LAYERS AND PHASES

Dating L	Mammals	Sorex sp.	Erinaceus europ.	Canis lupus	Canis familiaris	Vulpes vulpes	Ursus sp.	Meles sp.	Lutra sp.	Martes sp.	Mustela sp.	Lynx sp.	Lepus europ.	Sus scrofa	Transitional and Sus domesticus	Cervus elaphus	Capreolus capreolus	Ovis et / sive Capra	Ovis sp.	Capra sp.	Bos primigenius	Bos taurus domesticus	Equus caballus	Asinus asinus	Aves	Amphibia	Reptilia	Pisces	Invertebrates (Mainly molluscs)	Undeterminable	Splinters (groups of)	Total	BIND
I		1			1								3	4	34	2		87 (1)	3		8	17			4		1		147		9	322	1
I+II						2							1		12			36			1										5	189	
II					6	3							1	1	157	11		250	11	35	3	13			6		1	1	119		40	2247	
II+III					8	1							2	1	115	11		165	3	14	3	104			2		3	3	1613		52	2045	
III+S&M															1			3				97					3	1	1570		2	19	
III	2				25	4							8	18	236	20		284	4	52	7	169		2	6		25	5	620		84	1572	
III+IV					5	1							1	1	109	9		72	1	22		70		1	6		38		133		23	492	
III+Class															1															2		2	
IV		1			133	10		6	2	3			42	43	1135 (1)	75	4	982	18	297	3	1143 (1)		9	22		363 (1)	1	1729		317	6338	3
IV+V					19	1							6	1	149	12	1	75 (1)	3	73	5	162			1		50	1	96		40	695	1
IV+La					(1)										3							5							4		1	13	1
V	2			2	193	6	1	1	2		(1)	1	36	27	1539 (2)	264	12	995 (1)	167 (1)	293	5	1276	11		18	1 (1)	1094	2	1446		278	7672	6
V+VI					33										23	1		18	2	9		31					19		42		5	184	
V+VII					1								1	1	12	1		5		3		11	3				21		44		5	107	
V+La					1										2	1		2									4		19			29	
V+Class															1	1		2											3			7	
V+Class+S&M															1			1											1			3	
VI					33	5							11	27	407	48		416	10	19	1	125	1	3	3		15	1	660			1784	
VI+La															2	1		1				2							9			14	
VII													2		19	4		13	2	3		12	14	5			5 (1)		32		11	122	1
VII+V					4	3							2	1	42	6		40		5		29	1	2	1		2		90		4	232	
VII+LH+S&M						1									2	1		1				1		4	3		3		1		3	9	
VII+Class					142*										2	1		1				2		2	1		1		10		4	24	
Class														1	9	3		14		7		18					2		25		4	222	
Class+S&M					4										7			12				13							16		4	58	
Roman					16			4					5	1	127	19	1	107	1	28		134	3	2	8		26 (1)		7		1	14	
S&M															1			1										1	221		42	746	1
Unatt						1									3					3		1					2		49		3	62	
iHG	1				1										8			16				20					4		11		3	64	
Total	1 5	3	1	625 (1)	38	1	11	4	3	(1)	1	121	127	4158 (3)	491	18	3597 (3)	225 (1)	863	32	3456 (1)	33	30	78	1 (1)	1682 (3)	16	8729	2	936	25287 (14)	

* incl. 2 BIND   Figures within parentheses = BIND

MATERIAL AND METHODS

TABLE 4

DISTRIBUTION OF SEA AND LAND MOLLUSCS

Dating L	Glyphis italica Defrance	Patella coerulea L.	Patella ferruginea Gmelin	Monodonta fragarioides Lamarck	Cerithium vulgatum L.	Talparia lurida L.	Dolium galea L.	Murex trunculus L.	Murex brandaris L.	Triton tritonis L.	Thais haemostoma L. (Purpura)	Euthyria cornea L.	Conus mediterraneus Hwass.	Rumina decollata L.	Helix mazulii Jan.	Arca noae L.	Arca barbata L.	Glycymeris glycymeris L. (violaceus)	Mytilus edulis L.	Pinna nobilis L.	Spondylus gaederopus L.	Cardium edule L.	Venus rugosa L.	Tapes decussatus L.	Mactra stultorum L.	Pholas dactylus L.	Total
I					1			5							1	17		1			15	105		1			147
I + II						1		2								1					11	103	2	1			119
II	1				3	1	1	183			1		1		54	5		43		5	61	1204		53			1613
II + III	1							387							1	28	1	22	4	12	430	672		7	1		1570
II + S&M								5													3	4					12
III		5		1	2	1	1	212		1	4		3		1	21		9		9	84	260		4			619
III + IV		1		2	6	1	9	39			3		1	1		5		2		1	33	39					133
IV		51		3	102	8		444			15		5		22	128		31		11	344	543		9	1		1728
IV + V		4						23			1		1			9		5			37	16					96
IV + La								1														3		1			4
V		46		3	21	8	9	337			4		3	1	3	140		27		18	486	326	10				1443
V + VI							1	13								5				2	16	6					42
V + VII								11								1				2	8	22					44
V + La								7					1			4					5	2					19
V + Class				1				1													1						3
V + Class + S&M																					1						1
VI	1	7			16	1	3	259	3		4	1				44		4		97	217	4	1	1			660
VI + La							1	2													5	1					9
VII					1			9								3				3	5	10	1				32
VII + V					1			27								9		2		5	34	12					90
VII + LH + S&M																					1						1
VII + Class		1						2								1				2	2	2					10
Class					1		3	8										1		2	10	1					25
Class + S&M		1						2													10	3					16
Roman							1	4													1	1					7
S&M		4			7	2	4	57								17		1		2	51	73	2	47	1		221
Unatt		1												2		1					1	1					49
iHG								2													2	3					11
Total	1	123	1	10	161	23	31	2042	3	1	28	1	15	4	82	439	2	147	4	171	1874	3416	16	124	4	1	8724

TABLE 5

DISTRIBUTION OF IDENTIFIED BONE

	Antler Horn-core	Cranium*	Maxilla Premaxilla	Mandibula	Incisor	Canine	Premolar	Molar	Atlas	Axis	Other vertebra	Scapula	Coracoid	Furcula	Costa	Humerus
Mammals																
Sorex sp.																
Erinaceus europ.				3												
Canis lupus		1														
Canis familiaris		25	43	152		10	1	7	4	1	19	28			52	45
Vulpes vulpes			1	13												
Ursus, Meles, Lutra, Martes,																
Mustela, Lynx				4							1	2			1	2
Lepus europ.				5							5	12				9
Sus scrofa		20	18	23		8		1				14				11
Sus domesticus + trans.		272	691	1067	32	104	3	48		5	25	526			9	313
Cervus elaphus	190	12	15	74			4	17	1			25				6
Capreolus capreolus	14		1	2				1								
Ovis et sive Capra	108	41	134	982	1		8	385	5	6	26	406			31	253
Ovis aries	30	10	3	14				4	2		23	7			40	6
Capra hircus	337	20	23	203				79				34			10	21
Bos primigenius	2	5					1	5				1				
Bos domesticus + trans.	171	57	52	315	19		58	469	11	8	79	106			103	226
Equus caballus		1	1	2			2	4								1
Asinus asinus			1	7	1		2	3								2
Aves													4	2		15
Pisces		1		4							11					
Total	852	465	983	2870	53	122	79	1023	22	21	189	1161	4	2	246	910
In percent	6.1	3.3	7.1	20.6	0.4	0.9	0.6	7.3	0.2	0.2	1.4	8.3	—	—	1.8	6.5
Mammals %																
Sorex sp.																
Erinaceus europ.				60.0												
Canis lupus		33.3														
Canis famiiaris		4.0	6.9	24.3		1.6	0.2	1.1	0.6	0.2	3.1	4.5	—	—	8.3	7.2
Vulpes vulpes			2.6	34.2												
Ursus, Meles, Lutra, Martes,																
Mustela, Lynx				20.0							5.0	10.0			5.0	10.0
Lepus europ.				4.1							4.1	9.9				7.4
Sus scrofa		15.7	14.2	18.1		6.3		0.8				11.0				8.7
Sus domesticus + trans.		6.5	16.6	25.7	0.8	2.5	0.1	1.2		0.1	0.6	12.6			0.2	7.5
Cervus elaphus	38.7	2.4	3.1	15.1			0.8	3.5	0.2			5.1				1.2
Capreolus capreolus	77.7		5.6	11.1				5.6								
Ovis et/sive Capra	3.0	1.2	3.7	27.3			0.2	10.7	0.1	0.2	0.7	11.3			0.9	7.0
Ovis aries	13.3	4.4	1.3	6.2				1.7	0.9		10.2	3.1			17.8	2.7
Capra hircus	39.0	2.3	2.7	23.5				9.2				3.9			1.2	2.4
Bos primigenius	6.3	15.6					3.1	15.6				3.1				
Bos domesticus + trans.	4.9	1.6	1.5	9.1	0.5		1.8	13.6	0.3	0.2	2.3	3.1			3.0	6.5
Equus caballus		3.0	3.0	6.1			6.1	12.1								3.0
Asinus asinus			3.3	23.4	3.3		6.7	10.0								6.7
Aves													5.1	2.6		19.2
Pisces		6.2		25.0							68.8					

* including fragments of calvarium, frontal, infraorbital, lacrymal, occipital, parietal, petromastoid, and supraorbital.

MATERIAL AND METHODS

Fragments of Mammals, Birds and Fish

Radius	Ulna	Metacarpus Carpometacarpus	Phalanx I	Phalanx II	Phalanx III	Sacrum	Pelvis	Femur	Patella	Tibia, Tibiotarsus	Fibula	Talus + Centrotarsale	Calcaneus	Metatarsus Tarsometatarsus	Total
								1							1
	1									1					5
	1	1													3
25	34	72	3	1	1		14	12		22			9	45	625
1	2	13					2	1		1				4	38
3	3						2	1						1	20
15	6	6					21	17		20	2			3	121
4	13	8					1			4				2	127
232	246	174	15	8	3	1	84	58		155	3	33	17	34	4158
21	3	46	12	1			4	4		22		6	9	19	491
															18
227	72	228	23	3	2	1	105	58		294		41	35	122	3597
9	5	13	8	8	8		3	6		7		5	6	8	225
12	4	54	2	1	1		6	4		19		2	1	30	863
3		1	4	2	1			1				2	1	3	32
167	64	282	308	125	107	2	50	64	3	149		219	113	129	3456
2	1	1						12						6	33
3	1	2	4	1	1					2					30
8	19	4			1			6		12				7	78
															16
732	475	905	379	150	125	4	292	245	3	708	5	308	191	413	13937
5.2	3.4	6.5	2.7	1.1	0.9	—	2.1	1.8	—	5.1	—	2.2	1.4	2.9	

								100.0							
	20.0									20.0					
	33.3	33.3													
4.0	5.4	11.5	0.5	0.2	0.2	—	2.2	1.9		3.5			1.4	7.2	
2.6	5.3	34.3					5.3	2.6		2.6				10.5	
15.0	15.0						10.0	5.0						5.0	
12.4	5.0	5.0					17.4	14.0		16.5	1.7			2.5	
3.1	10.2	6.3					0.8			3.2				1.6	
5.6	5.9	4.2	0.4	0.2	0.1	—	2.0	1.4		3.7	0.1	0.8	0.4	0.8	
4.3	0.6	9.4	2.4	0.2			0.8	0.8		4.5		1.2	1.8	3.9	
6.3	2.0	6.3	0.6	0.1	0.1	—	2.9	1.6		8.2		1.2	1.0	3.4	
4.0	2.2	5.8	3.6	3.6	3.6		1.3	2.7		3.1		2.2	2.7	3.6	
1.4	0.5	6.3	0.2	0.1	0.1		0.7	0.5		2.2		0.2	0.1	3.5	
9.4		3.1	12.5	6.3	3.1			3.1				6.3	3.1	9.4	
4.8	1.9	8.2	8.9	3.6	3.1	0.1	1.4	1.9	0.1	4.3		6.3	3.3	3.7	
6.1	3.0	3.0						36.4						18.2	
10.0	3.3	6.7	13.3	3.3	3.3					6.7					
10.3	24.4	5.1			1.3			7.7		15.4				8.9	

THE FAUNA

TABLE 6

THE DISTRIBUTION OF MAMMALS, BIRDS AND FISH IN THE CONSECUTIVE UNMIXED LAYERS OF LERNA

	Dating L.	*Sorex sp.*	*Erinaceus europ.*	*Canis lupus*	*Canis familiaris*	*Vulpes vulpes Ursus, Meles, Lutra Martes, Mustela, Lynx*	*Lepus europ.*	*Sus scrofa*	Transitional and *Sus domesticus*	*Cervus elaphus*	*Capreolus capreolus*	*Ovis et Capra* (mixed)	*Ovis aries*	*Capra hircus*	*Bos primigenius*	Transitional and *Bos domesticus*	*Equus caballus*	*Asinus asinus*	*Aves*	*Pisces*	Total	In percent
No. of Fragments	I				1	2		3	4	34	2		87	3		8	17			4		165	1.3
	II				6	3		1	1	157	11		250	11	35	3	104			6	3	591	4.8
	III		2	1	25	4		8	18	236	20		284	4	52	7	169		2	6	5	843	6.9
	IV		1		133	10	11	42	43	1135	75	4	982	18	297	3	1143		9	22	1	3929	32.0
	V		2	2	193	6	5	36	27	1539	264	12	995	167	293	5	1276	11		18	2	4853	39.5
	VI				33	5		11	27	407	48		416	10	19		125	1	3	3	1	1109	9.0
	VII							2		19	4		13	2	3		12	14	5			74	0.6
	Class				142					9			14		7		18		2	1		193	1.6
	Roman				4					1			1									6	0.1
	S&M				16		4	5	1	127	19	1	107	1	28		134	3	2	8	1	457	3.7
	Unatt					1				3					3		1					8	0.1
	iHG	1			1					8			16				20					46	0.4
	Total	1	5	3	554	31	20	108	121	3675	443	17	3165	216	737	26	3019	29	23	68	13	12274	
	In percent	—	—	—	4.5	0.3	0.2	0.9	1.0	29.9	3.6	0.1	25.8	1.8	6.0	0.2	24.6	0.2	0.2	0.6	0.1		
In percent	Lerna I				0.6	1.2		1.8	2.4	20.6	1.2		52.8	1.8		4.9	10.3			2.4			
	II				1.0	0.5		0.2	0.2	26.5	1.9		42.3	1.9	5.9	0.5	17.6			1.0	0.5		
	III		0.2	0.1	3.0	0.5		0.9	2.1	28.1	2.4		33.7	0.5	6.2	0.8	20.0		0.2	0.7	0.6		
	IV		—		3.4	0.2	0.2	1.1	1.1	28.9	1.9	0.1	25.0	0.5	7.6	0.1	29.1		0.2	0.6	—		
	V		—	—	4.1	0.1	0.1	0.8	0.6	31.7	5.4	0.2	20.5	3.5	6.0	0.1	26.3	0.2		0.4	—		
	VI				2.9	0.5		1.0	2.4	36.7	4.3		37.5	0.9	1.7		11.3	0.1	0.3	0.3	0.1		
	VII							2.7		25.7	5.4		17.6	2.7	4.0		16.2	18.9	6.8				
	Class				73.6					4.7			7.3		3.6		9.3		1.0	0.5			
	Roman				66.8					16.6			16.6										
	S&M				3.5		0.9	1.1	0.2	27.8	4.2	0.2	23.4	0.2	6.1		29.3	0.7	0.4	1.8	0.2		
	Unatt					12.5				37.5					37.5		12.5						
	iHG	2.2			2.2					17.4			34.8				43.4						

MATERIAL AND METHODS

TABLE 7

WILD VERSUS DOMESTIC ANIMALS

NUMBER OF FRAGMENTS   MINIMUM NUMBER OF INDIVIDUALS

Dating L	Total Wild	Total Domestic	In percent Wild	In percent Domestic	Total Wild	Total Domestic	In percent Wild	In percent Domestic
I	19	142	11.8	88.2	11	21	34.4	65.6
I + II	2	61	3.2	96.8	2	11	15.4	84.6
II	19	563	3.3	96.7	11	57	16.2	83.8
II + III	15	402	3.6	96.4	5	47	9.6	90.4
II + S&M	—	5	—	100.0	—	3	—	100.0
III	60	772	7.2	92.8	16	77	17.2	82.8
III + IV	12	280	4.1	95.9	3	38	7.3	92.7
IV	189	3717	4.8	95.2	34	368	8.5	91.5
IV + V	26	481	5.1	94.9	8	72	10.0	90.0
IV + La	—	8	—	100.0	—	3	—	100.0
V	359	4474	7.4	92.6	45	533	7.8	92.2
V + VI	2	116	1.7	98.3	2	28	6.7	93.3
V + VII	2	35	5.4	94.6	2	13	13.3	86.7
V + La	1	5	16.7	83.3	1	4	20.0	80.0
V + Class	1	3	25.0	75.0	1	2	33.3	66.7
V + Class + S&M	—	2	—	100.0	—	2	—	100.0
VI	91	1014	8.2	91.8	15	197	7.1	92.9
VI + La	1	4	20.0	80.0	1	3	25.0	75.0
VII	6	68	8.1	91.9	2	15	11.8	88.2
VII + V	12	123	8.9	91.1	4	24	14.3	85.7
VII + LH + S&M	2	3	40.0	60.0	2	2	50.0	50.0
VII + Class	1	9	10.0	90.0	1	4	20.0	80.0
Class	—	192	—	100.0	—	19	—	100.0
Class + S&M	4	32	11.1	88.9	2	6	25.0	75.0
Roman	—	6	—	100.0	—	3	—	100.0
S&M	30	418	6.7	93.3	9	39	18.8	81.2
Unatt	1	7	13.0	87.0	1	4	20.0	80.0
iHG	1	45	2.2	97.8	1	32	3.0	97.0
Total	856	12987			179	1627		

THE FAUNA

TABLE 8

MIND OF TRANSITIONAL AND DOMESTIC PIG, SHEEP AND GOAT AND CATTLE
IN THE DIFFERENT LAYERS OF LERNA

Dating L	Transitional and Sus domesticus MIND	%	Capra et (sive) Ovis MIND	%	Transitional and Bos taurus domesticus MIND	%
I	4	20.0	12	60.0	4	20.0
I + II	3	27.3	6	54.5	2	18.2
II	11	20.4	35	64.8	8	14.8
II + III	12	27.3	24	54.5	8	18.2
II + S&M	1	33.3	1	33.3	1	33.3
III	23	32.4	33	46.5	15	21.1
III + IV	18	51.4	11	31.4	6	17.2
IV	121	35.9	159	47.2	57	16.9
IV + V	20	29.4	33	48.5	15	22.1
IV + La	1	50.0	—	—	1	50.0
V	203	43.1	184	39.1	84	17.8
V + VI	4	21.1	11	57.8	4	21.1
V + VII	5	45.5	4	36.4	2	18.1
V + La	2	50.0	2	50.0	—	—
V + Class	1	50.0	1	50.0	—	—
V + Class + S&M	1	50.0	1	50.0	—	—
VI	68	37.2	106	57.9	9	4.9
VI + La	2	66.7	—	—	1	33.3
VII	6	46.1	5	38.5	2	15.4
VII + V	12	60.0	6	30.0	2	10.0
VII + LH + S&M	1	50.0	—	—	1	50.0
VII + Class	1	33.3	1	33.3	1	33.3
Class	3	33.3	4	44.5	2	22.2
Class + S&M	1	16.7	3	50.0	2	33.3
Roman	1	50.0	1	50.0	—	—
S&M	11	31.4	14	40.0	10	28.6
Unatt	2	50.0	1	25.0	1	25.0
iHG	7	22.6	14	45.2	10	32.2
Total	545		672		248	

TABLE 9
Age Determination by Dental Status and Abrasion in Weeks, Months and Years
(after I.A. Silver, 1963)

Transitional and Sus domesticus L.

Dating L	No. of Ma	Side sin	Side dx	1—10 W %		6—12 M %		12—24 M %		3 Y %		More than 3 Y %		Total %	
I	4	2	1					66.7	2	33.3	1			75.0	3
II	22	10	7	5.6	1	44.4	8	11.1	2	38.9	7			81.8	18
III	45	18	16	2.5	1	20.0	8	5.0	2	72.5	29			88.9	40
IV	275	132	131	2.4	6	15.0	37	22.0	54	60.6	149			89.5	246
V	414	203	181	2.9	11	21.5	82	19.5	75	54.5	208	1.6	6	92.3	382
VI	135	66	64	7.4	10	23.0	31	6.7	9	62.2	84	0.7	1	100.0	135
VII	8	6	2			37.5	3	37.5	3	25.0	2			100.0	8
Class	4	1	2					25.0	1	75.0	3			100.0	4
S&M	23	13	10			19.0	4	33.3	7	47.7	10			91.3	21
iHG	4	2	2					100.0	4					100.0	4

Transitional and Bos taurus domesticus L

Dating L	No. of Ma	Side sin	Side dx	0—3 W %		5—6 M %		15—25 M %		17—36 M %		32—48 M %		More than 48 M %		Total %	
I	4	1		33.3	1			33.3	1	33.3	1					75.0	3
II	4		2							100.0	2					50.0	2
III	9	4	4					16.7	1	50.0	3	16.7	1	16.6	1	66.7	6
IV	92	51	35	1.3	1	4.0	3	13.3	10	72.1	54	4.0	3	5.3	4	81.5	75
V	138	77	52	5.3	6	7.0	8	5.3	6	68.4	78	14.0	16			82.6	114
VI	16	8	8	8.3	1			8.3	1	50.0	6	33.4	4			75.0	12
VII	3	1								100.0	1					33.3	1
Class	1	1								100.0	1					100.0	1
S&M	8	7	1					14.3	1	85.7	6					87.5	7

Ovis et (sive) Capra

Dating L	No. of Ma	Side sin	Side dx	6 W—3 M %		5—6 M %		12—18 M %		24—42 M %		More than 42 M %		Total %	
I	18	7	8	6.7	1	20.0	3	13.3	2	60.0	9			83.3	15
II	65	32	30	6.6	4	21.3	13	11.4	7	60.7	37			93.8	61
III	52	22	27			18.8	9	18.8	9	62.4	30			92.3	48
IV	333	163	165	2.2	7	12.7	41	17.7	57	65.5	211	1.9	6	96.7	322
V	349	156	187	1.8	6	15.6	53	12.4	42	68.1	231	2.1	7	97.1	339
VI	190	89	101	3.7	7	13.2	25	4.2	8	76.8	146	2.1	4	100.0	190
VII	5	2	3			20.0	1			80.0	4			100.0	5
Class	4	3	1							100.0	4			100.0	4
S&M	28	13	12			19.2	5	3.9	1	76.9	20			92.9	26
iHG	3	2	1	100.0	1									33.3	1

DESCRIPTIONS OF SPECIES WITH OSTEOLOGICAL AND CULTURAL INTERPRETATIONS

We will begin our discussion of the animal remains by presenting a list in concentrated table form of every species identified, and will follow this with the comments necessary to make the reader acquainted with the physical properties of some of the most important bones and fragments from each settlement. We will continue with a short summary of what we think is the importance of the various wild and domestic animals for the population of Lerna in the periods represented there. Last come the results of our investigations of the fauna in relation to its biotope.

We will deal first with the domestic animals and their wild ancestors, and then go on to the other mammals, the birds, fish, and lower animals.

The material description for each species begins with a list showing the number of fragments, the special physical properties observed, the calculated MIND, and the age distribution.

DOMESTIC DOG

The strata of Lerna I contain only one fragment of domestic dog, a left humerus, A456 (I:1)[1], of an adult individual. Its distal trochlea is fairly well preserved; the measurements are slightly larger than those of a "turf dog" (Canis palustris), or within the range of a modern schnauzer. The minimum breadth of the diaphysis shows it to be a gracile humerus.

From one of the six fragments of dogs from Lerna II, the mandible J855 (I:2, Measurement Table 2), it is possible to calculate the basi-cranial length *ad modum* Dahr (1937): 167.7 mm. The other mandible fragment, J862 (I:3), comes from a smaller dog with a molar row *ca.* 5 mm. shorter. J855 fits well with an individual about the size of a dingo, whereas J862 points forward to fragments G206 and G323 (I:13, II:4) in Lerna IV and Lerna V respectively.

In the mixed strata of Lerna II and III mandible fragment BD573 and 574 (I:4), the best preserved example found, belongs to a larger individual than J862 in Lerna II.

In Lerna III there are two left mandibles, A438 (I:6) and HTS61 (I:7), both well preserved, HTS61 being much the larger, and some fragments. Mandible A438 has a calculated basal length of 144.5 mm. which approaches B1515 (I:14) in Lerna IV, and gives an individual slightly larger than J862 in Lerna II. The other mandibular fragments belong to more heavily built individuals; HTS61, mentioned above as best preserved, gives a calculated basal length of between 168.3 and 170.8 mm. (the latter figure is a mean from 3 measurements *ad modum* Brinkmann, 1924). HTS61 reveals oligodonty, the first premolar (P_1) is missing, and the premolars are open-planted. This mandible is heavily built, and its corpus decreases distally in

---

[1] All such references are to Plate and number on the Plate.

height (height at P_2–P_3 as compared to height behind M_1 = 80.8%). Its type and proportions are for the most part the same as those of D253 (II:6) in Lerna V; also it shows marks of cutting.

From the same strata we have Mt4 J98 (I:5) which is much larger than any other metatarsal of a dog found in the excavation. Next in size is B1469 (II:8) from Lerna V. This is one proof

TABLE 10

Canis familiaris L.

Dating L	I	II	II+III	III	III+IV	IV	IV+V	IV+La	V	V+VI	V+VII	V+La	VI	VII+V	Class	Roman	S&M	iHG	Total
Cr						4	1		6				4		10				25
Mx		1	1		1	9	1		22	1			3		4				43
Ma		2	2	7	3	34	6		53	11	1	1	13	2	12	1	3	1	152
Tu			1	1		2			4								2		10
PM													1						1
Mo				3		2			1						1				7
At			1				1		1						1		1		4
Ax			1																1
Ve						1							1		17				19
Sc				1		6			11	6					2		2		28
Co						1									51				52
Hu	1		1	2		11	3		12	4			3		4		4		45
Ra						7	2		5	5			2	1	2	1			25
Ul			1			7			17	5			1		2	1			34
Mc		2	1	4		22	4		32				1		4	1	1		72
Ph I															3				3
Ph II															1				1
Ph III															1				1
Pe						3			4				2		4		1		14
Fe						5			2						5				12
Ti				4	1	5	1		5				1		4		1		22
Ca						1			3	1					4				9
Mt		1		3		13			15				1	1	10		1		45
Total	1	6	8	25	5	133	19		193	33	1	1	33	4	142	4	16	1	625
BIND								1							(2)				1
ctm		1		1		9	3		22	1	1		2						40
gn							1										1		2
burn						6			5				1				1		13
healed fracture													1						1
crtr				1									1						2
MIND	1	3	3	4	2	23	4	1	59	9	(1)	(1)	11	1	9	1	2	1	134
neo								1	1										2
y			1			2			1	1		(1)	1		3				9
subad						1			1						2				4
ad	1	3	2	4	2	20	4		56	8	(1)		9	1	4	1	2	1	118
sen													1						1
Tooth missing in:																			
Mx									$2P^2$										$2P^2$
									$2P_2$						$1P_1$				$3P_1$
Ma				$1P_1$					$1P_4$				$1P_2$	$1P_1$	$1P_2$				$4P_2$
																			$1P_4$

Measurement Tables 1–14

that the fragments of dogs found in these lower levels at Lerna are not representative of the species. Mt4 J98 has been compared with available skeletal material of wolves and dogs in the collections of the Museum of Natural History in Stockholm. In size it comes next to a cross between a wolf and a greyhound from the province of Jämtland, N. Sweden. This shows the presence in Lerna III of a race of dogs considerably larger than that represented by the stratified bones analysed above.

Among the bones from mixed Lerna III and IV the only measurable mandible, J475 (I:10), is to be compared, for size and form, with J855 in Lerna II; that is, it comes from a larger dog.

The dog bones from the House of the Tiles are too fragmentary to give any sure measurements.

The first bone to be mentioned in Lerna IV is a fragment of a maxilla, D786 (I:11), which can be certified as coming from the same individual as D781 (I:12). Most of the other fragments of upper jaws (B789, B1504, BC132) are much the same in form and measurements and also much like the corresponding examples in earlier layers. In dealing with the mandibles we may distinguish between two types, one smaller, with a calculated basal length of cranium of 133.7 mm. (Dahr) and 141 mm. (mean value *ad modum* Brinkmann) for B1515 (I:14), and one larger (B362, I:15, and G253) with a calculated basal length of 165.4 mm. and 164.8 mm. (Brinkmann) (cf. Measurement Table 2). The smaller type has been compared already with J862 in Lerna II. Among the humeri which were saved from these strata BD343 and BD617 (I:16) should be specially mentioned. BD617 is the smaller of the two and corresponds well to A456 in Lerna I (maximal length 139.5); that is, it comes from a dog approximately the size of a schnauzer. Lerna IV also has one measured distal part of a humerus, J250 (I:8), somewhat larger than A456 in Lerna I, and an ulna (I:9) going with it.

From the 7 metacarpals which were measured it becomes still clearer that in Lerna IV we have to deal with at least two, possibly three, different sizes of dog, a conclusion which is supported by a look at the rest of the fragments.

The mandibular fragment D781, mentioned above as coming from Lerna IV and belonging with the maxillary D786 to one individual, further D607 (I:19) and the mandibles in mixed Lerna IV and V, D22 and B324 (I:17, 18, respectively), represent different types. D607 (calculated basal length 158.4 mm., Brinkmann) has a short tooth row, densely planted premolars and teeth, overlapping between P_4 and M_1; it decreases considerably in height distally.

D22 is relatively large (calculated basal length of the cranium 169.0 and 170.6); it has a long tooth row which is open planted in the premolar region and its corpus slightly decreases in height distally. Mandible B324 has a short tooth row with open planted premolars (calculated basal length 150.5 and 153.2) and its corpus scarcely decreases in height distally. It seems most probable that these three mandibles represent three different types, or possibly races, of dog: D22 being the same as, for instance, B362 in Lerna IV, B324 the same as DE483 (II:5) in Lerna V, and D607 the same as the much later B334 (II:16) in Classical Lerna (cf. below and Measurement Table 2). The sample in Lerna IV plus Later which contains the fragments of a puppy does not contribute to the picture.

Among the numerous dog bones of Lerna V maxilla B1472 (II:2) comes from the same individual as does one mandible from the same lot (II:3). In two maxillae, A325 and B1472, both P_2s are missing (oligodonty). There are six fragments from skulls, none measurable, but the maxillae show only small differences in measurements. Of the 53 fragments of mandibles 20 have marks of cutting and 5 show traces of burning (BE420, DE490). The calculated basal length for the smallest individual is 134.4 mm. (mean of the 3 calculations after Brinkmann/ *ad modum* Dahr for the same jaws give the values 138.7 and 141.6; cf., for instance G323, II:4). The bulk, however, of jaws (cf. Measurement Table 2) of type DE490 (= 2 individuals) and D253 (II:6) fall within the calculated range of basal lengths 151.0–175.0 mm.

(for both methods), and one single specimen, BE198 (II:7), corresponds to a basal length of 181 mm. (Brinkmann) and 188 mm. (Dahr).

The measured fragments of humeri, the metacarpals and metatarsals and pelves, as well as the other measurable parts strengthen my opinion that in Lerna V we are dealing with at least two, possibly three, different types of dog. In mixed Lerna V and VI measurements and calculated length for one measurable mandible, B735 (II:9), 153.2 mm. *ad modum* Dahr, suggests mandible G206 in Lerna IV for instance; that is, it comes from an individual slightly larger than a modern schnauzer. The only fragment of dog in Lerna V and VII, mandible D565, belongs to a small type of dog which we will find, for example, in Lerna VI exemplified by mandibles in B733 (II:10), the measured length of the molar row being 30.2 and 32 mm. Mandible D565 is characterized by a corpus which is thin behind M_1; its ascending part goes up more steeply than in the other mandibles of the collection; also its corpus is more twisted along its long axis than are the others. The consequence of this is that the molar row is less straight (more S-formed) as seen from above (from the chewing surface) than in the others. The molar row is also short, and P_4 overlaps M_1 at its proximal end. The few fragments from Lerna V and Surface and Mixed and from Lerna V and Later do not require any comments.

In Lerna VI again we observe three different types of dog: one smaller, mandible DE456 (II:11), calculated basal length 130 mm. (Dahr), one medium or rather larger, DE452, basal length 173.5 mm., and one still larger, B733 (II:12) and B1536 (II:13). The length of both of the carnassials of the last two mandibles is 22.3, and in the whole collection this is surpassed only by BE198 (II:7) in Lerna V with its 23.2 mm. (cf. Measurement Table 2). Furthermore it should be mentioned that oligodonty is found in one mandible in Lerna VI, F18–19, which has no P_2. In mandible D243 from Lerna VII and V P_1 is missing, and this affects the calculation of its basal length, 141.6 mm. (Dahr). Its corpus is robust and decreases only slightly in height distally.

In the Classical strata we meet a new size of dog, a small type with oligodonty (P_1 and P_2 missing) exemplified by B334 (II:14 and 15). The state of preservation does not allow any calculation of the basal length. Another type of mandible, also B334 (II:16), has a considerably higher corpus behind M_1, and its distal part decreases more rapidly and strongly (distally). Its basal length is calculated as 176.4 mm. (Dahr) and its buccal region just at M_1 is clearly concave. Its corpus is longitudinally twisted, and as a result, the tooth row becomes S-formed (cf. D565 in Lerna V and VII, II:1, or B733 in Lerna VI, II:10, both of these, however, being much more gracile). In Classical times we certainly must reckon with at least one (possibly two) new races of dogs which will, of course, show combinations with the types known earlier.

The few fragments of dog bones from Roman times do not give any additional information, but from Surface and Mixed we have the medial part of a mandible, BE37 (II:17), of the same type as B334 (II:16) from Classical Lerna, with the corpus height decreasing strongly distally. However, its concavity of the buccal surface at M_1 is not as obvious as in B334.

COMMENTS:

The distribution of the total of 625 fragments of dog bones from the different strata is to be found in Table 10. In my opinion the most notable feature in this material, which represents a minimum number of 134 individuals, is that no single complete cranium could be found, nor even one intact neurocranium (brain-pan). Nor is it possible to make a reconstruction of a skull from well preserved parts of one individual. This fact and the presence in almost every stratum of marks of cutting on the mandibles and other bones (cf. Table 10), as well as the absence of most of the ascending processes of the lower jaws, forces us to conclude that the fur of the dogs was used, and that the meat and the brains made a desirable contribution to the food supply for considerable periods. It is known from earlier observations on skeletal material that dog meat was highly esteemed. We will not discuss this matter in detail here, but the reader is referred to Boessneck (1956, 1963, and his bibliographies), Oberdorfer (1959), Petri (1961), and Lepiksaar (1962).

The marks of cutting on the dog mandibles and the distal parts of the extremity bones must not necessarily be interpreted as proof that the meat was eaten. In our material, however, we also have marks of cutting on humeri and pelves, that is in the parts of the body where the large muscular concentrations are found, which makes it seem most probable that the meat was cut from the bones to be used for food. It is also clear that no special kind of dog was preferred for food; bones from the small, medium, and larger specimens show marks of cutting.

Careful observation with a magnifying glass of the mandibles with marks of cutting shows that the knife usually penetrated just below the outer side of the articular process (cf. A345 in Lerna V, III:1). In some cases marks could be seen also on the ascending processus muscularis mandibulae (A345) and in a few specimens also in more distal parts of the jaw, either on the lingual side (G323 in Lerna V, III:2, a young animal), or on the buccal side (DE497). Usually it is not difficult to distinguish between such lesions and those that have been made during excavation and transportation. Nor could these marks be confused with the worm-like, winding, sometimes net-like grooves that were caused by the erosive action of acids in penetrating rootlets in the soil which are often to be seen in bone material from excavations, cf. mandible BD343 in Lerna IV (III:3). Occasionally traces of gnawing may also be found on dog bones.

WOLF

Table 11

Canis lupus L.

Dating L	Lerna III	V	Total
Cr		1	1
Ul		1	1
Mc	1		1
Total	1	2	3
MIND; ad	1	1	2

Measurement Tables 15–16

Of these three fragments only two, the metacarpus 5, HTJ14 (XVIII:1), in Lerna III, and the ulna D595 (XVIII:2), in Lerna V, could be measured. The skull fragment, B766 of Lerna V (XVIII:3), includes part of the left zygomatic and temporal and the left parietal bone. In comparison with the Neolithic fragments of wolves that are published by Boessneck (1963, pp. 24, 25) the measured fragments from Lerna come from more heavily built individuals. This is especially true for our metacarpus (Mc5) which surpasses the maximal length of the corresponding part in the material cited by 7 mm., while the minimum breadth of its diaphysis is 1.5 mm. larger. Also the Lernaean skull fragment B766 gives the impression of coming from a larger specimen. No regular measurements could be obtained from this fragment. In Ellerman and Morrison-Scott's *Checklist* (p. 53) the present occurrence of the wolf in Europe and the course of its gradual disappearance from this continent is followed. The western boundaries of its appearance in Russia are said to show much variability while there are mentions of its temporary occurrence in areas south of Roumania-Bulgaria-Jugoslavia as well as in Greece and northern Turkey. Papadopoulo (1934, p. 295) in his survey of the fauna of Greece reports that the wolf is very rare in the Peloponnese and extinct on Crete, but that it still kills many thousands of sheep and goats, cattle and other domestic animals in northern parts of the kingdom. In connection with this point we should not forget the statements quoted by Boessneck (1958, p. 53) about the increasing appearance and more settled character of the wolf in East Germany after World War II.

Thus it seems most natural to find specimens of this dreaded carnivore in prehistoric layers at a site of the type and extent of Lerna.

WILD BOAR AND DOMESTIC PIG

TABLE 12

Sus scrofa L.

Dating L	I	II	II+III	III	III+IV	IV	IV+V	V	V+VI	VI	VII+V	Class S&M	S&M	Total
Cr	2	1		1		4		8	1	2	1			20
Mx				1		10	1	1		5				18
Ma	1			2		11		3		6				23
Tu				3		1		3		1				8
Mo						1								1
Sc						4		5		5				14
Hu				2	1	3		3		2				11
Ra				2						2				4
Ul	1			1		7		2		2				13
Mc			1	5		1		1						8
Pe										1				1
Ti								1		1		1	1	4
Mt				1		1								2
Total	4	1	1	18	1	43	1	27	1	27	1	1	1	127
ctm						1								1
gn						1		1						2
wkd								1						1
MIND	1	1	1	2	—	8	1	3	1	4	1	1	1	25
y	1					2		1					1	5
subad						2				1				3
ad		1	1	2		4	1	2	1	3	1	1		17

Measurement Tables 17–27

The distinction between wild and domestic pig in a collection such as this one, with the kind of fragments which make it up, is inevitably somewhat arbitrary. It is a characteristic of pig bones that they are more crushed, more fragmentary, with fewer measurable pieces, and more gnawed than are those of any other species. The numerous marks of gnawing and their peculiar appearance are partly the result of the activities of dogs which found these bones and the fat that adhered to them attractive. Strong fragmentation occurs in all layers and affects all parts of the skeleton; for instance, very often the small metapodial bones of young animals may have been completely consumed, as has been said to be the case in the Northern countries (cf. Lepiksaar, 1965). As a result of this we have in all the layers and phases a very small

TABLE 13

Sus domesticus and transitional

Dating L	I	I+II	II	II+III	II+S&M	III	III+IV	IV	IV+V	IV+La	V	V+VI	V+VII	V+La	V+Class	V+Class+S&M	VI	VI+La	VII	VII+V	VII+LH+S&M	VII+Class	Class	Class+S&M	Roman	S&M	Unatt	iHG	Total
Cr	8	2	26	16		10	6	72	15		94	6					12		1		2					7		1	272
Mx	1	1	17	10		20	15	187	33		320	6	2				57		1	5						16			691
Ma	4	1	22	24	1	45	25	275	38	1	414	6	8				135		8	22		2	4	2		23	1	4	1067
Inc	1					5	2	11			8	1												1		1			32
Tu			3	2		9	2	29	3		45	2		1			1						1	1	1	5			104
PM											2																		3
Mo	1		3	1		3	1	14			23													1		2			48
Ax	1					2					2			1															5
Ve		1				3		7			10						3									1			25
Sc	1	2	19	11		30	23	162	19		188	3	2				44		2	1				2		17			526
Co						1		8			2																		9
Hu	4		12	17		18	13	87	15		98	1					25	1	2	3						16		1	313
Ra		1	15	5		21	6	58	3	1	74	1					33		1	1			3	1		8	1		232
Ul		1	11	7		11		83	8	1	88	1					20	1		3			1			9	1		246
Mc	2	1	7	10		15	4	46			63						15			3						6		1	174
Ph I	1					3		4			7																		15
Ph II							1	1			4															1		1	8
Ph III								1			2																		3
Sa											1																		1
Pe	2		4	3		6	2	17	2		32						16							1		2			84
Fe		1	3	5		5	2	8	3		12						14			2						5			58
Ti	1	1	8			18	6	36	9		36						24		4							6	1		155
Fi						1					2																		3
Ta	4	1		1		2	4	14			9						1			1						1			33
Ca	1					4		7			4															1			17
Mt	2		7	1		4	1	8			1	1					7											1	34
Total	34	12	157	115	1	236	109	1135	149	3	1539	23	12	2	1	1	407	2	19	42	2	2	9	7	1	127	3	8	4158
BIND								1			2																		3
ctm								1			1						2												4
gn								1			8															1			10
path	1		1			1					1						1												4
burn				1		14	1	8	3		7															1			36
wkd																													1
bronze								1																					1
MIND	4	3	11	12	1	23	18	121	20	1	203	4	5	2	1	1	68	2	6	12	1	1	3	1	1	11	2	7	545
Neo	1	1	1			1	1	5			4			1	1		5	1	1			1							22
y	1	1	4	3		4	4	18	2		37	1	1	1			16		2	3		1	1			2	1		100
subad	1		1	3		2	2	24	9		41	3	1	1		1	5	1	2	3						4		2	104
ad	2	1	5	5	1	16	10	72	7	1	118	3	3	1			41		1	6	1	1	2	1	1	5	1	5	310
sen				1			1	2	1		3						1												9

number of measured fragments of pig bones used in this study in comparison with the total number of pig bones examined and identified.

Our division of the pig bones depends in the first place on tracing the subadult, the adult and the older specimens of the two categories from the bottom to the top layers and strata. Only in cases where newly born and young individuals are found in the same samples as adult specimens of either wild or domestic pig have they been registered as one or the other on the grounds of probability. For this reason very few younger individuals have been registered as *Sus scrofa*. Of course this does not give a really accurate picture of the distribution, but we have chosen this way of publishing the material from the purely practical point of view.

In Table 3 the number of fragments of pig which were originally assigned as wild and domestic can be readily seen. They are 127 and 4,386 respectively, but it should be mentioned that the latter figure includes 228 unidentifiable splinters of bone which, because of their size, the appearance of the section, and the thickness of their walls, have been classed as domestic without more exact identification. Here as always when this kind of work is to be done for a difficult collection of bones one has to make a decision weighing time against results, keeping in mind the fact that indefinite time can be devoted to any osteological material with a very slight improvement of the results. We have chosen the less time consuming method of grouping together the smaller fragments and splinters after having determined more accurately the category of as many as possible of the larger fragments. This makes our total figure of identified bones and fragments lower, but makes for greater reliability in the results, which could be seriously distorted if every little splinter were given the same value in the calculation of the minimum number of individuals as we give to a larger fragment in species whose bones are less damaged or even complete.

Furthermore we have tried to note for each mandibular or maxillary fragment as well as for loose teeth, which could be identified, the approximate age of the individual. The estimation of the approximate age at slaughtering or killing has been done according to the method of Silver (1963), and both groups of pigs, wild and domestic, have been treated the same way. The result of this investigation is seen in Table 9.

In all the phases which have many pig bones it can be said that the percentage of newly born and very young pigs is small, not over 4%, though this figure is probably a little too low as a result of the loss of more fragments of young individuals than of adults. For individuals aged from about half a year to one year, the percentage of slaughter increases to well over 35%, and during periods which are the best represented, that is Early Helladic II, III and Middle Helladic (Lerna III, IV, and V) it amounts to around 15% to 20% of the minimum number of mandibles registered. During these three periods approximately the same percentage of pigs one to two years old were slaughtered, while animals two to three years old formed more than half of the total. The estimated number of individuals older than three years from Lerna IV and V is between 0 and 2% of the total for these settlements, leaving aside the fact that not all, but 95.6% and 92.8%, of the mandibular fragments have been determined according to side.

The attempt to find fragments suitable for tracing the domestication of the pig in Lerna has been concentrated, during the primary registration, on the search for intact lacrymal bones. This was done because, in the study of animal domestication (cf. Hilzheimer, 1926), it was observed long ago that the lacrymal bone was affected by the shortening of the snout which took place during the domestication of the pig. We have tried to exclude the lacrymals of younger individuals in order to have a series of fully grown adult lacrymals from different settlements for our special purpose of measuring their height-length index. This is shown in Diagram no. 2. Morphologically the lacrymals may be divided into two groups, one larger, flatter, oblong to rectangular, with a height-length index of *ca.* 54 (cf. D652 in Lerna IV,

IV:14), and the other smaller, less flat, usually more rugged, with more pronounced ridges and pits, more quadratic in form and with breadth-length index ranging from *ca.* 60–85 (cf. D591 in Lerna V, IV:15).

It is obvious that the lacrymals which were saved must include those of both wild boar and pigs in a state of primitive and full domestication. The first important thing we find from these bones and their measurements, as well as from the other bone material investigated, is that the people of Lerna II, that is the Middle Neolithic period, already had the domestic pig.

By separating the lacrymals of young, subadult and adult individuals of wild and domestic pig we have made clear some of their characteristics which should be mentioned briefly: a) Lacrymals of infantile and young individuals are naturally much smaller in size, they have much thinner walls, and they are somewhat shorter than in adults, at least when measured at the facial surface. But they already show the form they will achieve in the full-grown state. On the other hand the deeper portion of the distal end often stretches farther out than does the superficial portion. Between the superficial and deeper portions is a groove which receives the maxillary bone. The form of this groove is variable.

b) In adults of both wild boar and domestic pig the lacrymal bone has its maximum extent in the superficial area, the form of the bone in adult wild males being mostly rectangular with the height less in proportion to the length. The bone shortens from the state of primitive to full domestication, and its form changes from triangular or tetrahedric to being more or less quadratic.

In Diagram 2 it is perhaps impossible to discern the limits between individuals in a primitive state of domestication and those that were fully domesticated. This is especially true since other measurable fragments (cf. Measurement Tables 18–27) of domestic pig also occur from Lerna II onwards while wild boar probably existed in all layers and is still to be found in the Peloponnese. However, as the same diagram shows, the proportion between maximum length and height of the lacrymals seems to follow a slightly different pattern in domestic specimens from that in the wild with the result that the main type of spread in the measurements of domestic specimens has a steeper angle than it has in the wild. The differentiation between wild and domestic pig in the list of our material must therefore be arbitrary to a certain extent, a point which has been stressed by various authors dealing with other material of this kind. Instead of dealing in detail here with all the work that has been done we will refer to the work of Opitz (1958) and his review of the literature.

To return again to the picture given in Diagram 2 one would like to assume that the two individuals at the upper right, which are from Lerna IV, were adult wild boars, that the medial group of individuals, mostly from Lerna V, were wild and primitively domesticated pigs, and that the rest of the specimens in the left section of the diagram were domestic pigs. A further division is hardly possible.

It was mentioned above that the domestic pig occurs already in Lerna II. In this Middle Neolithic settlement its size has greatly decreased from that of the wild pig, as can be seen in Measurement Table 17 (cf. upper jaw J855 in Lerna II, IV:9). Other examples of the large difference in size between wild and tame specimens are the third metacarpal bone BD312 in Lerna IV (IV:1), which measures 98.2 mm. in maximal length, and the second metacarpal from a domestic animal B1536a in Lerna VI (IV:13), maximal length 63.0 mm. Corresponding figures will be given in the monograph on the bones from Troy which is in preparation. In both cases we are dealing with adult specimens.

At first glance the existence of widely differing types of tear bones of *Sus* gives the impression of two different "races," and the conclusion which we have outlined above must be taken as a conjecture. But there are other possible interpretations of Diagram 2 which must be discussed at this time. In the literature on the lacrymal bone in the pig it is often mentioned that the form, especially the proportion between height and length, is different in the two types of wild boar, the European *Sus scrofa* L. and the eastern Asiatic *Sus vittatus* (Müller and Schlegel), which are usually supposed to have participated in the formation of the domestic pig, although the details of the development are still far from clear. There is also in the Mediterranean a group of wild specimens (*Sus meridionalis*, Major) which is believed to be intermediate between the European and the East Asiatic groups. In addition we must mention the opinion advanced by many students and summed up, for instance, by Zeuner (1963, pp. 256 ff.) that the domestic pig is nearly everywhere derived from local wild forms.

But if to this is added the fact that two different types of domestic pig occurred together with wild boar in middle and south Europe during the Neolithic period, one the small turbary pig (*Sus palustris*, Rütimeyer) believed to have been introduced from the East, and the other, somewhat later, the result of domestication of the local wild boar (*Sus scrofa*), we may begin to look at our Diagram 2 from another point of view. Is it perhaps possible that our shortest lacrymal bones in the left part of the diagram ranging between Lerna IV and Lerna V represent the domestic breed introduced from the East?

Before we leave the question of the pigs in Lerna let us glance at the other measurable pig bones from the site (Measurement Tables 18–27).

Maximal length and breadth could be obtained from three upper tusks of wild boar, one from Lerna IV, BE559 (IV:2), and two from Lerna V, DE221 (IV:4) and DE548. From Lerna V comes a third tusk, a lower, B1472 (IV:5) which has been worked.

We have only one measurable third molar from the lower jaw of a wild boar, G276 in Lerna IV (IV:6), with a maximum length of 48.2 mm. and a distal breadth of 19 mm. These measurements fit almost exactly with those of the wild sows in Boessneck's (1963) material from Burgäschisee-Süd.

One distal part of a humerus, D563 (IV:3), comes from Lerna IV, and its dimensions are somewhat smaller than those of the wild specimens in the Argissa Magula material from Thessaly (Boessneck, 1962). There is, however, no doubt about its character. Turning to the ulna we find one proximal end from Lerna IV, B1466 (IV:7), with the same dimensions as an example in the Argissa Magula material from Early Thessalian II. Finally, in the case of the two remaining measurable bones, one Mc3, BD312 (IV:1), and one Mt4, J229 (IV:8), both from Lerna IV, the measurements indicate large beasts of the *Sus scrofa* group, larger in fact than any in the series published by Boessneck in 1963.

The first appearance of the domesticated pig as shown by this material had already taken place in Lerna II whence comes the upper jaw fragment J855 (IV:9) of the same size as those, for instance, from Middle Thessalian I onwards in Argissa Magula (*op. cit.*, p. 95). Domestic pigs of the same size occur in Lerna IV and Lerna V as seen in our Measurement Tables 24 and 26 for humerus and tibia. Also in Lerna VI we have domestic pigs, partly of small size, as seen in the metapodials B1536 b and a (IV:12,13).

Two pathological changes must be mentioned, both in tibiae of domestic pigs, one from Lerna III and IV, A445 (IV:10), and one from Lerna V, B1461 (IV:11), both of which seem to be the result of fractures showing large callous formations as sequelae. Cf. also X-ray, Plate XXV:1,2.

SHEEP AND GOAT

TABLE 14

Ovis et Capra

Dating L	I	I+II	II	II+III	II+S&M	III	III+IV	IV	IV+V	V	V+VI	V+VII	V+La	V+Class	V+Cl+S&M	VI	VII	VII+V	VII+Class	Class	Class+S&M	Roman	S&M	iHG	Total
Hc	2		5	2		6	3	38		48	1					1								2	108
Cr	1		10	1		2		9		9						6	1	1					3	1	41
Mx	1		6	4		2	1	45		55						14	5	7	1				3	3	134
Ma	18	9	51	40		45	16	256	23	276	13	1		2	1	189				2	4		20	3	982
Inc							1																		1
PM								1																	8
Mo	18	3	18	5	1	35	12	105	7	154	1	3				4	1	4		3			8	3	385
At			1													3								1	5
Ax	1			1		2		1								1								1	6
Ve			3			2		2		6						12							2		26
Sc	7	3	38	9		27	8	173	12	88			1			31	1			2	3		4	1	406
Co			10			1		4		12															31
Hu	5	4	10	22		23	5	74	6	64	1					19		5		1			14		253
Ra	6	1	12	14	1	26	8	58	2	60	1	1				15		5		2	2		12	1	227
Ul	1	1	4	3		5	2	22	2	17		1				11		1					2	1	72
Mc	6	5	24	14		28	5	55	6	55		1	1			14	2	4		1			7	1	228
Ph I	2	1	4	2		1	2	2		7						1									23
Ph II	1							2																	3
Ph III										2															2
Sa								1																	1
Pe	7	3	18	4		6		18	3	16						25							3	1	105
Fe	3		4	7		8		5		15						13		8					3		58
Ti	7	4	18	28		35	7	60	8	59	1					36	1			1	2	1	18		294
Ta			4	1		3		18	1	13						2		4					1		41
Ca	1		1	3		5		9	5	8						2	1	1					7		35
Mt		2	8	4	1	17	2	24		31		1				17	2			2	1	1			122
Total	87	36	250	165	3	284	72	982	75	995	18	5	2	2	1	416	13	40	1	14	12	1	107	16	3597
BIND	1								1	1															3
ctm	1					1																			2
path						3		4																	7
burn		3	1	2		6	1	7	1	13													8		44
wkd			1																						1
MIND	11	6	25	19	1	26	8	119	20	137	7	2	2	1	1	94	3	5	1	3	3	1	10	14	519
neo	2	1	2	1		2		3		3						4							1	1	19
y	1	3	10	6		6	1	14	2	20	1	1		1		12	1	1		1	1		1	1	84
subad	2		1			3	2	26	3	20		1		1		6		1	1	1			1		67
ad	6	2	12	12	1	14	5	74	15	89	6		1		1	70	2	3		2	2	1	8	11	339
sen						1		2		5						2									10

Measurement Tables 28–45

TABLE 15

Ovis aries L.

Dating L	I	II	II+III	III	III+IV	IV	IV+V	V	V+VI	VI	VII	S&M	Total
Hc			1	2	1	5	3	15		1	1	1	30
Cr		1				4		4	1				10
Mx						1		2					3
Ma		2				4		7	1				14
Mo		2						2					4
At								2					2
Ve								23					23
Sc		2				1		4					7
Co								40					40
Hu				2				4					6
Ra			1					6		2			9
Ul								4		1			5
Mc		1				3		5		4			13
Ph I								8					8
Ph II								8					8
Ph III								8					8
Pe								3					3
Fe		1						5					6
Ti	1	1	1					4					7
Ta	1							4					5
Ca	1							5					6
Mt		1						4		2	1		8
Total	3	11	3	4	1	18	3	167	2	10	2	1	225
BIND								1					1
ctm								2					2
gn					1								1
MIND	1	2	1	1	1	3	2	9	1	4	1	1	27
y		1				1		1					3
subad								1					1
ad	1	1	1	1		3	2	7	1	4	1	1	23

Measurement Tables 28–45

It is not an overstatement to say that, in regard to sheep and goats, osteology has until recently been moving along the wrong roads. For the correction of this error we are all deeply indebted to three European scientists, J. Boessneck, H.-H. Müller, and M. Teichert. It is to be regretted that the monograph by these three authors which recently appeared (1964) was not at hand for the study of all the bone collections previously excavated, including the Lerna collection. This splendid work makes it possible to separate morphologically almost every bone of sheep and goat, and to learn to do so in a relatively short time. It ought to be translated into a number of other languages and, above all, its original drawings which are masterpieces of precision and skill (which is not to be seen in the publication) should be printed on paper of a much better quality.

The fact that this publication was not available during the first phase of our work affects our records of identified bones of sheep and goats in this way: the greater number of them were registered under the headings for "sheep and goat," and only certain fragments, especially horn-cores, and some distinguishable metacarpals and metatarsals, have been assigned to the proper species from the beginning.

If we look at Table 3 (p. 6) for the material from each settlement we find that the figures for both absolute and relative numbers of identified sheep and goat bones and the certified bones of

TABLE 16

Capra hircus L.

Dating L	II	II+III	III	III+IV	IV	IV+V	V	V+VI	V+VII	VI	VII	VII+V	Class	S&M	Unatt	Total
Hc	4	6	21	8	115	30	120	6	2	10	2	2	2	8	1	337
Cr	11		1		3	3	1							1		20
Mx			1	2	7	3	10									23
Ma	12	8	7	2	73	18	66	3	1	1		2	2	8		203
Mo			3		32	8	31			1			1	2	1	79
Sc	2		2	3	8		16							2	1	34
Co					10											10
Hu	1		2	1	3	3	6						2	3		21
Ra	1		1		3	2	4				1					12
Ul					2		2									4
Mc	2		5	3	17	3	18			5				1		54
Ph I					1		1									2
Ph II							1									1
Ph III							1									1
Pe	1				3					2						6
Fe			1		1		2									4
Ti			4	1	6		7							1		19
Ta					2											2
Ca			1													1
Mt	1		3	2	11	3	7					1		2		30
Total	35	14	52	22	297	73	293	9	3	19	3	5	7	28	3	863
ctm		1			1		1	1	3							7
path			1		3		5									9
burn					6		1									7
MIND	8	4	6	2	37	11	38	3	2	8	1	1	1	3	1	126
neo					1		1									2
y	1		3		5	2	5	1	1	1	1			1	1	22
subad	3	2	1		5	1	4							1		17
ad	4	2	2	2	24	7	27	2	1	7		1	1	1		81
sen					2	1	1									4

Measurement Tables 28–43

each species follow the same pattern throughout the whole collection, at least in general lines, and that the most striking difference between them is the high frequency of horn-cores of goat and the low frequency of sheep. The explanation of this may be the normal one that some, perhaps many, of the sheep were hornless, and that a great many of the young males were killed before their horns had appeared. In the same table we see that of all the identified fragments in the group more than one-third were registered as "*Capra* and *Ovis*." If we trace both species from Lerna I on (excluding uncertified strata) we will find their relative frequency as follows:

Lerna	I	II	III	IV	V	VI	VII
Percentage of caprovines in each settlement	54.6	50.1	40.4	33.1	30.0	40.1	24.3
Percentage of total material in each settlement	1.3	4.8	6.9	32.0	39.5	9.0	0.6

The caprovine bone pieces from Lerna I consist of 90 fragments, most of which are tiny splinters and slivers designated as *Ovis* and *Capra* in the list referred to above. However, the few bones that can be measured and come from the same animal (Measurement Tables 39–41), i.e. one distal end of a right tibia, one talus and one calcaneus, all A462, probably on the basis of the new criteria (Boessneck *et al.*, 1964) belong to a sheep (V:1,2,3).

From mixed layers of Lerna I and II we have registered 36 fragments and small splinters as belonging to the group of sheep and goat.

Although there are no less than 250 fragments registered as sheep and goat in Lerna II, and only 11 fragments which for stratigraphical reasons have been taken together as sheep and 35 which, for the same reason, have been counted as coming from goats, we have no measurable pieces which could shed any light on the types represented.

The same thing is almost true of the mixed layers of Lerna II and III from which we have only three measurable fragments: one horn-core of a *Capra*, BD581 (VI:1), one radius and one distal part of a tibia of *Ovis*, both BD577 (V:8,9). The ovine character of the radius was certified by comparison, and the tibia probably belongs to the same individual. The goat is represented by a reconstructed horn-core, with a sharp frontal edge and with marks of cutting, from an adult male, BD581. It is a solidly built moderately twisted horn-core measuring 60 mm. near the base with a minimum diameter of 31 mm. at the same place.

In Lerna III (EH II) the goat is represented by two measurable fragments of horn-cores, A476 (VI:2) which is cut off before the base, long, thin and slightly twisted, and which comes either from a castrate or a female, and D743 (VI:3), even more heavily built than BD581 in Lerna II and III but less crested, from an adult animal, probably a male.

The sheep is also found in the material from this settlement, but there are very few fragments that could be used for comparison. Two distal parts of humeri, one left and one right, A477a and b (V:10,11), both came probably from the same individual. From Lerna III we have a distal end of a tibia with heavy sequelae of arthrosis or arthritis deformans, G43 (V:4). Its deformation makes it impossible to determine it more accurately (cf. X-ray, Plate XXV:3).

Mixed layers of Lerna III and IV have contributed to the picture one horn-core of a young animal, J268 (V:5). Its distal end has been gnawed and its form is rather goatlike, but it is not impossible that it belongs to the sheep group. The same thing is true for the horn-core G65 (V:6) from Lerna IV which comes from a still younger individual and is also rather goatlike.

Lerna IV is rich in remains of sheep and goat; 982 fragments and splinters have been assigned to the mixed group, 297 fragments to goat including no less than 115 fragments of horn-cores, and 18 to sheep. It is, however, most probable, because of the difficulty of distinguishing small fragments and broken pieces of shaft bones, that the mixed group contains a great many sheep.

A selection of measurable fragments of horn-cores of goats from Lerna III and IV, IV, IV and V is to be seen in Measurement Table 28; it shows a rather striking conformity. The first example, A38 (VI:4, Lerna III and IV), comes from a young male, while the rest, A361 (VI:5), B1507 (VI:6), BD625 (VI:7), BE558 (VI:8), D787a (VI:9), D787b and D21 (VI:10, Lerna IV and V) are from females, BE558 a young animal, the others adults. They are all saber-form and, except for D787b, very slightly twisted.

Measurement Tables 36, 37, 42 and 43 show the rest of the measurable goat bones from Lerna IV: two metacarpalia, A445 (VII:10, Lerna III and IV) and A447 (VII:12), the latter with a pathological change in the diaphysis; one metacarpal, D607 (VII:11); one proximal part of a metatarsal with heavy medial pathological changes, D784:II (VII:13); one phalanx I B329 (VII:14), also with pathological changes in the distal part; a distal left part of a mandible which is so seriously changed by a pathological alteration in the premolar alveolar region that it is impossible to tell whether it comes from a sheep or goat, J465 (V:7); two halves of pelves, both from lot A479, one left and one right but from different individuals, have been registered as goat.

Sheep are represented by one right mandible and one metacarpal, both from lot B1507 and from the same individual, and one left metacarpal, BD308, and one small horn-core of a young animal, D21 (V:12, Lerna IV and V).

From certified Lerna V come no less than 1455 identified fragments of sheep and goat, exclusive of a sample of fragments of one separate individual (BIND). The estimated minimum number of individuals and the age distribution can be seen in Table 14.

From the sheep in Lerna V we have a relatively well preserved left side horn-core, DE496(V:13), of a ram; there is also a left mandible, DE497 (VII:2), probably not from the same individual, but the radius DE497 (VII:4) and the metacarpal DE496 (VII:5) may belong to the same animal as this mandible. There is also a skull fragment from a young individual, B1471 (VII:1), and a humerus, DE533 (VII:3), the measurements of which can be seen in Measurement Table 33.

Turning to the goat in Lerna V we find three horn-cores, DE496, DE532, and DE543, all from she-goats, with the same sabre-form as the horn mentioned in Lerna IV but without any twisting. In mixed Lerna V and VII there is one horn-core of a he-goat with strong twisting. This specimen probably comes from a larger animal but it is cut off *ca.* 14 cm. from the tip so no measurements can be made. The extremity bones of goat are represented in this period by one metacarpal and a pair of metatarsals of a ram(?), all B1481 (VII:15, 16, 17). A proximal end of a metatarsal, B1472 (VII:20), a phalanx I and a fused phalanx II and III, all B1481 (VII:18,19), have the most developed and strongly deforming sequelae of arthritic disease found in the whole collection, and must belong to the same individual (X-Ray, Plate XXV:4,5,6).

The number of bones from Lerna VI is much smaller than from earlier periods and comes from less diversified finding places; most of it is from DE452, DE456, and lots B733 and B1536, that is from bothroi and the Shaft Graves. One would, therefore, not be inclined to pay as much attention to it or to attach the same value to the results that come from studying it. It is, however, notable that in Lerna VI the sheep bones as well as the cattle bones are smaller than in the earlier settlements. In Lerna VI sheep is represented by one horn-core, one ulna, B733 (VII:6), two radii, B1536 (VII:7), three right and one left metacarpus (of three individuals) and one complete and one damaged right metatarsal of B733 and B1536 (VII:8,9). One of these metacarpals, B1536a, is probably from a ram, the others from ewes.

Of the remaining caprovine material one skull fragment, J455 (V:14, Surface and Mixed) is well enough preserved to deserve mention. It is a left horn-core base of a sheep, probably a ram. Its form is very much the same as that of the wild sheep in Cyprus, the mufflon, *Ovis ammon ophion* Blyth, but it is of much smaller dimensions. It is just a few mm. larger in maximal diameter at the base than is Boessneck's specimen (1962, p. 30, plate 12, fig. 2) from the prepottery pit (Grube a⁰) in Argissa Magula in Thessaly.

To conclude this short summary of the material from the small ruminants we can say that the increase in the total number of sheep and goats in Lerna bears a normal relation to the increase in the total quantity of bone material, but that during Lerna IV and V there is a trend towards more goats and fewer sheep, and in Lerna VI a trend to a smaller race. We will return later to possible reasons for this and its implications.

WILD OX AND DOMESTIC CATTLE

TABLE 17

Bos primigenius Boj.

Dating L	I	I+II	II	III	IV	IV+V	V	Total
Hc				1	1			2
Cr	3				2			5
PM				1				1
Mo				3		2		5
Sc			1					1
Ra		1				1	1	3
Mc				1				1
Ph I	2					1	1	4
Ph II						1	1	2
Ph III			1					1
Fe	1							1
Ta	1						1	2
Ca			1					1
Mt	1			1			1	3
Total	8	1	3	7	3	5	5	32
ctm	1	1	1	1	1			5
MIND	5	1	3	3	2	1	4	19
subad	1			1				2
ad	4	1	3	2	2	1	4	17

Measurement Tables 46–48, 50, 51, 53, 55, 57–61.

In bone samples which are like those from Lerna in size and composition and which include successive layers from the Neolithic period onwards from a continent closely connected to the European mainland, one can always expect to find both wild and domesticated cattle, as well as different stages of domestication in individuals. The problem, however, with the bones of such animals has always been to separate the wild group from the primitively tamed.

For reasons which are self evident, we must expect to find all transitional stages of size and form from the large bulls of the wild cattle that strayed in the mighty woods and open fields of the Peloponnese and constituted the most desirable game (which produced the most meat) of the early settlers of Lerna to the tiny short-horned and probably inbred domestic cattle that were associated with the densely populated settlements of the late Middle Helladic and early Late Helladic and later periods.

Our enumeration and assignment of the cattle fragments to the wild or domestic breeds must for various reasons be arbitrary, especially when it comes to younger individuals of wild ox; and it will always be difficult, not to say hazardous, to tell whether a horn-core or a third molar (to take just two examples) of large size from Lerna V belongs to a small specimen of wild or a large specimen of domesticated cattle. Hence we have registered no neonatal or young individuals as wild, and very few subadults (cf. Table 17), so that these age groups will be overrepresented in our lists of domestic cattle.

This problem has been dealt with extensively by Boessneck (1963) and the authors he has cited (B. K. Hescheler and J. Rueger, 1942; M. Degerbøl, 1942; E. Drottens, 1947; G. Nobis, 1943; J. Boessneck, 1957, and others). The result of their studies is that for a series of important collections of material the transitional group between wild and domesticated animals has been somewhat diminished.

TABLE 18

Bos domesticus and transitional

Dating L	I	I+II	II	II+III	II+S&M	III	III+IV	IV	IV+V	IV+La	V	V+VI	V+VII	VI	VI+La	VII	V+VII	VII+LH+S&M	VII+Class	Class	Class+S&M	S&M	Unatt	iHG	Total
Hc			2	2		5	3	65	14		67	1	1	3		1	1			1		5			171
Cr		2	2	3		5	2	16			20		1	1			1				1	4		1	57
Mx	1	1		1		1		26	2	1	10	1		8						1	1	1			52
Ma	4		4	9		9	3	92	18		138	1	2	16		3	5					8			315
Inc			1			2	1	7	2		4											2			19
PM				1		3	2	19	4		23	1					1					5			58
Mo	1	2	14	10		15	9	165	28		186	2	1	6		3	1			1	2	18	1	4	469
At								5	1		3			2											11
Ax								3	1		2			1											8
Ve	1		11	1		12	6	21	1		26		1	1								1		4	79
Sc		1	5	2		7	1	39	3	1	31	1	1	6						1				2	106
Co		1	16	6		8	4	42	6		20									1					103
Hu	4	1	8	4	1	15	4	61	9	1	86	2	3	11		1	1			2	5	6		2	226
Ra		1	13	6		12	2	56	6		52	3		5		1				2	1	8		2	167
Ul			3	3		3	1	22	2		23			4						1	1	1			64
Mc	1		4	9		12	5	111	19		80	7	1	11		1	2			1	1	16		1	282
Ph I	1		5	7		11	9	98	18		121	3		9			8		1	3		13		1	308
Ph II			2	4		4	1	43	2		51		1	2			1					12		1	125
Ph III			3	3		3	4	41	2		44			2								4			107
Sa							1	1																	2
Pe	1		2	5		7		12	4		11	2		8											50
Fe		1	3	2		5	1	17			23		3	5		3	1			1					64
Pa																									3
Ti		2	2	7		8	5	51	4	1	50	2		6			3			1		6		1	149
Ta+Ce	1	2		4		10	3	55	6		118	5	1	3							1	10			219
Ca	1		2	1		6	4	41	6	1	38	1		6			1					6			113
Mt	1		2	6		6	3	31	4		49		1	9			4			2		8		2	129
Total	17	13	104	97	1	169	70	1143	162	5	1276	31	11	125	2	12	29	1	2	18	13	134	1	20	3456
BIND								1																	1
ctm			1	3				3			13	1		2								1			24
gn											3			2											6
path								1	1		3														4
burn		3		1		1		12			11	1										3			33
wkd											1			1											2
bronze								2																	2
MIND																									
neo	4	2	8	8	1	15	6	57	15	1	84	4	2	9	1	2	2		1	2	2	10	1	10	248
y	1	1		1		1	1	4	1		4	1	1	1		1								1	16
subad	1	1	1	1		3	1	7	1		5	1	1	1		1	1		1		1	2		2	28
ad	1		1	1	1	2	2	11	3		8	3		6		1	2					1			33
sen	1	1	5	5		7	1	32	9	1	63	3	1	6		1		1		2		6	1	7	158
			1			2		3	1		4														13

The underlying problems of distinguishing between the wild and tame species in neonatal and young individuals are, to be quite honest, completely unsolved. When this was written (September, 1965) a new publication had just appeared (Bökönyi et al., 1965), in which the claim is made that under certain conditions it may be possible to separate wild and domestic specimens in cattle by densitometry in X-ray, but we are still a very long way from being able to distinguish between young individuals of these two categories.

The first evidence of wild cattle on our site comes from Lerna I; from lot J894 come one supraorbital and two maxilla fragments (VIII:1) from the same adult individual, and one phalanx I probably also from the same individual (VIII:2; Measurement Table 59). In our opinion these bones belong to a cow.

From mixed Lerna I and II we have a proximal part of a heavy radius, J893 (VIII:4), measuring no less than 107 mm. proximally (maximal breadth of articular surface 97 mm.). It is possible that this fragment could come from the cow just discussed, but it probably belongs to a larger specimen so we have counted it as coming from another animal. It is further characterized by a series of marks of cutting around the metaphysis, ca. 65 mm. from the proximal end, made by some very primitive kind of tool (cf. Plate IX), which also stresses its Neolithic origin. It should be mentioned that the phalanx I, J894, could possibly go with the radius J893 rather than with the skull fragments J894, which would still give us two individuals. Lot J894 also includes a caput femoris (VIII:3) with marks of gnawing which comes from a younger specimen and measures 53 mm. in diameter. According to Boessneck (1963) an adult bone of this size is large enough to have come from wild oxen; since our caput femoris has been diminished in diameter by gnawing as well as coming from a subadult or even younger animal, we have included it among the *Bos primigenius*.

There were in Lerna I three other fragments of wild cattle: one distal end of a metatarsal, BE594 (X:2), one damaged talus (astragalus), J889 (VIII:5), with marks of cutting, and one phalanx I from a front leg, BD615 (VIII:6), the metatarsal having a distal breadth of 66 mm. and the phalanx I measuring 71 mm. at the outer (lateral) part. For three reasons we have counted these fragments as remains from different individuals: the relative differences in their measurements, their different places of origin, and the fact that BE594 must come from a younger specimen than BD615, though a connection between BE594 and J889 is not impossible.

Since it is impossible to separate the remaining bovine fragments from Lerna I into wild and primitively domesticated, and moreover these fragments could not be used for measurements, we have listed them as domesticated with a question mark. It is to be noted in the table of the calculated MIND that the four individuals calculated from a total of 17 fragments include only one adult. The same observation must be made for the bovine fragments in mixed layers of Lerna I and II.

The existence in Lerna II of wild cattle could scarcely be proved by the measurable fragments listed in Measurement Table 47, namely two last mandibular molars (transitional?) from J624 and J741 (measuring 40 and 42 mm. in length); but their presence is clearly attested by one fragment of an articular part of a scapula, J667 (VIII:8; cf. Measurement Table 48), one calcaneus, BD602 (VIII:9), which can be certified as belonging to the same individual as the talus J889 (VIII:5) from Lerna I, and also from one phalanx III from a hind leg, BE567 (VIII:7). The relationship of the talus from Lerna I and the calcaneus from Lerna II means one individual less in Lerna II. The relationship is very clearly seen if the two bones are put together in their normal positions. Clear marks of cutting go over from the medial region of the talus to the corresponding processus of the calcaneus (Pl. IX). These cuts were made across the leg in order to carve off the strong tendons that unite these two bones; the position of the marks shows that the animal was lying on its back with its legs upward. With a magnifying glass one can see that the cuts must have been made with a blunted blade and with a sawing motion.

There is more doubt about the origin of the distal end of a humerus, BE575, from Lerna II. Its measurements (maximal distal breadth 84 mm., breadth of the trochlea 80 mm.; cf. Measurement Table 49) would suit as well for wild as for domestic cattle (cf. Boessneck, 1963, p. 168 and the bibliography cited there). We have classed it among domestic with some hesitation. It is probably transitional.

From Lerna II and mixed II and III we have the first reliable occurences of bovine fragments that, to judge by their size, must be from domesticated animals. The following fragments may be mentioned: one phalanx II of a left hind leg, BD591 (XI:1) from Lerna II, two astragali, A469 and A470 (XI:2,3) both from Lerna II and III, and one phalanx I and one phalanx II, both BD577 (XI:4,5) from Lerna II and III, and coming from the hind leg of one individual. If we place the measurements and indices of these five bones in the available diagrams of comparative material we will find that there is no doubt that they belong not to the aurochs but to cattle of much smaller size.

In Lerna III, we find a series of four teeth from the mandible of one individual, all BE564 (XI:10). Although they belong to a subadult we can rely on the measurements of the third molar which is illustrated; it has a maximal length of 43 mm. and maximal breadth of 17 mm. This should place it among the wild specimens.

From the same period we have a horn-core, BA-BB219 (XII:1), rather damaged but partly reconstructed, which could possibly belong to a subadult wild cow. We have placed it in the list of the *primigenius* with some hesitation.

Two other bone specimens from this period, one well preserved left metacarpal and one damaged proximal end of a metatarsal of the same individual, A438 (X:1 and 3), are typical wild ox bones both in form and measurements.

From this settlement we have no less than 169 fragments and small splinters which we have classed as domestic cattle or transitional forms, and these represent a calculated minimum number of 15 individuals. Examples of fragments that are more or less transitional are the third molar (M_3) A414 (XI:11; maximal length 39.5 mm., breadth 15 mm., Measurement Table 47) and the phalanx III A474 (XI:12; Measurement Table 61); an example of the domesticated form is one phalanx I, A475 (XI:6; Measurement Table 59).

The bovine fragments and splinters from Lerna IV, Early Helladic III, amount to 1.146, and those from mixed layers of Lerna IV and V to 167, but only 8 (3 from Lerna IV, 5 from Lerna IV and V) of these could be classified as wild cattle. The rest are uncertain, transitional or clearly domestic.

Typical of the wild cattle are the following fragments: the third molar BD423 (XI:13; Lerna IV and V, Measurement Table 47), length 47.5 mm., and the phalanx I and phalanx II from the same lot (XI:14, 15), all from the same individual. More uncertain is the horn-core A353 from Lerna IV (XII:2).

From the measurable horn-cores of Lerna IV we have the impression of both short-horned cows, A479, BE558 and G158 (XII:3,4,7; Measurement Table 46) and of castrates, D787a and D787b (XII:5,6). Probably from the same individual as A479 are the following bones: a right distal part of a mandible of a mature (possibly senile?) individual, one phalanx I (XI:7) and two phalanges II (one = XI:8), one proximal fragment of a left metatarsal (X:8), one left centratarsal going with it, one right *os carpi radiale* and one right *os carpi intermedium*. A second right *os carpi intermedium* of the same size from another individual comes from the same lot A479. A calcaneus, also from this lot, is, however, from a subadult (VIII:10). With the horn-core BE558 (XII:4) go the distal part of a left lower jaw, BE559, a phalanx II from the same lot and a phalanx I, BE560. There is also a phalanx I from lot BE559 belonging to a somewhat more heavily built animal (cf. Measurement Table 59).

Among the rest of the bones of domestic cattle are two almost undamaged metacarpals, D799 (X:5; left and more slender) and BE332 (X:6; right, just 1 mm. shorter and somewhat broader). The first certainly comes from a cow; BE332 might be from a castrate which is not adult. Both these bones represent a height at the withers of between 123 and 129 cm. (cf. Boessneck, 1956, tab. 1, p. 76).

The proximal fragment of a sacrum is difficult to assign either to a wild or domestic specimen. A proximal part of a tibia, D563, from Lerna IV is probably from a tame animal.

The number of bone fragments assigned to domestic cattle reaches its maximum in Lerna V with 1.276 fragments. Wild ox still occurs but is very rare. Only 5 fragments, radius distal G302 (XI:18), metatarsus proximal A207 (X:4), astragalus A321 (XI:17), one hind leg phalanx I D602 (XI:16), and one phalanx DE550, calculated as MIND 4, may without hesitation be labelled as coming from wild ox (cf. Tables 17, 18). Metatarsus A207 is interesting as it was shaped to a point at the distal end and used as a tool.

The domestic breed is represented by a large number of fragments but very few can be measured. We may mention three horn-cores of cows (three individuals), B1467a and b, D568 (XIII:1,2,3; all from short-horns), two horn-cores from castrates, DE543 and DE537 (XIII:4,5); from mixed Lerna V and VI a third from a castrate may be added, DB1–9 (XIII:6). The character of these cores does not differ very much from the still shorter ones we will find in Lerna VI. From one metacarpus in Lerna V, B1474 (X:7), we get a height at the withers of *ca.* 125 cm.; it is possible but not certain that the left medial mandibular fragment B1472, the metacarpus just mentioned, B1474, and the horn-core B1467 mentioned above all come from the same individual. The distal end of the phalanx I, DE537 (XI:9), shows sequelae of a severe joint disease (XXV:7).

It is interesting to note that the horn-cores B1467a and 1467b are connected stratigraphically with a proximal metatarsal fragment from the same lot and of small dimensions and gracile build (X:10). This small domestic cow occurs first in Lerna V, and can be followed through the later layers of the site. Another example of the same size is the distal end of a metatarsal A347 (X:9) also from Lerna V. A very informative series of measurements on the metatarsal bone fragments is found in Measurement Table 58: those that were saved have a maximal proximal breadth of 44.6 (Lerna IV), 42.0 (Lerna V), 40.3 (Lerna VI), and the maximal distal breadth from Lerna V is 48.0, from Lerna VI 44.0, 49.0 and 47.0, and from Lerna VII and V 41.3. For the measurements of the remaining fragments from Lerna V see the Measurement Tables.

From the horn-cores of Lerna VI and also from the other fragments that are well enough preserved to allow an estimate of size we can see that the domestic cattle had further decreased in size during this period (late Middle Helladic to early Late Helladic), and that it was a typical short-horn race. The horn-cores B733, B1536a and B1536b (XIII:7,8,9), all from cows of this period, are noted with their measurements in Measurement Table 46; B1536a is from a young animal, the two others from adults. Other parts of the skeleton also, for instance the mandible B1536, indicate cattle that were small and of slender build (Measurement Table 47), while the complete and well preserved metatarsus B733 (X:11) of a cow gives us a low estimated height at the withers of 110 to 120 cm.

This is not the most slender bone of this kind that has been observed in Lerna. From mixed Lerna VII and V we have a still thinner metatarsal fragment, D245 (X:12), with a maximum distal breadth of only 41.3 mm. We here approach the size of the cattle from Argissa

Magula investigated by Boessneck and published in 1962. His cow "XV⁰" from Middle Thessalian II has a metatarsal of only 188 mm. maximal length (Boessneck, p. 83) corresponding to a height at the withers of less than 110 cm. It is not possible to measure the maximum distal breadth but its minimum diaphysal breadth is 19 mm., i.e. 1 mm. less than our D245. The same small size of cattle is also reported from the large samples of bones from La Tène Oppidum Manching (Schneider 1958) as well as from other places in Europe.

In the Lerna material there are few measurable and useful bovine bones from periods later than Lerna VI. We have, however, observed that the size of domestic cattle continued to decrease after Lerna VI, and parallels to this are known from other parts of the world. Iron Age and Medieval cattle in Scandinavia, for instance, tend to decrease in size in more densely populated areas and cities, and in districts where undernourishment and inbreeding resulted from the year-round open air and uncontrolled life of the herds. From the Neolithic period onward in North and Middle Germany Nobis (1954, p. 188) has shown clearly the process of dwarfing, probably by a process of selection, and also the possibility of a relatively quick return to a larger size in periods of better nourishment and breeding. Probably this was also true for the cattle in Bökönyi's (1962, pp. 5,13) bovine material from Medieval Hungary where they increased in size during this time. On the question of decrease in size we may also compare Bergquist and Lepiksaar (1957).

ASS AND HORSE

TABLE 19

Asinus asinus L.

Dating L	III	III+IV	IV	VI	VII	VII+V	VII+ Class	Class	S&M	Total
Mx		1								1
Ma			1		5	1				7
Inc			1							1
PM			2							2
Mo			2						1	3
Hu	1							1		2
Ra			1	1			1			3
Ul				1						1
Mc			1				1			2
Ph I	1					1	1		1	4
Ph II							1			1
Ph III			1							1
Ti				1				1		2
Total	2	1	9	3	5	2	4	2	2	30
ctm	1		1		1					3
gn			1			1				2
burn			2							2
path			1							1
MIND	2	1	8	2	1	2	1	1	1	19
y						1				1
ad	2	1	7	2	1	1	1	1		16
sen			1						1	2

Measurement Tables 62–65, 67–68, 70–72

TABLE 20

Equus caballus L.

Dating L	V	V+VII	VI	VII	VII+V	S&M	Total
Cr		1					1
Mx				1			1
Ma	1			1			2
PM						2	2
Mo		2			1	1	4
Hu	1						1
Ra	2						2
Ul				1			1
Mc				1			1
Fe	2			10			12
Mt	5		1				6
Total	11	3	1	14	1	3	33
burn	5						5
MIND	3	2	1	1	1	1	9
ad	3	2	1		1	1	8
sen				1			1

Measurement Tables 62, 63, 65–67, 69.

The equine bones in the Lerna material form but a minor part of the total, while the fragmentary character of the bones and their state of preservation has, in many cases, made it extremely difficult to make an accurate determination of species. Of 63 identified fragments of equine bones (only *ca.* 0.3% of the total) 47 specimens come from certified layers, and the rest are from mixed strata. To this we must add one sample of splinters belonging to an ass in Lerna VII.

From the Neolithic layers of Lerna I and Lerna II not a single equine bone has been identified. The first occur in Lerna III, only two fragments, a medial part of a humerus, and a phalanx I, J485 (XIV:3) and HTS73 (XIV:4), both certainly from asses. Lerna III and IV contain one maxilla, A445 (XIV:5), of an ass. The distal ends of the second and third incisors in this fragment have been burnt and thus have lost most of their enamel surface. Their roots are intact, as is also the alveole of the I^1 (dx).

Early Helladic III (Lerna IV) strata have produced nine equine bone fragments, two burnt, one of a mandible, B348 (XIV:6), one upper incisor, J833 (XIV:7), two second upper premolars, G74 (XIV:8) and G288 (XV:1), one second and one third upper molar, G82 (XIV:9) and J470 (XIV:10), one distal end of a radius, D707 (XIV:11), one proximal part of a metacarpus, A363 (XIV:12), and one phalanx III, J470 (XIV:13). Eight of these fragments, all except the upper incisor J833, can without hesitation be determined to have come from Asinus. True ass characteristics, except size which is small in the mandibular fragment B348, the metacarpal fragment A363 and the phalanx III J470, are found also in the uncomplicated enamel pattern of the premolars G74, G288, and the molars G82 and J470. The distal end of a radius D707 (XXV:8), which has suffered pathological changes, presents some difficulty. The author has discussed it with Professor J. Boessneck, and was also able to compare it with a series of corresponding equine bones in the Bayerische Zoologische Staatssammlungen in Munich. Dr. Boessneck came to the conclusion that from a morphological point of view—especially in the form of the distal joint and of the dorsal side—and disregarding the pathological changes, D707 must come from a representative of the asses, and not from a true horse. The remaining fragment, one second upper incisor, J833, is more problematic. It is well preserved in its distal part while its root is damaged and broken. In section one can say that the size of J833 and of the two incisors in A445 (Lerna III and IV) above, was almost the same. It is, however, difficult to arrive at any decision about the determination of the species of the two fragments, especially as there exist asses and horses with this part of the skeleton of the same size. We have, in view of these facts and lacking any evidence of true horses in the layers up to this date, placed the two fragments, A445 and J833, among the asses.

Eleven fragments of equine bone from Lerna V were originally registered as *Equus caballus* L. in our material, but a careful investigation of the material that was saved reveals that only one can be used for the discussion, namely the proximal part of a rather heavily built radius D241 (XVI:1). We have compared it with the material available from asses and true horses in the collections of the Museum of Natural History in Stockholm, and have come to the conclusion that, in view both of size and form, it probably comes from a horse.

Three other equine fragments should be discussed here: two second (?) upper molars, D244 (XVI:5) and D565 (XVI:4), and one much damaged third upper molar D237 (XVI:6). The two first come from layers of Lerna V and VII, the last from Lerna VII and V. We would not hesitate to place all three teeth among true horses except that D565 differs greatly from the two others in its fully developed enamel plications on both the protocone and the metacone, and in its development of the oblique valley. D244 and D237 have much in common in regard to the different enamel plications already mentioned, but they definitely come from a smaller race. At this stage of the study we would like to label D565 as the first occurence of a cold-blooded "occidental" horse, whilst the two other teeth may represent the "oriental" type, which occurs somewhat earlier, and is already represented by the radius fragment D241 from certified Lerna V.

From Lerna VI layers only four fragments of equine bones have been found; two of them, B733 (XV:2), join to make one, a proximal radius with a part of its ulna adhering. B733 is certified to come from an ass. The next fragment in this series is a distal end of a tibia, B1536 (XV:3), the size of an ass or a small horse. After comparison with several individuals in the collections mentioned above we have, for morphological reasons, listed it as from an ass. The third fragment is a proximal end of a metatarsal bone, DE456 (XVI:2), which in size and form is from a true horse.

Late Helladic (Lerna VII) equine finds may be handled in two groups according to provenience, and consist of both true horse and ass. The find numbered F7, 15, 20 (XVI:3,7,8,9,10) is a sample of more or less crushed bones, badly amalgamated with soil, which come from one individual, a horse of a little over medium height at the withers. The parts which were measurable after attempts at restoration are listed in Measurement Tables 62, 63, 66, and 67; they show that we have to deal with a horse *ca.* 145 cm. in height at the withers (cf. Frank, 1962, and the literature cited there). The teeth that go with this find are unfortunately very badly worn down. The size and enamel pattern of the best preserved of the four, the third and fourth upper premolars, definitely show marks of "oriental" type, and differ considerably from the molar D244 discussed above from Lerna V. Both enamel pattern and size suggest that we may be dealing with a cross-breed (or hybrid) ass-horse.

Strata of Lerna VII with V have given us one medial fragment of a left mandible of a young ass, D264 (XV:4), and one phalanx I, D240 (XV:5), also from a young ass, possibly the same individual.

There are also asses from mixed Archaic and Classical strata with coherent finds, as for example BA224 which has one distal end of a radius, one proximal part of a metacarpus, one phalanx I and one phalanx II (XV:6,7,8,9 and Measurement Tables). From classical times in a well we have one almost complete right tibia, Well A1 (XV:10), from an ass.

Our description of the material will end with the few equine bones found in surface and mixed layers. Of *Equus caballus* we have three teeth from a mandible, one P_3, one P_4, and one M_1, all from the same adult individual and numbered BE14a, b, and c (XVI:11, 12, 13). There is also one third lower molar, J75 (XV:11), from an ass.

In summing up we must make some generalizations. It is as a rule difficult to make a definitive statement about the absence or presence of asses and horses in an area of excavation (or investigation) and to fix the time of their introduction. In some places we have very few equine bones, in others they are abundant, as is the case with dog bones also. Dogs, horses and asses are not normally expected to be found in the debris of slaughter and meals as are the other species of wild and domesticated animals which usually make up the meat production in a community, though we have seen in this and other similar studies that dog bones from various strata and epochs frequently show signs of cutting; the number of marks of cutting on the ass bone fragments so far detected is only three.

On the other hand, had wild asses or horses been present and hunted in the Peloponnese during the time covered by the excavations at Lerna we would probably have found some bone evidence for them also in the earlier layers of the site. The first occurence of the ass in Lerna III and of the true horse in Lerna V may thus give us the approximate time for the introduction of both these animals even better than does the occurrence of the other wild and domesticated animals which were originally eaten.

VOLE

TABLE 21

Sorex sp.

Dating L	iHG
Fe	1
MIND; ad	1

From Human Grave 193 one fragment of a vole was registered.

HEDGEHOG

TABLE 22

Erinaceus europaeus L.

Dating L	III	IV	V	Total
Ma		1	2	3
Ul	1			1
Ti	1			1
Total	2	1	2	5
ctm		1		1
MIND; ad	1	1	2	4

Measurement Tables 73, 74

38 THE FAUNA

The remains of this little insectivore will often be overlooked during excavation (this is in no way a criticism) and the occurence at a site of only a few of its bones cannot indicate much more than its presence. It proves nothing or very little about its commonness in the pertinent phases, for it is more or less by chance that its small bones are found amongst the masses of remains of larger animals.

As in many other cases we find the most important and detailed information for comparative purposes in Boessneck (1963, p. 18). According to this author the hedgehog has not been found in Neolithic layers in any excavation except at Burgäschisee-Süd, where it was comparatively frequent.

We have compared the measurements of the mandibles from Lerna V with the corresponding measurements in Boessneck's Neolithic material; our specimens seem to be somewhat larger, and are thus nearer the specimens which he has used for comparison. The difference in size between Middle Bronze Age and Neolithic specimens seems to the author probably to be of ecological significance, with the expectation that, if we had any Neolithic examples from Lerna, we would find them nearer in size to these Neolithic specimens from Middle Europe. It is most likely that the increased size in Lerna V is the result of ecological change in the region of Lerna.

If the marks of cutting on the corpus of one of our lower jaws, GQ57 in Lerna IV (XVII:1), are really a proof of skinning, the questions immediately arise: How was the skin used? How was the rest of the animal used? Was it eaten? The conjecture may be made that the sharp pointed spines of this animal would be a good source of supply for making pricking tools for fine handicrafts.

The hedgehog is common in Greece today (Ondrias, 1965).

RED FOX

Table 23

Vulpes vulpes L.

Dating L	I	II	II + III	III	III + IV	IV	IV + V	V	VI	VII + V	VII+ LH+ S&M	Unatt	Total
Mx								1					1
Ma		2	1		1	3		3	2	1			13
Ra						1							1
Ul						1			1				2
Mc				4		4		1		2	1	1	13
Pe		1				1							2
Fe									1				1
Ti	1												1
Mt	1						1	1	1				4
Total	2	3	1	4	1	10	1	6	5	3	1	1	38
ctm								1					1
MIND	2	2	1	2	1	3	1	2	2	1	1	1	19
y	1				1				1				3
subad				1		1							2
ad	1	2	1	1		2	1	2	1	1	1	1	14

Measurement Tables 75-79

When we turn to other comparatively small animals which are also sparse in Lerna it is obvious in the case of the red fox that the number of fragments cannot give any certain information about the minimum number of individuals. Moreover the variation in MIND from one settlement to another should lead us to believe there was a corresponding variation in the frequency of foxes in the fauna of the different eras. The relatively few measurements that could be obtained from the fragments we saved must be regarded only as a complement to the description of the material.

If we turn again to Boessneck (1963, pp. 34 ff.), we find an excavation group of Neolithic fox bones next to a comparatively modern group. Our measurements, which include scanty information about the Lernaean foxes from Lerna II up to the Surface and Mixed lots, partly agree with Boessneck's Neolithic material and partly fall within the measurements of his recent specimens.

An important contribution to the study of fossilized and recent carnivores has been made by Kurtén in a book which has just appeared (1965). We have used our measurements for a statistical comparison with Kurtén's figures for foxes from the Palestine Caves (Shukbah level A and others) from postglacial and recent times; the comparison had validity since this is an adjacent region. Of course the Lerna bones are too few for statistical significance, but nevertheless the comparison has some importance. The variability is very low within Kurtén's series, and he has been able to show by means of biometrics and statistics a trend in the species *Vulpes vulpes* to "a slow gradual growth throughout the Main Würm period up to and including the Mesolithic" as well as a dwarfing in post-Mesolithic times. The variability within our fox material is slightly higher, but in fact not more than could be expected in view of the few individuals involved and the fact that it comes from different strata.

A cautious interpretation of the result we obtain when we compare our material with that of Boessneck (1963) and Kurtén (1965) would be that at Lerna we are dealing with a local type or "race." In spite of the few individuals involved and their different dates, measurements, such as the length and breadth of the carnassial, show a low dispersion value, low enough to allow the theory of a local type, but statistically sufficiently separated from the populations discussed by these two authors to deny biometrical conformity with either of their groups.

It is to be noted that the mandibular fragments of the fox (Lerna V and Lerna VI) and one femur fragment (Lerna VI) show the same kind of marks of cutting as we found in dogs. It seems probable that both the fur and the meat were carefully removed and used.

The best preserved fragments of red fox are three mandibles (J666, Lerna II, XVIII:4; B733, Lerna VI, XVIII:5; D240, Lerna VII and V, XVIII:6) and one ulna, B733 from Lerna VI (XVIII:7).

The red fox is common on the Greek Mainland today, but is not found on Crete (Ondrias, 1965).

BROWN BEAR

TABLE 24

Ursus arctos L.

Dating	Lerna V
Mt2	1
ctm	1
MIND; ad	1

Measurement Table 80

The occurrence of this species which is still reported from Greece and near-by countries (*Checklist*, p. 236) is quite natural. It is also natural that we should find it only in Lerna V, the settlement which produced the bulk of the bone material largely because it was most extensively excavated. The tiny fragment which we have says very little about the size of its owner. It is, however, to be supposed that in Early and Middle Helladic times here as, for instance, in Troy brown bears were held in captivity and that furs may sometimes have been merchandise. In such a fur one can expect parts of phalanges or even metacarpals or metatarsals to have been left behind when it was pulled off the carcass. The presence of bear skins in Iron Age burials (cremation graves) from North Europe would never have been proved if it had not been for the remnants of the phalanges, especially the claw-phalanges, in the burnt remains. Although in fresh skins it is almost impossible to take the last phalanges out of the horn claw, after cremation they come out, can be detected and determined (e.g. Gejvall, 1948).

BADGER

Table 25

Meles meles L.

Dating L	IV	V	S & M	Total
Ma	2	1		3
Ve			1	1
Sc	1			1
Co			1	1
Hu	1			1
Ra	1		1	2
Ul			1	1
Pe	1			1
Total	6	1	4	11
ctm	1			1
gn	1	1		2
MIND; ad	2	1	1	4

Measurement Tables 81–86

Like other small mammals represented by very few fragments in our material the badger first occurs in Lerna IV, and is represented in Lerna V, and in Surface and Mixed. The best preserved bones come from Lerna IV and from Surface and Mixed, but the total material is too small for a statistical evaluation. We may simply refer to Measurement Tables 81–86; it can also be said that our identified and measured badger bones, when compared with Boessneck's (1963) Neolithic badger bones from Burgäschisee-Süd, give a picture of a somewhat more gracile animal.

We have also made a comparison with Kurtén's (1965) measurements of the lower jaw carnassial of the badgers of the Palestine Caves from the Würm and Mesolithic periods and up to recent times. Our mandible G81 from Lerna IV (XVIII:10) is more robust than the other two, TrBcut8 from Lerna IV (XVIII:9) and DE544 from Lerna V (not measurable). This robusticity is noticeable both in the thickness of the ramus and in the height at P_4–M_1.

It is interesting to note that the *Checklist* (p. 271) in its detailed description of the occurrence of the badger in Europe does not mention it for Greece, although it is clearly reported here in other works (cf. Ondrias, 1965, p. 122). The *Checklist* reports it in both Crete and Asia Minor; the exclusion of Greece must be an oversight.

As with the other small mammals our great problem is whether the occurence of the badger is significant, that is whether its first appearance in Lerna IV is simply a result of the much greater number of animal bone fragments than in Lerna III due to the greater area excavated, or whether it indicates alterations in the ecology or other environmental factors in favor of the species.

The marks of cutting and traces of gnawing on the bones of the badger make it clear that its fur and meat too were used.

COMMON OTTER

TABLE 26

Lutra lutra L.

Dating L	IV	V	Total
Sc	1 (XVII:13)		1
Ul	1 (XVII:12)	1	2
Pe		1	1
Total	2	2	4
MIND	1	1	2
y		1	1
ad	1		1

Measurement Tables 87, 88

Of the four fragments found, only two, the scapula C33 (XVII:13) and the ulna BE419, could be measured, and the latter gave only one measurement.

It should be mentioned that in the *Checklist* (p. 275) the common otter is not reported as found in Greece, surely an oversight. In other handbooks (e.g. *The Mammals of Europe*, original edition; Brehm-Ekman, 1938, p. 308; Ondrias, 1965) this mammal is listed and mapped in larger rivers throughout the Balkan peninsula including the Peloponnese.

BEECH MARTEN

TABLE 27

Martes foina Erxl.

Dating L	IV
Ma	1 (XVII:14)
Hu	1 (XVII:15)
Fe	1
Total	3
MIND ; ad	1

Measurement Tables 89–91

The few fragments of this small carnivore were assigned to the beech marten and not to *Martes martes*, the Pine Marten, partly because of Lerna's geographical position and partly because of the small size of the bones. This is especially true of the humerus BE355 (XVII:15) which is rather gracile. Compare the measurements given by Boessneck (1963) and Kurtén (1965) and also Ondrias (1965).

WEASEL

Mustela sp. (cf. nivalis L.)

Lerna V = 1 BIND, y.

In Lerna V, according to label "when clearing burial DE36 between bothros 3 and bothros 4," a whole skeleton of this carnivore was found. A selection of its bones is shown in XVII:16.

The subspecies *Mustela nivalis galinthias* (Bate, 1905) is believed to be spread over large parts of Greece, and is reported from the Peloponnese (1963), Ondrias (1965).

LYNX

TABLE 28

Lynx lynx L.

Dating L	V
Ra	1
MIND; ad	1

Measurement Table 92

One fragment of a radius, DE496 (XVIII:14), from Lerna V is the only fragment of this species we have been able to find; this merely introduces it into our list. In Measurement Table 92 we have compared its measurements with those of four radii of lynxes from the collections of the Museum of Natural History, Stockholm.

We have reason to suspect that the fur of the lynx was used as may have been the case for domestic dog, fox, and brown bear.

Today the lynx is reported from the Pindos Mountains, but its distribution is unknown (Ondrias, 1965).

EUROPEAN HARE

In citing earlier workers Boessneck (1958, pp. 55 and 147) has emphasized the extreme scarcity of hare bones in Neolithic layers, and has given the measurements available for material in Bavaria. Our fragments are so few and in such small pieces that the measurable pieces do not suffice for a statistical analysis.

The first measured fragment comes from Lerna I, a distal part of a tibia, A456 (XVII:2) which is burned. Its measurements fall just below the corresponding measurements in Boessneck's material (1956). Lerna III–IV and Lerna IV are the first layers from which we have any number of measurable fragments, also of tibiae and three in number, A446, D798 (XVII:3), G278 (XVII:4). Maximum lengths of these bones differ slightly from those in Boessneck, but it is obvious that the Lernaean hares of this period, at least to judge by these three specimens, were slimmer and more gracile than those from Bavaria.

In Lerna V we find the only measurable fragment of a mandible in the collection, DE497 (XVII:5); other measurable bones are: 2 scapulae, DE497 (XVII:6); 3 humeri, A320 (XVII:9), DE531 (XVII:10); 2 radii, A320 (XVII:8); and one ulna, A320 (XVII:7). The distal breadth of two humeri from Lerna V is 12.0 mm. and 13.0 mm. If we compare these with Boessneck's corresponding measurements (1963, p. 19) for his only Neolithic find from Burgäschisee-

Süd (10.4 mm.) and for four modern humeri from Schweizer Jura (11.5 mm., 11.8 mm., 12.4 mm., 12.6 mm.) we find the Lerna V humeri fall within the range of the modern material to slightly higher.

TABLE 29

Lepus europaeus, L.

Dating L	I	I+II	II	II+III	III	III+IV	IV	IV+V	V	V+VII	VI	VII	VII+V	S&M	Total
Ma					1		1		2		1				5
Ve							3				1		1		5
Sc					1		5		6						12
Hu					1		5		3						9
Ra				1	1		5	2	4		1			1	15
Ul					1		2	1	2						6
Mc							3	1	2						6
Pe		1			1		4	1	7		4		1	2	21
Fe	2		1	1			2		7	1	2			1	17
Ti	1				2	1	9	1	2		3			1	20
Fi							1					1			2
Mt							2		1						3
Total	3	1	1	2	8	1	42	6	36	1	11	2	2	5	121
ctm									1		2				3
burn	1				2		1								4
MIND	1	1	1	1	2		4	1	4	1	4	1	1	2	24
y							1							1	2
subad									1						1
ad	1	1	1	1	2		3	1	3	1	4	1	1	1	21

Measurement Tables 93–100

As can be seen in Table 29 above the greater number of fragments and bones in Lerna IV, V, and VI involves only slight increase in the calculated minimum number of individuals. It is thus hardly advisable to draw any extensive conclusions from the greater number of bones. If the species had really increased in number during these periods, or more accurately, if the hare had been more common in the menu of the population during Lerna IV and V this would have been reflected in a larger number of individuals because the total number of bone fragments from Lerna IV and Lerna V exceeds one-third of all the hare bones from the site. It is certainly not an exaggeration to say that the hare has not played an important role as game in any of the settlements excavated at Lerna. Possibly some of the individuals in our samples were caught and brought home by the numerous dogs. We must also point out that the occurrence of this rodent gives us information about the type of landscape since it prefers the open fields.

Hare bones from excavations are usually, like the bones of other small animals, in a better state of preservation than those of large animals, and their representation in the different strata is, therefore, not to be compared with that of larger species. It is of interest to note from what part of the carcass these bones come. Tibiae, humeri, ulnae and radii are usually well preserved and often found whole. Femora, on the other hand, since they come from regions with much meat and muscle (17 femora of hare are registered for Lerna), have produced only one measurement.

The subspecies of hare found in the Peloponnese today is, according to Ondrias (1965), *Lepus europaeus Niethammery*, Wettstein 1943.

RED DEER

TABLE 30

Cervus elaphus L.

Dating L	I	II	II+III	III	III+IV	IV	IV+V	V	V+VI	V+VII	V+La	V+Class	VI	VI+La	VII	VII+V	VII+LH+S&M	VII+Class	Class+S&M	S&M	Total
An	1	5	3	4	2	26	2	108	1	1	1		23	1	1	5		1	1	4	190
Cr						3		8					1								12
Mx						3		12													15
Ma				1	1	17	4	39					3		1		1		1	6	74
PM								4													4
Mo		1						15								1					17
Ax								1													1
Sc	1	1	3	4		4	2	7												3	25
Hu				1				5													6
Ra				2	1	6	1	5					3						1	2	21
Ul				1									1		1						3
Mc		1	2	4	3	7	1	24					3							1	46
Ph I				1			1	8					2								12
Ph II								1													1
Pe								2					2								4
Fe				1		2							1								4
Ti		2	2			1	1	11					3							2	22
Ta			1			1		4													6
Ca		1		1	1	1		2					3								9
Mt					1	4		8				1	3	1						1	19
Total	2	11	11	20	9	75	12	264	1	1	1	1	48	1	4	6	1	1	3	19	491
ctm			1	1		3		5					7								17
gn								1					2								3
ansh								1													1
path								3													3
wkd							1	7					2		1					1	12
burn				2		6		9													17
MIND	2	4	2	5	2	9	3	20	1	1	1	1	5	1	1	1	1	1	1	4	66
y	1	1		2		2		2				1	1							1	11
subad		2				1		1					1	1							6
ad	1		2	3	2	5	2	14	1	1	1		3		1	1	1	1	1	3	43
sen		1				1	1	3													6

Measurement Tables 101–113

The list of material in Table 30, as well as the calculated minimum number of individuals, age distribution and so on, makes it clear that bone fragments of red deer occur in all layers of the site and that, as is to be expected, they are more numerous in settlements IV and V (75 and 264 fragments or 15% and 54% respectively of the total number of red deer bones).

This table also gives us an idea of the distribution of kinds of deer bones identified. Obviously the fragments and splinters of antlers are most numerous, and are followed by jaws and teeth (if upper and lower jaws are taken together), while metacarpals and metatarsals come next in number. In all, just under 500 pieces of bone of this species have been identified, including 8 small groups of splinters.

From Table 6 (p. 10) we may get an idea of the percentual distribution of the red deer bones in the different settlements (mixed layers, except Surface and Mixed, excluded). It is of interest to note that, regardless of the great variation in the total number of bones in the different eras and the increase in the total numbers in Lerna IV and Lerna V, the relative percentage of deer bones stands at a rather low level (minimum 1.2% in Lerna I, maximum 5.4% in Lerna V and Lerna VII). From pure Classical and Roman strata we have no bones of *Cervus* but this is just chance. It is probably also simply chance that this animal appears in four fragments of one individual in Lerna VII, a settlement which produced a total of only 74 bone fragments, less than 1% of the identified bones of vertebrates in the whole collection.

The figures make it clear that from Neolithic times on deer-hunting played a definite though subordinate role in the lives of the inhabitants of Lerna. Most of this game was made up of adult individuals, but young and subadult specimens appear also, although to a lesser degree and in a way that cannot be statistically certified because of the relatively low number of fragments of this species.

A short description of some of the fragments that were saved follows. It is advisable that the reader compare this with Measurement Tables 101–113 and with the corresponding plates and figures.

Of antlers 6 specimens were in a condition that permitted measurement. They range from Lerna II to Lerna V and VI. Four of them, BD575 from Lerna II (XIX:1), B1472 (XIX:5) and D below Wall O (XIX:3) from Lerna V and B735 from Lerna V and VI (XIX:6), come from rather heavily built adults with the circumference of the pedicle under the burr ranging from 134 to 147 mm. The other two, D563 (XIX:2) from Lerna IV and BE398 (XIX:4) from Lerna V, belong to younger animals. D563 has been used as a tool of some kind, and BE398 is atypical in that it has an extra tine just at the level of the burr pointing out and up and bending slightly to the side. Their circumference below the burr is 79 and 75 mm. They are characterized by long, smooth and thin pedicles; it has not been easy to separate them from those of fallow deer (cf. Lotze, 1963, and Hansen, von Bülow, Lotze, 1964).

Obviously red deer belongs to the class of game that was relatively hard to get at and rather sought after. We have already stated that the remains of such species are usually more fragmented, more crushed and include very few measurable fragments compared to those of domestic cattle, sheep and goat. We have very few measurable fragments of red deer bones; those we have are listed in Measurement Tables 101–113.

In his extensive work of 1963 on the bones from Burgäschisee-Süd Boessneck deals with more than 9,500 bones (representing a minimum of 120 individuals) of red deer from the Neolithic period. He also thoroughly reviews all the literature concerning the size of red deer from Neolithic onwards, and gives the measurements of material from Bialowieza in Poland, Siebenbürgen and Roumania from recent times. These investigations have shown, among other important results, that the disappearance in Middle Europe of the biotopes specially suited for the red deer as well as the extensive hunting of this game are two of the main reasons for a certain decrease in its size from Medieval times onwards. A comparison of metapodials of present-day deer from East Europe, where its normal ecological environment still exists, and the corresponding bones from Neolithic sites shows no essential difference.

Although the measured deer bones from Lerna are very few, we have tried to correlate our figures with Boessneck's own and his comparative tables in order to find out whether it is possible that there is a trend towards larger or smaller size in our specimens. Most of our measurements fall within the boundaries of those of the Neolithic material from Burgäschisee-Süd, i.e. the following: cranium, upper jaw, mandible, antler, scapula, humerus, radius, metacarpus, tibia, astragalus, metatarsus and phalanx I. But there is an interesting fact about the position of our measurements within the ranges of the corresponding measurements from the Middle European Neolithic. Except for the few measurements of the skull (neurocranium), the radius, the ulna and metacarpus, which lie close to the middle of the range, the rest, much the larger part of the material, obviously falls within the lower third of the figures for the Neolithic material, showing that the size of our red deer from the Peloponnese was on the average somewhat smaller. It is the opinion of the author that the Peloponnesian red deer may very well, for ecological reasons and due to selection (cf. Huxley, 1944, p. 121), already in early times have developed into a local slightly diminished form (there are very few specimens left today). This may have been caused by the beginning of deforestation already during Lerna IV, perhaps in connection with climatic changes from then on; these we will deal with later.

Our material is not sufficient for sex determination of the various bones, but the ratio of fragments of antlers seems to be very high for such a small total number of fragments, no less than 38%. Boessneck (1963, p. 103) found in his Neolithic material a sex ratio of 7:3 which he considers to be unnatural. It seems that at Lerna we have even more males in proportion to females, though this possibility is only partly supported by our measurements. It is the author's opinion that the large antlers of the male constitute its natural handicap against man during hunting; whether the hunting was done with short range implements (spears) or those with longer range (snares) the final capture and killing of the male animal, probably easier during the rut, was much easier because of its antlers, and certainly happened more often than the capture of the shyer females.

Finally, it should be emphasized that from Lerna V we have three fragments of red deer extremity bones with severe pathological changes; two are illustrated here: one tibia, BE168 (XIX:7), and one metacarpus, BE395 (XIX:8). The nature of these two grave arthritic deformations with large extoses is more likely to have been the sequelae of earlier lesions (bites of dogs or other hunting beasts, injuries made by hunting implements, or lesions incurred during pursuit) than a sign of infectional polyarthritis or of ageing; cf. X-ray, Plate XXV:9, 10.

The red deer found in Greece today belongs to the subspecies *Cervus elaphus hippelaphus*, Erxleben, 1777, and is reported in "the Sidonia peninsula, Chalkidiki, Macedonia" (about 15 individuals). It has been established in the woods of Tatoi and on Parnes in Attica. According to Heldreich (1878) it lived on Penteli (Attica), Euboia, and Akarnania, and according to Zerva (1927) in the Pindos, on Olympos, and in Chalkidiki (Ondrias, 1965).

ROE DEER

Table 31

Capreolus capreolus L.

Dating L	IV	IV+V	V	S&M	Total
An	3	1	9	1	14
Mx			1		1
Ma	1		1		2
Mo			1		1
Total	4	1	12	1	18
ctm		1			1
gn		1			1
ansh	2		1		3
MIND	3	1	4	1	9
ad	2	1	4	1	8
sen	1				1

Measurement Tables 114–115

Although the roe deer was identified only in Lerna IV, Lerna IV and V, Lerna V and Surface and Mixed we have reason to believe that it was present also in the other settlements of the site. Its representation in Lerna IV and Lerna V is consonant with the large number of bone fragments from both these periods, and does not tell us much more than that roe deer existed in the surroundings of the site and were hunted by its inhabitants.

From Table 31 we can see that the total of 18 bone fragments gave a calculated minimum number of no less than 9 individuals, 8 of which are adults and one senile, and that 3 of the 14 antlers had been shed. Only one antler, BE284 from Lerna V (XIV:1), is well enough preserved to justify a picture. BE284 is a typical but rather large specimen with the circumference of the burr measuring 155 mm., of the pedicule 79 mm., and above the burr 85 mm., considerably larger than the measurements of the individuals published in Boessneck (1963). On the other hand the only other measurable fragment, mandible A18 in Lerna V (XIV:2), falls well within the boundaries of the Neolithic material from Burgäschisee-Süd and the recent mandible cited there from the Tieranatomisches Institut of Munich.

There is no possibility of sexing the material from the different strata, but the fact that 14 of the identified fragments of roe deer bones were antlers makes it seem most likely that roe bucks were more easily obtained than were the females or (as other students have put it) they were in greater demand. If this was true it presents a parallel to the sex distribution of red deer which we discussed above.

The presence of roe deer in Lerna does not give us any more information about the character of the biotope beyond what is known from the occurrence of the red deer. Both belong to landscapes with forests as well as those with scattered clumps of trees, while the roe deer also likes open fields and cultivated areas. Its scarcity in our material is probably to be interpreted as being the result of its swiftness and the undeveloped hunting methods rather than as giving a real picture of its rarity.

Today the roe deer is found in the woods of the Pindos, on Olympos, and in the Rhodope Mountains (Ondrias, 1965).

BIRDS
AVES
TABLE 32
FRAGMENTS

Dating L	Cormorant	Heron	Mallard	Garganey	Wigeon	Duck sp	Tufted Duck	Gray Lag Goose	Whooper Swan	Crane	Goshawk	Peregrine	Rock Partridge	Domestic Fowl	Great Bustard	Pigeon	Eagle Owl	Raven	Hooded Crow	Undeterminable	Total
I			2					1		1											4
II	1	1	2	1							1										6
II + III			1							1											2
III			2		2			1			1										6
III + IV				1				1			3									1	6
IV		1	7			1		3	2	1			1			1	1	1	2	1	22
IV + V			1																		1
V	1		1		1		1				1	3	1	1	3		1		1	3	18
VI		1									2										3
VII + V														1							1
Class																				1	1
S & M			1			1					1			5							8
Total	2	3	17	2	3	2	1	6	2	3	9	3	3	6	3	1	2	1	3	6	78

TABLE 33

MIND

Dating L	Cormorant	Heron	Mallard	Garganey	Wigeon	Duck sp	Tufted Duck	Gray Lag Goose	Whooper Swan	Crane	Goshawk	Peregrine	Rock Partridge	Domestic Fowl	Great Bustard	Pigeon	Eagle Owl	Raven	Hooded Crow	Undeterminable	Total
I			1					1		1 cut											3
II	1	1	1	1							1										5
II + III			1								1										2
III			2	1							1										4
III + IV				1				1			2									1	5
IV		1	5			1		1	1	1			1			1	1	1	1	1	16
IV + V			1																		1
V	1		1		1		1				1	2	1	1	1		1		1	1	13
VI		1									1										2
VII + V													1								1
Class																				1	1
S & M			1		1					1				2							5
Total	2	3	13	2	2	2	1	3	1	3	7	2	3	3	1	1	2	1	2	4	58

Measurement Table 116
Plates XX–XXI

In Lerna I we find only four fragments representing three species, the mallard (*Anas platyrhynchos*), the gray lag goose (*Anser anser*), and the crane (*Grus grus*), i.e. one swimming duck, mostly confined to shallow lakes or marshes, another swimmer which finds its biotope in wet, grassy places, and one wader, which finds its food in marshes or water-rich meadows.

Lerna II has given us in all six bone fragments of five different species of bird: one cormorant (*Phalacrocorax carbo*), a sea bird with one race living on lakes, a good swimmer; one heron (*Ardea cinerea*), a stork-like wader; 2 bones of a mallard; one garganey (*Anas querquedula*), a swimming duck; and one goshawk (*Accipiter gentilis*) which usually hunts in surroundings with scattered trees and brushwood.

In Lerna III, and mixed Lerna III and IV we have identified bones of two mallards, one wigeon (*Anas penelope*), a swimming duck that usually takes its food in shallow waters, muddy shores and pasture land close to water, one garganey, one gray lag goose and three goshawks (one from Lerna III and two from Lerna III and IV). One of six small undeterminable fragments also comes from Lerna III and IV.

With Lerna IV a change can be seen in the composition of the avian fauna. The following species (with minimum number of individuals) have been identified: one heron; five mallards (and one in Lerna IV and V); one duck which could not be more closely identified; one gray lag goose; one whooper swan (*Cygnus cygnus*); one crane; one rock partridge (*Alectoris graeca*); one pigeon (*Columba sp.*); one eagle owl (*Bubo bubo*), the largest of European owls; one raven (*Corvus corax*); one hooded crow (*Corvus cornix*); and one undeterminable fragment.

Lerna V has yielded 13 different individuals of a dozen different species. We will list first the species which have appeared earlier: one cormorant, one mallard, and one wigeon, to which we can now add one specimen of the tufted duck (*Aythya fuligula*), a diving duck which often lives in the company of mallards, for instance, and which likes various biotopes in coastal or inland water districts. Turning to the predatory birds we find one goshawk (cf. Lerna II, Lerna III and Lerna III and IV above) and two peregrines (*Falco peregrinus*). The rock partridge is represented by one individual, and we have — the first appearance in European prehistory as far as the author has been able to find[1] — also one individual of domestic fowl (*Gallus gallus*). One great bustard (*Otis tarda*) could be identified with the help of comparative material made available by Dr. J. Lepiksaar in Gothenburg. *Otis tarda* is represented by three fragments, A332 (XX:15), of the distal end of a tibiotarsus. This very large land bird lives on wide treeless grass steppes and in cultivated fields. It is a good runner and has a powerful flight. The bustards are extremely shy birds. The remaining bird bones from Lerna V belong to one eagle owl, one hooded crow, and one undetermined species (possibly a duck).

There are very few bird bones from Lerna VI. Species represented are one heron and one goshawk.

In mixed layers of Lerna VII and V one individual of rock partridge was identified, while from Classical times our collection includes only one unidentified species of bird. Finally, Surface and Mixed layers have yielded four species of bird: one mallard, one unidentified duck, one goshawk, and two of domestic fowl.

We will deal in more detail in the discussion below with the change in the composition of the avian fauna between Lerna III and Lerna IV (cf. Table 33). Here we will simply point out that the bird bones from the periods earlier than Lerna IV include only swimming birds and waders plus one raptor (goshawk), whereas the later periods include a series of additional species of typical rock (and stepp) dwellers and some domestic birds (?) as well.

AMPHIBIANS

As can be seen in Table 3 (p. 6) there are several fragments from Lerna V belonging to a large specimen of toad (*Bufo sp.*).

REPTILES

The only species of reptile which occurs in Lerna is the tortoise, *Testudo hermanni hermanni*. Numerous fragments of its carapace and also a series of other parts of the skeleton have been collected from all the excavated layers at the site except a few mixed layers. A total of 1682 fragments of this species and three BIND are recorded (but we do not know surely whether these remnants have been collected systematically throughout the excavation). After Lerna V a very few fragments of this turtle have been registered, as can be seen in Table 3 (p. 6).

FISH

Every fragment of fish bone in the collection was saved, and all of them, very few in number, are listed in Tables 3, 5, and 6 (pp. 6, 8–10).

The identifications given below are those of Dr. J. Lepiksaar of the Natural History Museum of Gothenburg, who very kindly studied the material for us.

From Lerna I and II comes the premaxillary bone, J886 (XXII:1) of a fish of the Croaker family, *Johnius hololepidotus* Lac. (= *Sciaena aquila*). This bone is from a large specimen *ca.* 1.3 m. in length.

Lerna II has produced two vertebrae of one individual of the tuna (*Thynnus thynnus*), HTN130 (XXII:2). One fragment coming from a basioccipital and parasphenoideum bone, HTN141 (XXIII:3), possibly belongs to the croaker species *Johnius* like J886. The small and more caudal vertebra J843 from Lerna II and III come from the tuna.

---

[1] The earliest finds of domestic fowl reported hitherto are published by Schweizer (1961) and are dated to the Late Hallstatt period.

Lerna III has contributed to the picture four vertebral centers of one individual of the Great Blue Shark, *Carcharhinus glaucus* L., J480 (XXII:4), and a fragment of a vertebra of the same species.

From Lerna IV comes a small vertebral center of another shark, the Gray Shark, *Galeorhinus galeus* L., A360 (XXII:5). One fragment of a vertebra from Lerna IV and V is too small and damaged to be identified.

From Lerna V comes a large left dentale of the Gold Brass, *Sparus auratus* L. (= *Chrysophrys aurate* or *Aurata aurata*), DE497 (XXII:6), which has recently been reported in a Neolithic context from the Black Sea region by O. Necrasov and S. Haimovici (1959). Lerna V also contains a skull fragment which cannot be identified.

In Surface and Mixed layers was unearthed a very much worked fragment of a vertebral center of the shark family. Deformation through working makes closer identification impossible.

MOLLUSCS

Professor Emeritus Nils Odhner of the Section of Invertebrate Zoology, the Museum of Natural History in Stockholm, has kindly identified the marine and land molluscs as well as the few small fragments of other invertebrates. Professor Odhner's list of identifications may be found on Table 4 (p. 7), and the reader will have no difficulty finding the names of all the species and their pictures if he compares this table with Plates XXIII and XXIV and their legends.

An important observation was made by Professor Odhner concerning the land pulmonate (*Helix mazulli* Jan.) which occurs from Lerna I through Lerna V, being common in Lerna II and Lerna IV and very rare in Lerna V. There it disappears from our list. It is said that this snail is indigenous in Italy (especially in Sicily), and it ought to have been (must have been?) introduced from that part of the Mediterranean. There is no other record of its existence in Greece, there are no other sources of knowledge of this period, but surely we must now say that it did once exist in Greece! One small fragment of a common sea-urchin (*Sphaerechinus granularis* Lamarck) comes from Lerna V, and is common in the sea now; two fragments of claws of crabs and two small young specimens of land molluscs cannot be identified without a great expenditure of time on this relatively unimportant detail.

THE IMPORTANCE OF THE FAUNA

In Table 7 (p. 11) we have presented the statistics for wild and domestic animals and we have shown the same points diagrammatically in Diagram 3 for each of the settlements at Lerna from I to VII, excluding the Classical and Roman eras for lack of sufficient material. The results illustrated are:

a) The total number of fragments of wild and domestic animals.
b) The percentage of the total number of fragments represented by each of these.
c) The total calculated MIND of wild and domestic animals.
d) The percentage of the total MIND represented by each of these.

Diagram 3, a) shows clearly that throughout the history of Lerna game played a definite but, except for Lerna I and perhaps Lerna III, a subordinate role; to put it another way, the earliest community which the excavators encountered already got some of its meat by hunting.

Diagram 3, b) shows the low and almost even level of the relative frequency of wild animal bones through the different settlements.

We get a more accurate picture when we turn to Diagrams 3, c) and d), which show the frequencies of calculated MIND, absolutely and relatively. In Diagram 3, d) we find that in Lerna I about 35% of the calculated individuals were wild animals against about 65% domestic (and transitional). The figures go down to 15% and 85% in the following period, Lerna II, Middle Neolithic, while they are 22% and 78% for Lerna III, indicating an increase of game again. From Lerna IV on the MIND for the wild species lies between 7.1% and 11.8%. It is important to remember that the bones of game animals are more fragmentary than are the domestic throughout the whole collection; as mentioned above (pp. 4,40) one fragment of a bear, for instance, had to be registered as one individual in the lists of MIND, whereas for the domestic and transitional species the MIND is calculated on the number of mandibles or maxillae, of horn-cores and of some other fragments. So we must acknowledge that even the figures for MIND in Diagram d) overestimate the number of wild animals. We should also add that birds and fish are not included in these calculations.

We can without hesitation conclude that game played a definite role in Lerna during Early Neolithic, that its importance was considerably less during Middle Neolithic, that its importance increased again during Lerna III, and that after that it kept a relatively inferior position, so far at least as we can tell from excavation.

Table 7 gives a more varied picture of the whole situation since it contains also the mixed layers and strata and their bone material calculated in the same way as are the certified layers in parts a) through d) of Diagram 3.

Among the domestic animals cattle were no doubt the most important meat producers. This can be seen in our Diagram 4 giving the distribution of MIND of domestic pig, sheep, goat, and cattle in the different settlements from Lerna I to Lerna VII. A parallel to this diagram, showing in addition the situation in the transitional and mixed strata, is found in Table 8 (p. 12). The MIND for cattle in Lerna I through Lerna V is calculated to be between 15% and 21% of the total number of domestic individuals. We must remember also the meat volume of this animal in comparison with the more numerous caprovines and pig.

Diagram 4 also shows a very interesting change in the MIND from Lerna I to Lerna V. Contemporary with a slight decrease in the MIND of the caprovines we see a steady increase in the MIND of the domestic pig, while the MIND of cattle remains fairly constant. Sheep and goat increase during Lerna VI, and in Lerna VII they still show a high level of MIND. Cattle has decreased sharply during Lerna VI, but increases again in Lerna VII. Since the total number of fragments from Lerna VII is very small our observations here are of little value, but they are more reliable for Lerna VI; this is especially important for the cattle. The only real trend in the MIND of domestic animals is the decrease of sheep/goat from Lerna II to Lerna V and the accompanying increase of the domestic pig.

In Diagram 1 we are struck by two clear deviations from the normal relationship between the number of identified fragments and MIND. Both occur in Lerna VI[1] and concern sheep/goat and domestic pig. MIND for these animals in Lerna VI is unusually high for a relatively small number of fragments; there may be some special explanation for this. Perhaps these animals were slaughtered or prepared as food in the area excavated for Lerna VI, or perhaps because of a food shortage the other parts of the skeleton were smashed into small pieces, so the number of mandibles and upper jaws seems to increase. Cattle, on the other hand, decreased in number during this period. Only 9.0% of the total number of identified fragments come from Lerna VI. The relative increase of mandible fragments of sheep/goat from Lerna V to Lerna VI makes 17.2%, and of pig 6.3%. In Lerna V sheep/goat constitute 39.1% of the MIND of domestic animals (cattle, sheep/goat, pig), but in Lerna VI they make 57.9%. The corresponding figure for pig in Lerna V is 43.1% and in Lerna VI 37.2%.

Table 9 (p. 13) shows the results of the investigation of the ages shown by the bone fragments of the domestic animals. The righthand column of the table shows the number of mandible fragments for which an age determination could be made, i.e. fragments which had preserved teeth.

According to this table the pigs were killed shortly after they became adult or even as subadults. From Lerna II on a certain percentage of young animals was killed; for Lerna II no less than 50% were killed before they were one year old. In Lerna III this figure decreases to about 23%, during Lerna IV it goes down again to about 17%, in Lerna V it increases to about 24%, in Lerna VI it is more than 30% and in Lerna VII it is more than 37%. The accompanying decrease in the number of wild boar is typical for the beginning of domestication which obviously took place during Lerna II; there are also possible indications of the import of a smaller domestic pig (sty pig?) during Lerna VI. It is remarkable that we have found individuals more than three years old only in Lerna V and Lerna VI.

Before Lerna IV we have too few mandibles of domestic cattle to form any clear picture of age of slaughter. However, Lerna IV, Lerna V, and Lerna VI show for the first time fragments of very young calves (newborn to six months old), and Lerna III, Lerna IV, Lerna V and Lerna VI have examples of cows that were kept alive more than three or four years; the bulk were slaughtered as young adults or adults of 1.5 to 3 years old. Table 9 indicates here that already in Lerna III a developed breeding system had been put into operation for cattle.

From the osteological part of our study we may remember that the cattle were very small in stature in Lerna VI (p. 51). Our fragments from this settlement come from a small, shorthorned race (XIII: 7, 8, 9). The explanation for the appearance of these small animals may be either importation or that they were the result of a diminished selection through linked inbreeding; this is the commonest explanation for the decrease in body size during domestication (Müller, 1964, and his bibliography).

[1] Most of the animal bones and other objects from Lerna VI were found not in habitation-deposits of the usual sort but in the earth which filled two large shaft graves. It is possible though not ascertainable that circumstances of the burials may account for a measure of variation in the statistics (Caskey).

To sum up the information we get from age determination: the killing of really young pigs began with Lerna II and continued thereafter; the same thing is substantially true for cattle, though it may have begun a little later; with sheep/goat this practice seems to have begun during Lerna I. The same tables show a trend toward keeping the animal stocks alive longer; this may indicate some development in breeding and keeping the animals, but may also be partly the result of changes in the biotope and composition of the fauna.

We have already spoken of the many cuts and marks of gnawing on the fragments of dog bones from the different settlements. Tables 3 (p. 6) and 6 (p. 10) give an indication of the distribution of dog bones throughout the excavated area. They show the very low frequency of occurrence in Lerna I and Lerna II, and a steadily increased percentage of 2.9%–4.1% during Lerna III, Lerna IV, Lerna V and Lerna VI, while also clarifying the wrong impression given by the high percentage of dog bones in Classical and Roman times which is due to the low totals of fragments preserved or found (Roman) and the presence of two BIND (Classical).

It is true that during Lerna III through Lerna VI the domestic dog occurs in numbers of fragments and MIND sufficient to attract our attention beyond the fact that it was a companion to man and was an item of food. Lerna IV, Lerna V, and Lerna VI give examples of young animals being killed, but there is only one senile dog in the whole collection, somewhat the same picture as for the other domestic animals. Dog bones are more frequent than those of fox, hare, wild boar, red deer, roe deer, wild ox, horse, ass, birds and all other wild species in the total number of fragments from the site. There must be an explanation for this, and the first question to ask is what kind of dogs we find in the material. Because the animal was eaten we do not have a single complete skull of a dog in our collection; the best preserved fragments are halves of mandibles, from different strata, from which we have tried to calculate the basicranial lengths of the dogs (cf. pp. 14, 16, 17). From the comparatively modest number of individuals covering the time from Lerna III to Lerna VI we can hardly expect to do more than divide the material into three or four different sizes (or races?). Very few characteristics, as for instance the cases of oligodonty from Lerna III, Lerna V, Lerna VI, Classical, and Surface and Mixed give hints of the course of development. If we study the frequency of MIND of dogs in relation to the frequency of wild and domestic animals as a whole (Table 9), we do not find an answer because the relative total of the wild species decreases as time goes on while the frequency of MIND of dogs increases at the same time. It is the author's opinion that it is rather dangerous to make very much of the statistical possibilities arising from the frequencies of domestic and wild species. But the fact that 17.2% of the total MIND of dogs comes from Lerna IV and 44% from Lerna V, the two settlements from which we have the largest number of fragments and the highest MIND of sheep and goat, makes it at least possible that most of the dogs were shepherd dogs or house dogs rather than hounds used in hunting.

In the records of pathologically altered bones there is a high percentage of healed fractures and sequelae of arthrosis from external violence. When these characteristics occur in adult sheep and goat or in small adult specimens of domestic pig they corroborate the conclusion reached by Müller (1964), namely that domestic animals were not killed as a result of such an injury until the normal time came for slaughtering them. One severe case of deformative arthrosis occurs in red deer in Lerna V, the only example in a specimen of a wild species. Probably these injuries are the results of the bites of the watch dogs of the herds of sheep, goat, and pig; they are observed mainly on the hind legs of the animals. One cannot exclude the possibility that wild species of caprovines existed in the Peloponnese during the time covered by this excavation, and that these arthritic sequelae represent animals that escaped in the hunt and later more easily fell into the hands of the hunter or were taken by dogs since they were handicapped in this way. However, from the osteological point of view we cannot get enough information from our material to solve this problem.

As far as we can tell from the relatively few identifiable fragments the ass was the first of the equines to be introduced into the region of Lerna. This happened sometime during the Early Helladic period (Lerna III) while the real horse first came later in the Middle Helladic period (Lerna V). For parallels see, for instance, Boessneck (1962) who has in his whole material from Argissa Magula only one horse molar from "Planum XXa of the lowest Bronze Age I", i.e. from Middle Thessalian I.

There are still many important questions to be solved before one can make a sure statement about the earliest occurrence of the ass and horse in the Balkans. When we presented our material we mentioned one of the great difficulties; the ass and horse should not normally occur among the bones of other domestic animals since they were normally not eaten. According to Antonius (1922) the horse was introduced into the Peloponnese during the Middle Bronze age; his evidence was the representation of the animal on the stele of the fifth Mycenaean Shaft Grave. Boessneck (1962, p. 39) suspects that the absence of horse bones in the later strata of the Middle Bronze age may be due to the feudal connections of this animal. We first find the horse in the Troad during Troy VI (Gejvall, 1943, publication in preparation). Professor O. F. Gandert has made a very useful collation of all sources dealing with the earliest appearance of the horse; this is published by Boessneck (1962, p. 39), to whom we refer for details of this very important problem. Of great interest for the present material is the recent discovery, first in Hungary, later also in N. E. Yugoslavia and Roumania, of the original Pleistocene *Equus hydruntinus* (Bökönyi, 1954, and Necrasov and Haimovici, 1959). We have checked very carefully for this equine in our material, but have found no sign of it.

The question of the introduction of the horse into this part of Europe is still far from being answered, but the first real horses in Lerna V fit well into the picture drawn by other students and with our results from Troy.

FAUNA AND BIOTOPE

The composition of the fauna at Lerna during the time from Early Neolithic to the Roman era as revealed by the study of the bone fragments must be due partly to environmental, partly to cultural, changes. This is certainly true for the relative decrease in number of wild ox from Lerna III to Lerna IV, the contemporary decrease of the wild boar (cf. Tables 3 and 6, pp. 6, 10), and the permanent high frequency of sheep and goat throughout the excavated area. Of these, the great number of caprovines and especially of the goat must have been particularly important in the destruction of valuable pasture land and trees. However, on this question there has been during the last decades a considerable change of opinion about the importance of climatic changes as opposed to grazing.

Signs of climatic changes in this area have been reported by Butzer (1957, p. 33). His Neolithic "Subpluvial II (ca. 5000–2400 B.C.)" is said to have been a "moist interval" with somewhat more rainfall than today and a higher rate of evaporation, a situation on a plane "halfway between that of the pluvial and modern conditions, and with temporary decreases in the rainfall shortly before and after 4000 B.C. and again about 3000 B.C." Butzer then continues with a "Postpluvial III (ca. 2400–850 B.C.)" with "renewed decrease in precipitation," leading to a longer period of arid conditions, probably accompanied by greater warmth, with an average rainfall below that of the present. At least one moister interval is reported in the 12th century B.C. During the following "Postpluvial IVa (ca. 850 B.C.–700 A.D.)" (note the misprint Postpluvial III) the situation is said to have been more like the present with slightly warmer winters and "very severe droughts between perhaps A.D. 590–645," only a minor climatic fluctuation.

We have no reliable evidence to assist us in making a decision about the effect of climatic fluctuation of this sort on the biotope as compared with other influences. But we must refer to another author (Brentjes, 1965) who feels very strongly that the influence of climatic changes has been greatly overestimated, and that the greatest devastator of pastureland, the bush, and many trees has been the goat.

In our material, however, we have found a change in the composition of the avian fauna (Table 33, p. 48) which strongly suggests an environmental change sometime between Lerna III and Lerna IV, which could be connected with the arid conditions mentioned above during Butzer's Postpluvial III period. Among the bird bones before this time we find a predominance of bone fragments of grallatorial and swimming birds, whereas from Lerna IV on in addition to these species (cormorant, heron, mallard, garganey, wigeon, tufted duck and another unidentified duck species, gray lag goose, whooper swan, and crane) we find rock partridge, domestic fowl, great bustard, one species of pigeon, i.e. birds more confined to cultivated and arid fields, and also scavengers like the raven and hooded crow. There are also goshawk from Lerna II, Lerna III, Lerna III and IV, Lerna V, Lerna VI, and Surface and Mixed, peregrine from Lerna V, and eagle owl from Lerna IV and Lerna V. This trend is typical for a biotope which changes from humid conditions with high level ground water or temporarily submerged areas to drier or more extensively cultivated fields with greatly lowered ground water.

On the side of cultural development we must take into account the effect of man on the biotope of wild and domestic animals. Man makes his effect first by hunting, later by cultivating the soil and introducing primitively and fully domesticated animals. In this connection we may quote Brentjes, "A hunter inhabits the land together with the game, the farmer inhabits the land from which he drives away the animals." In our case we must not underestimate the effect on the biotope of an increasing population with its more and more extensive hunting and the opening up of larger cultivated areas and severe deforestation.

The picture is, of course, more complicated than it has appeared in our rough estimate compiled through the study of some few tens of thousands of bone fragments. There are details in our lists of bone frequencies which may shed light also on cultural breaks, details which, when studied with archaeological and paleobotanical evidence, may shed more light on importations and immigrations from other districts and countries. Although the evaluation of such evidence falls outside the scope of this study and the author feels he is not the person to make such a synthesis, he may be permitted to point out some trends and peculiarities in the frequency lists which seem to give us a little information of this kind.

There was a striking decrease in the relative number of MIND of wild species between the Early and the Middle Neolithic periods probably as a result of an increase in primitive agriculture. With the beginning of Early Helladic II game again seems to have played a more important part, the MIND of the large game animals, wild boar, red deer and aurochs, increasing considerably more than might be expected with the very moderate increase in the total number of bone fragments excavated. At the same time we find an increase in game which is small but swift and harder to catch. These two circumstances, along with the introduction of the ass to the plains of the Argolid, must indicate improved hunting methods and cultural influences from abroad, possibly from the Near East.

The consistently low level of game from Early Helladic III on and the simultaneous increase in the total and relative number of domestic animals show that another step has been taken towards a settled agricultural and greatly increased population.

We are very puzzled about the frequency of the land snail, *Helix mazulli*, which decreased after Lerna IV at the beginning of Lerna V, as far as can be seen from the shells and fragments that were collected. Since we have been told that not all shells of molluscs were collected from every part of the excavation we cannot rely completely on the disappearance of *Helix mazulli* from Lerna V onward, but it would be very odd if this snail only was not collected after Lerna V; we come then to the conclusion that probably it had disappeared from the Argolid. The sudden decrease and disappearance of the shells of the only land snail in our list recalls to our minds the discussion of the dry Postpluvial III period posited by Butzer.

During the Middle Helladic period, Lerna V, or possibly already in Lerna IV (above, p. 36), we have the first appearance of real horses, probably of oriental type; this may involve other cultural revolutions at this time.

There is one final observation to be added to this discussion. In spite of extensive and intensive agriculture and extensive grazing by large herds of cattle, sheep, goat and pig, and in spite of the almost total deforestation which began early in prehistoric times (there may have been periods of recovery), Lerna is still today a very rich and fertile land, producing two or three crops a year in some fields and suitable for the cultivation of olive and fruit trees. The presence of acorns in the ancient debris suggests that oaks grew near the site; they are rare or altogether lacking today (Hopf, 1962). This means that changes in climate and cultural changes could have taken place with little perceptible effect on the biotope of the animals dealt with here. This, in turn, may give support to our conclusions drawn from the more obvious alterations in the composition of the fauna that we have discussed.

The bones give us details about the consumption of land mammals and birds, but tell us very little about fishing, since fish bone debris is rare and was probably eaten by many animals, pigs, dogs, foxes and other scavengers. We do not get any definite information about the part of the food that was made up of vegetables, fruit, and cereals. Here Hopf's work will partly fill the gap in our information since it gives a complete list of the botanical finds from the site. There are still many problems to be solved before we can make a quantitative evaluation of the animal-vegetable balance of the food in prehistoric Lerna.

SUMMARY

A collection of 2,390 lots, of different sizes, of animal remains — mostly bone fragments and shells of sea molluscs — all from the Excavations of the American School of Classical Studies at Lerna in the Argolid from 1952 to 1958, and representing most of the archaeological periods from the Early Neolithic to Roman times, has been carefully studied and identified from the osteological point of view.

Every fragment was registered, a preliminary identification was made, and a series of notes was recorded on various physical properties of the material in a special list. All information was then punched into 80-column punch cards with the aid of codes and subcodes worked out for this purpose. The material was later processed with an IBM 1401 computer according to three programs. The results, which have been of great value for the scientific treatment of the problems inherent in the material, are reported in this work and its 125 tables, 116 of which handle the osteometrics, 4 diagrams and 25 plates, showing the most important sequences of bone fragments necessary to follow the investigation.

A total of 25,287 fragments (units) have been identified, including 936 samples of small bones which contain many thousands of infinitesimal splinters which could not be further evaluated. One species after another of wild and domestic animals has been followed from the most ancient strata on; the minimum number of individuals has been calculated, and age distribution has been observed. The material description for each species presents all available information concentrated in a usable table.

The inhabitants of *Lerna I, Early Neolithic*, were to some extent dependent on big game, wild ox, wild boar, and red deer, but birds, fish and bivalves were also on the menu. The domestication of the pig and possibly also of the sheep may have taken place already.

Lerna II, Middle Neolithic, was characterized by a slight but marked decrease in the game as well as by certified evidence for domesticated pig, cattle, and caprovines. The number of small game, such as fox and hare, was still very small.

With *Lerna III, Early Helladic II*, came the introduction of the first equine animal, the ass; there was also a slight increase in game during this period. From this settlement on we may speak of a more systematic breeding of domestic pig, sheep/goat, and cattle. In almost every period domestic cattle continued to be the most important meat producer in Lerna. Along with the increase in the number of individuals of domestic animals we see a gradual decrease in size of pigs and cattle. This is well documented by the measurements, and can be seen clearly in the pictures of the bones of these species.

Lerna IV and *Lerna V, Early Helladic III* and *Middle Helladic*, account for well over 70% of the total number of fragments, and so give a more varied picture of the animal life. Bear, badger, common otter, beech marten, and lynx are represented by very few fragments; the first appearance of true horses is certified in Lerna V, but may have taken place already during Lerna IV.

The first specimen of domestic fowl was identified in Lerna V. As far as the author can find this is its earliest occurence in Europe.

SUMMARY

Lerna IV also shows a most interesting change in the avian fauna, which was earlier characterized only by waders and ducks, plus a goshawk. These species still continue to appear in small numbers, but from now on the layers also include a series of birds confined to drier soils (rock partridge, domestic fowl from Lerna V, great bustard, pigeon) and scavengers (like ravens and hooded crows). The peregrine and eagle owl are also newcomers in Lerna V and Lerna IV.

Other game animals in Lerna IV and Lerna V are roe deer and hare. A peculiarity, reported by earlier students, is the common use of the meat of the domestic dog through the different strata. The dogs of Lerna were probably for the most part shepherd dogs or watch dogs with very few hounds for hunting.

Lerna V marks the end of the occurrence of wild cattle in the material, and also shows a marked decrease in wild boar.

In *Lerna VI, late Middle Helladic to early Late Helladic*, which produced only 9.0% of the total number of fragments, some very striking changes could be seen. First of all, we must point out the great decrease in size of both domestic cattle and pig. There was also a slight decrease in size in the sheep. But a considerable increase in the relative number of individuals as calculated from the fragments of mandibles of both pig and sheep/goat seems to be a compensating trend in the Sixth Settlement.

The *Late Helladic, Classical and Roman* strata which follow have given us too few bones to serve as the basis for any significant conclusions.

We have made a quantitative evaluation of the material from the statistical point of view. We have also devoted much time and space to age determination of the domestic animals, which has shed light on the gradual development of more linked breeding and more planned households. A special chapter has been given to the interrelation between the fauna and increasing population and the possible effects on the fauna of climatic changes as opposed to deforestation and other activities of man and goat during the time covered by the excavations.

Finally some connections between cultural changes or breaks and the results of the osteological study have been suggested.

MEASUREMENTS

CANIS FAMILIARIS

Measurement Table 1

Maxilla

Canis fam. Mx	BD591 L. II	A445 L.III+IV	B789 L. IV	B1504 L. IV	BC132 L. IV	D786 L. IV	A325a L. V	A325b L. V
1. Nasal length				78.0	76.0	78.2		76.0
2. Maximal breadth over condyli occipitales								
3. Frontal breadth								
4. Minimum orbital breadth								
5. Length from proximal edge of M²-alveole to proximal edge of C-alveole					66.0	66.2		
6. Length of total tooth row (alveolar)						60.5		
7. Length of molar row (alveolar)		22.0	15.5	18.5	20.0	18.0		
8. Length of premolar row (alveolar)			44.5	50.0	45.5	48.0		
9. Length of carnassial		20.0	17.5	17.2		20.0.		
10. Breadth of carnassial	9.2	10.1		9.9	9.1	9.0		
11. Maximal length of M¹		13.2		12.2		11.5	12.0	
12. Maximal breadth of M¹		16.2		16.0		15.0	17.0	
13. Maximal length of M²	6.4	7.1	6.0				6.1	
14. Maximal breadth of M²	9.5	10.3	8.3				10.0	

Canis fam. Mx	B1467 L. V	B1472 L. V	DE483 L. V	DE499 L. V	DE529 L. V	DE531 L. V	DE538 L. V	DE543 L. V
3. Frontal breadth							49.0	
4. Minimum orbital breadth							36.0	
5. Length from proximal edge of M²-alveole to proximal edge of C-alveole			63.0				65.0	
6. Length of total tooth row (alveolar)			62.0	65.0			60.7	
7. Length of molar row (alveolar)	16.0	20.0	17.5	17.6	18.0	17.5	18.5	
8. Length of premolar row (alveolar)			50.0	49.0	51.0		46.0	47.0
9. Length of carnassial	17.5	20.0			20.0		18.0	18.5
10. Breadth of carnassial	10.0	10.0			10.5		9.7	9.4
11. Maximal length of M¹		12.5			12.8	11.1		
12. Maximal breadth of M¹	17.5	17.5			17.0	13.8		
13. Maximal length of M²	6.1	7.8			7.2	7.2		
14. Maximal breadth of M²	10.0	10.0			12.0	9.7		

MEASUREMENTS

Canis fam. Mx	G323 L. V	B733 L. VI	B1536a L. VI	B1536b L. VI	B1536c L. VI	BD10a Class	BD10b Class	BD10c Class
2. Maximal breadth over condyli occipitales		32.0						
3. Frontal breadth	36.0							39.0
7. Length of molar row (alveolar)			17.0	19.0	17.5			
9. Length of carnassial			17.0	19.0	19.0	19.0	18.8	
10. Breadth of carnassial			9.0	8.2	8.2	10.0	9.4	
11. Maximal length of M^1				11.0	11.8	13.0	13.0	
12. Maximal breadth of M^1				14.2	14.1	16.5	15.7	
13. Maximal length of M^2				6.2	6.9			
14. Maximal breadth of M^2				9.1	9.9			

MEASUREMENT TABLE 2

MANDIBULA

Canis fam. Ma	J855 L. II	J862 L. II	A469 L. II+III	BD573 L. II+III	A438 L. III	A440a L. III	A440b L. III	BE565 L. III
1. Length from middle of condylus to I_1-alveole								
2. Length from processus angularis to I_1-alveole								
3. Length from incisura between condylus and processus angularis to I_1-alveole					104.0			
4. Length from middle of condylus to proximal edge of C-alveole								
5. Length from processus angularis to proximal edge of C-alveole								
6. Length from incisura between condylus and processus angularis to proximal edge of C-alveole					91.0			
7. Height of ramus from lower edge of processus angularis to highest point of processus coronoideus		48.2						
8. Height of corpus behind M_1 medially	23.0				20.0	23.0		
9. Height of corpus between P_2 and P_3	18.0			17.8	16.0			18.0
10. Length from proximal edge of M_3-alveole to proximal edge of C-alveole	77.0				67.0			
11. Length from P_1–M_3	73.0				65.0			
12. Length from P_2–M_3	69.0							
13. Length of molar row	38.0	33.0						
14. Length of premolar row	37.5							36.1
15. Length from P_2–P_4	33.5							

Canis fam. Ma	J855 L. II	J862 L. II	A469 L. II+III	BD573 L. II+III	A438 L. III	A440a L. III	A440b L. III	BE565 L. III
16. Length of carnassial		20.2					23.0	
17. Breadth of carnassial		8.0					9.5	
18. Maximal breadth of corpus	12.1		13.0	10.5	10.0	11.0		
19. Meas. 2 × 1.21 Basal length after Brinkmann								
20. Meas. 4 × 1.37 Basal length after Brinkmann								
21. Meas. 6 × 1.46 Basal length after Brinkmann								
22. Meas. 11 × 2.9–44 Basal length after Dahr	167.7				144.5			
23. $\overline{X}$								

Canis fam. Ma	HTS61 L. III	J475 L. III+IV	A447 L. IV	B431 L. IV	B362 L. IV	B749a L. IV	B749b L. IV	B749c L. IV	B1497 L. IV	B1504 L. IV
1.	139.0				132.0					133.0
2.	139.0				133.5					133.0
3.	134.0				128.4					127.0
4.	121.0				118.0					116.0
5.	122.0				120.0					116.0
6.	117.0				114.0					110.0
7.			53.5		56.0	57.0				53.2
8.	24.5	23.0	25.0	20.0	24.8					24.2
9.	19.8				19.1		18.2	17.1	18.0	18.0
10.	78.6				77.2					76.5
11.					72.2					70.6
12.	69.0									66.0
13.	36.0	38.7								34.0
14.									42.5	40.5
15.	33.0						35.0	37.0	37.0	35.0
16.	21.3						20.0			
17.	9.0						7.4			7.5
18.	12.5	12.5		10.0	12.0		11.1	11.0	10.5	11.1
19.	168.2				161.5					160.9
20.	165.8				161.7					158.9
21.	170.8				166.4					160.6
22.					165.4					160.7
23.	168.3				163.2					160.1

Canis fam. Ma	B1515 L. IV	BD343 L. IV	D607 L. IV	D781 L. IV	DE577 L. IV	G206 L. IV	G253 L. IV	B324 L.IV+V	Dcut13 L.IV+V	B22 L.IV+V	G110 L. V	A345 L. V	B740 L. V
1.													
2.									140.0				
3.									133.0				
4.	95.0							108.0					
5.	100.0								122.0				
6.	94.0							105.0	115.5				
7.		51.5						49.0					
8.	20.0	21.5	22.9			19.5	21.5	22.3	25.0	22.0		24.0	24.0

MEASUREMENTS

Canis fam. Ma	B1515 L. IV	BD343 L. IV	D607 L. IV	D781 L. IV	DE577 L. IV	G206 L. IV	G253 L. IV	B324 L.IV+V	D cut 13 L.IV+V	B22 L.IV+V	G110 L. V	A345 L. V	B740 L. V
9.	16.3		20.5			17.2	18.0	19.0	19.4	18.5		20.2	17.8
10.	66.5		74.0			68.3		71.0	80.0				
11.	64.0		69.8			67.0	72.0	68.0	74.0	75.0			
12.	61.0		66.0			62.0	67.0	65.0		70.5			
13.	34.0	35.4	33.7			33.0	34.0	33.0		39.0	37.0		
14.	34.0		37.0		40.4	35.0	39.0	36.0		38.0			40.0
15.	29.0		34.0	34.0	32.0	30.0	34.0	32.0		34.0			36.0
16.		23.0	22.0								24.0		
17.		9.0	9.0		8.4						9.2		
18.	10.5	12.0	11.3			10.3	10.0	11.9	11.8	12.0	11.9	12.1	
19.									169.4				
20.	130.2							148.0					
21.	137.2							153.3	168.6				
22.	141.6		158.4			150.3	164.8	153.2	170.6	173.5			
23.	133.7							150.5	169.0				

Canis fam. Ma	B1458 L. V	B1469 L. V	B1472 L. V	B1483 L. V	BD422 L. V	BE172 L. V	BE198 L. V	BE394 L. V	BE420 L. V	BF56 L. V
1.		126.0					146.0			
2.		128.0								
3.		122.0					142.0			
4.		110.0					130.0	118.0		
5.		111.0						116.0		
6.		105.0					126.0	111.5		
7.		50.0	57.5		53.0		62.5	55.0		
8.	22.4	20.3				22.6	28.4	23.0	22.8	23.0
9.		16.3		19.0			20.5	20.0	19.8	19.5
10.	74.0	73.0					86.0	79.0	81.6	
11.	71.0	69.0					80.0	75.5	75.6	72.0
12.	66.0	65.0					74.0	72.0	68.0	66.0
13.	37.0	34.5					38.0		35.5	35.3
14.	37.0	38.0							41.0	39.0
15.	32.0									33.2
16.							23.2		21.8	
17.							10.1		8.6	
18.	12.0	10.2				11.8	14.2	11.4	11.0	11.1
19.		154.9								
20.		150.7					178.1	161.7		
21.		153.3					184.0	162.8		
22.	161.9	156.1					188.0	175.0	164.2	164.8
23.		153.0					181.0	162.3		

Canis fam. Ma	C11 L. V	D253 L. V	D405 L. V	DE482a L. V	DE482b L. V	DE483a L. V	DE483b L. V	DE490a L. V	DE490b L. V	DE493 L. V
1.										
2.										
3.										
4.		121.0	117.0			110.8				
5.										

Canis fam. Ma	C11 L. V	D253 L. V	D405 L. V	DE482a L. V	DE482b L. V	DE483a L. V	DE483b L. V	DE490a L. V	DE490b L. V	DE493 L. V
6.		114.0	112.0			108.0				
7.										
8.	23.6	26.0	22.5			20.5	23.0	22.0	20.0	23.3
9.		20.0	18.0			16.2	18.6	16.3	16.5	21.5
10.		76.5	77.0			74.5	77.5	75.0	75.0	
11.		73.5	71.8			72.5	71.5	68.6	69.0	
12.		69.0	67.0			65.4	67.0			
13.		34.0	35.5			34.0	34.5	33.0	33.0	36.0
14.		41.5	39.0			40.0	39.0	37.0	38.3	
15.		36.0	34.3			33.0	34.0		33.0	
16.								19.0		
17.								7.1	7.3	
18.	12.1	11.9	11.6	10.2	10.1	9.9	11.8	10.5	10.2	11.8
19.										
20.		165.8	160.3			151.8				
21.		166.4	163.5			157.7				
22.		169.2	164.2			166.3	163.4	154.9	156.1	
23.		166.1	161.9			154.8				

Canis fam. Ma	DE497a L. V	DE497b L. V	DE528 L. V	DE531 L. V	DE536 L. V	DE538a L. V	DE538b L. V	DE538c L. V	DE538d L. V
1.		125.0							
2.		124.8							
3.		120.0							
4.		109.0							
5.		109.0							
6.		104.0							
7.	50.5					51.5	56.5		
8.	19.8	18.9	23.0			23.2	22.0	21.8	
9.	17.8	17.0	19.5		17.7			17.2	19.0
10.	73.5	74.0	81.0					75.6	
11.	69.0	69.0	73.0					68.6	
12.	64.0	64.0	68.0					64.0	
13.	34.0	33.5	35.5			33.0		32.2	
14.	37.0	37.0	39.0	37.6	39.0			37.3	38.4
15.	32.0	33.0	34.0	33.0	34.0			32.5	33.0
16.	21.0	21.3	21.0					18.8	21.5
17.	8.0	7.8	9.1					7.6	8.8
18.	9.8	10.0	12.2	11.1	11.1	11.4	11.2	10.4	11.4
19.									
20.									
21.									
22.	156.1	156.1	167.7					154.9	
23.									

MEASUREMENTS

Canis fam. Ma	G323a L. V	G323b L. V	B735a L.V+VI	B735b L.V+VI	D565 L.V+VII	B733a L. VI	B733a L. VI	B733c L. VI
1.	109.0							
2.	109.0							
3.	105.5							
4.	98.0							
5.	97.5							
6.	94.0							
7.	43.0		51.0					
8.	19.5	19.0		20.0	20.0	21.0	21.0	25.0
9.	15.0	16.3		17.0	15.5			
10.	66.0	69.0		72.0				
11.	63.0	64.0		68.0				
12.	57.0	60.5		63.0				
13.	32.0	32.0		33.2	30.2	32.0	32.0	38.0
14.	34.0	34.3		36.0				
15.	28.0	30.6		31.0				
16.				20.0	18.1			22.3
17.				7.3	7.5			9.0
18.	10.2	9.7		11.1	10.5	10.1	10.0	12.2
19.	131.9							
20.	134.3							
21.	137.2							
22.	138.7	141.6		153.2				
23.	134.4							

Canis fam. Ma	B1536a L. VI	B1536b L. VI	B1536c L. VI	B1536d L. VI	B1536e L. VI	DE452 L. VI	DE456 L. VI	F1819 L. VI	D243 L. VII + V
1.		129.0							
2.									
3.		124.0							
4.		112.0							
5.									
6.		108.0							
7.		53.0							
8.		21.0		20.0	21.0			19.1	22.0
9.		18.0		17.0	17.2			16.1	17.8
10.		74.0		71.0					74.0
11.		69.0		67.0		75.0	60.0		64.0
12.		65.0		63.0		70.0	56.0		65.0
13.		34.0		35.0	33.5	38.5	30.0		36.0
14.		37.0				40.5	31.5	33.5	31.0
15.		31.2				34.5	27.3		31.0
16.		21.0	22.3		20.0			19.6	
17.	9.0	8.1	8.4		8.1			7.6	
18.		11.1	13.0	10.0	11.0	12.1	11.0	11.4	10.4
19.									
20.		153.4							
21.		157.7							
22.		156.1		150.3		173.5	130.0		141.6
23.		155.6							

Canis fam. Ma	B334a Class	B334b Class	B334c Class	B334d Class	BD7a Class	BD7b Class	BD10a Class	BD10b Class	BE37 S&M
1.									
2.									
3.									
4.									
5.									
6.									
7.									
8.		26.3			19.2	21.0	22.0		22.8
9.	21.0	17.8	14.1				19.0		17.2
10.							77.5		
11.		76.0	63.5				72.0		
12.		70.5	58.0				67.0		67.0
13.		34.0	28.0				35.5		34.4
14.		41.3	37.0				39.0		
15.		36.0	31.0						34.0
16.		19.3	18.5	20.8	19.4	19.0	22.2	22.8	21.0
17.		7.5	7.0	9.1	8.3	8.2	8.8	8.9	8.0
18.		10.0	8.6		11.4	10.0	11.0	11.0	11.4
19.									
20.									
21.									
22.		176.4	140.2				164.8		
23.									

Measurement Table 3

Atlas

Canis fam.	BD7 Class
Breadth of cranial articular surface	35.5
Maximal length from cranial to caudal articular surfaces	26.0

Measurement Table 4

Vertebra

Canis fam.	B1536 L. VI
Maximal length	22.0
Maximal diameter of corpus	10.7

Measurement Table 5

Scapula

Canis fam.	A334 L. V	A345 L. V	B1469 L. V	BD422 L. V	DE507 L. V	BD7 Class
Length of articular processus	29.4	30.0	26.2	29.1	28.8	26.0
Minimum breadth of 'neck'	25.0	25.0	20.0	25.8		17.7
Length of articular surface	25.3	25.0	24.0	25.0	24.5	23.0
Breadth of articular surface	17.1	17.0	16.0	17.2	17.0	15.2
Diameter at minimum breadth of 'neck'	10.2	10.2	9.0	11.2	10.8	10.1

MEASUREMENT TABLE 6

HUMERUS

Canis fam.	A456 L.I	BD343 L.IV	BD617 L.IV	D607 L.IV	J250 L.IV	BE198 L.V	DE483 L.V	DE510 L.V	DE520 L.V	DE538 L.V	B1536a L.VI	B1536b L.VI	B1536c L.VI	BD7a Class	BD7b Class	BD10 Class	J831 S&M
Maximal length			139.5														
Maximal proximal diameter		36.0	33.2	41.0		42.0		32.2	36.0			34.0					
Maximal distal breadth	27.0		27.3		29.0		31.0	32.2		31.0	27.2		28.0	29.4	30.3		28.6
Minimum breadth of diaphysis	9.3		10.2				12.0			11.9			10.1	12.0	11.8	11.5	12.3
Breadth of trochlea	17.0		17.5		19.0		20.0	21.0		21.0	17.0		18.0	18.6			18.0

MEASUREMENT TABLE 7

RADIUS

Canis fam.	A427 L.IV	B1504 L.IV	J151 L.IV	DE481 L.V	DE483 L.V	B1536 L.VI	DE452 L.VI	BD10a Class	BD10b Class
Maximal length		154.0							
Maximal proximal breadth	16.1	17.0		16.0	18.7		18.3		
Maximal distal breadth		22.0	22.0			20.1			
Minimum breadth of diaphysis	10.4	11.4	13.5			10.0	10.3	12.5	12.5
Maximal proximal diameter	10.9	12.0		10.3	11.4				
Diameter at minimum breadth of diaphysis	5.4	7.0	10.0			6.3	7.1		6.0
Maximal distal diameter		12.5	13.0			11.2	11.0		

MEASUREMENT TABLE 8

ULNA

Canis fam.	J250 L. IV	DE529 L. V	DE534 L. V	DE546 L. V	B735 L.V+VI	B1536 L. VI	BD7a Class	BD7b Class
Length of olecranon	26.0	22.5	18.5	21.4				
Minimum diameter of olecranon		18.5	19.6	18.5	17.5			
Diameter of processus anconaeus		22.5	24.5	22.6	22.0	19.1	21.3	
Maximal breadth of articular surface		14.3	16.2	13.1	15.8	13.5	13.9	15.6	15.5

MEASUREMENT TABLE 9

METACARPUS

Canis fam.	Mc2 B1504a L. IV	Mc2 B1504b L. IV	Mc2 B1536 L. VI	Mc3 B1504c L. IV	Mc3 DE503 L. V	Mc4 B1504d L. IV	Mc4 DE481a L. V	Mc4 DE536a L. V	Mc4 DE536b L. V	Mc5 B369 L. IV	Mc5 B1504e L. IV	Mc5 BE559 L. IV	Mc5 DE481b L. V	Mc5 DE481c L. V
Maximal length	55.0	55.0		63.0	55.8	63.0	63.3	60.0	59.0	71.0	54.0	50.0	53.0	52.4
Maximal proximal breadth	6.2	6.4	7.1	7.8	7.4	6.5	7.0	7.7	6.0	8.1	10.0	10.2	9.5	9.9
Maximal distal breadth	8.7	8.6		7.9	7.8	7.9	8.2	8.0	7.9	11.3	9.6	8.4	9.0	8.6
Minimum breadth of diaphysis	6.1	6.2	5.3	6.1	5.3	6.1	6.2	5.7	5.1	7.4	7.0	6.3	6.8	6.2
Minimum diameter of diaphysis	5.0	5.0	4.1	4.8	4.6	5.2	5.1	5.0	5.1	6.1	5.0	4.7	5.0	5.0

Measurement Table 10

Pelvis

Canis fam.	A32 L. IV	B1504 L. IV	BE558 L. IV	B1467 L. V	DE481 L. V	B1536a L. VI	B1536b L. VI
Maximal length of one half			121.0			133.0	
Length of acetabulum	15.0	20.4	23.0	20.5	18.6	18.3	21.0

Measurement Table 11

Femur

Canis fam.	B1504a L. IV	B1504b L. IV	DE545 L. V	BD7 Class	BD10 Class
Maximal proximal diameter	36.0	36.5	35.0		
Breadth (diameter) of caput	18.0	18.2	17.0	17.0	
Maximal distal breadth	30.0				31.5
Minimum breadth of diaphysis			11.8		12.2

Measurement Table 12

Tibia

Canis fam.	A446 L.III+IV	J250 L. IV	DE538 L. V	BD7a Class	BD7b Class
Maximal length				188.0	188.0
Maximal distal breadth		19.5	21.8	21.2	21.2
Minimum breadth of diaphysis		10.3	12.5	12.4	12.2
Maximal proximal diameter	34.0				
Diameter at minimum breadth of diaphysis		10.0	11.0	12.5	11.6
Maximal distal diameter		15.5	15.5	15.3	14.9

Measurement Table 13

Calcaneus

Canis fam.	DE497 L. V	BD7a Class	BD7b Class
Maximal length	39.5	42.3	41.5
Length of tuber calcanei	27.5	26.0	26.0

Measurement Table 14
Metatarsus

Canis fam.	Mt2 B1504a L. IV	Mt2 DE481a L. V	Mt2 DE528 L. V	Mt2 B1536 L. VI	Mt3 A472a L. III	Mt3 A472b L. III	Mt3 B1504b L. IV	Mt3 B1504c L. IV	Mt3 DE481b L. V	Mt4 J98 L. III	Mt4 B1504d L. IV	Mt4 B1469 L. V	Mt5 DE481c L. V	Mt5 DE481d L. V
Maximal length	61.5	63.0	56.6				70.0	70.0	71.0	77.5	71.5	74.0	65.0	
Maximal proximal breadth	7.2	5.0	4.5				8.9	8.8	8.8	9.2	6.1	6.2	6.0	
Maximal distal breadth	8.0	8.2	7.6	8.4	8.0	7.9	8.8	8.8	8.3	9.5	8.1	8.4	7.8	7.3
Minimum breadth of diaphysis	5.5	5.6	5.5	6.1		6.0	7.0	6.9	7.0	8.0	6.1	5.7	4.9	4.9
Diameter at minimum breadth of diaphysis	6.0	6.1	5.5	5.1	5.5	6.0	6.0	5.5	5.4	6.2	5.5	5.6	7.1	6.8
Maximal proximal diameter	12.3	13.0	11.6				13.6	13.2	14.0	15.0	11.8	12.2	10.8	
Maximal distal diameter	7.9	7.7	7.0	9.1		9.0	9.8	9.1	8.6	10.2	9.1	8.8	7.6	7.4

CANIS LUPUS

Measurement Table 15
Ulna

	D 595 L. V
Length of olecranon	39.0
Maximal breadth of articular surface	21.0
Minimum diameter of olecranon	29.5
Diameter of processus anconaeus	34.0

Measurement Table 16
Mc 5

	HTJ 14 L. III
Maximal length	77.0
Maximal proximal breadth	14.0
Maximal distal breadth	12.4
Minimum breadth of diaphysis	9.0
Minimum diameter of diaphysis	7.0

SUS

MEASUREMENT TABLE 17

CRANIUM

Sus scrofa

	BD612 L. II	B1509 L. IV	D652 L. IV	B1472 L. V	BE172 L. V	D171 L. V	DE503 L. V	DB124 L. V+VI	B1536 L. VI	D240 L. VII+V
1. Maximal length of os lacrymale	29.5	44.0	44.5	37.0	34.0	35.0	35.0	39.0	35.0	32.0
2. Maximal height of os lacrymale	21.0	25.0	24.0	22.0	22.0	21.0	23.0		21.3	20.6
3. Index	71.2	56.8	53.9	59.5	64.7	60.0	65.7		60.9	64.4
	n 9	Range 53.9 — 71.2		M±εm 61.9+1.94		S.D. 5.82	Var. 9.41			

Transitional and Sus domesticus

	J862 L. II	J882 L. II	A361 L. IV	G57 L. IV	G281 L. IV	J179 L. IV	A14 L. V	BE428 L. V	D591 L. V	DE462 L. V	DE483 L. V	DE536 L. V	DE543 L. V	D155 L. VII
1.	27.0	26.2	25.0	25.0	27.0	30.0	30.0	26.7	25.0	32.0	27.0	24.0	28.0	29.0
2.	21.5	20.9	19.0	21.2	21.0	22.0	25.0	21.0	20.5	23.0	22.0	18.5	23.0	20.5
3.	79.6	79.8	76.0	84.8	77.8	73.3	83.3	80.8	82.0	71.9	81.5	77.1	82.1	70.7
	n 14	Range 70.7 — 84.8		M±εm 78.62+		S.D. 4.14	Var. 5.26			1.11				

MEASUREMENT TABLE 18

MAXILLA

	Transitional and Sus domesticus			
	J855	D781	B1536a	B1536b
	L. II	L. IV	L. VI	L. VI
Length of total tooth row	103.0			
Length of molar row	61.0	68.5		
Length of premolar row	42.0			
Length of diastema	10.5			
Maximal length of C^1			23.0	22.0
Maximal breadth of C^1				18.0
Maximal length of P^1				12.0
Maximal breadth of P^1				6.5
Maximal length of P^2				13.0
Maximal breadth of P^2				9.1
Maximal length of P^3				13.0
Maximal breadth of P^3				12.0
Maximal length of M^1			15.0	
Maximal breadth of M^1			14.0	
Maximal length of M^2			21.0	
Maximal breadth of M^2			17.0	
Maximal length of M^3	28.0	33.0		
Maximal breadth of M^3	18.0	19.0		

MEASUREMENT TABLE 19

MANDIBULA

	Transitional and Sus domesticus G167 L. IV
Height of corpus behind M_3	50.0
Length from angulus mandibularis to proximal edge of M_3-alveole	71.0
Length of tooth row (P_1–M_3)	120.0
Length from P_2–M_3	103.0
Length of molar row	68.0
Length from P_2–P_4	38.5
Length of M_3	33.0
Breadth of M_3	18.0

MEASUREMENT TABLE 20

C^1

	Sus scrofa		
	BE559	DE221	DE548
	L. IV	L. V	L. V
Maximal length of C^1	28.2	31.0	26.5
Maximal breadth of C^1	22.0	21.0	21.0

MEASUREMENT TABLE 21

C_1

	Transitional and Sus domesticus B1536 L. VI
Maximal length of C_1	20.5
Maximal breadth of C_1	10.0

MEASUREMENT TABLE 22

M_3

	Sus scrofa G276 L. IV
Maximal length of M_3	48.2
Maximal breadth of M_3	19.0

MEASUREMENT TABLE 23

SCAPULA

	Transitional and Sus domesticus B1536 L. VI
Minimum breadth of 'neck'	17.2
Diameter at minimum breadth of 'neck'	7.2

MEASUREMENT TABLE 24

HUMERUS

	Sus scrofa D563 L. IV	Trans. and Sus domesticus A479 L. IV
Maximal distal breadth	54.0	40.0
Breadth of trochlea	39.0	

Measurement Table 25

Ulna

	Sus scrofa B1466 L. IV	Trans. and Sus Domesticus		
		B1508 L. IV	B1536a L. VI	B1536b L. VI	B1536c L. VI
Diameter of processus anconaeus	53.0	37.8	22.2	37.0	35.0
Minimum diameter of olecranon	43.0	29.3	20.0	28.2	27.2
Maximal breadth of articular surface	30.0	21.5	16.0	21.0	20.0

Measurement Table 26

Tibia

	Trans. Sus and domesticus B1461 L. V
Maximal distal breadth	30.5
Maximal distal diameter	26.0

Measurement Table 27

Metapodials

	Sus scrofa		Trans. and Sus domesticus	
	Mc3 BD312 L. IV	Mt4 J229 L. IV	Mc2 B1536a L. VI	Mt3 B1536b L. VI
Maximal length	98.2	115.0	63.0	70.0
Maximal distal breadth	22.6	22.8	16.0	14.0
Minimum breadth of diaphysis	17.0	17.2	12.0	10.5
Maximal proximal breadth	21.0	21.0	20.0	14.0
Minimum diameter of diaphysis	14.0		8.5	
Diameter at minimum breadth of diaphysis		14.5		8.0
Maximal proximal diameter		32.0		18.2
Maximal distal diameter		21.0		15.0

OVIS ARIES AND CAPRA HIRCUS

Measurement Table 28

Horn-core

	Ovis aries Dcut12					Capra hircus	
	J268 L.III+IV	G65 L. IV	B21 L.IV+V	DE496 L. V	J455 S&M	BD581 L.II+III	A476 L. III
1. Circumference of base	72.0	82.0	81.0	132.0	141.0		[100.0]
2. Maximal diameter at base	28.0	33.0	29.5	50.5	51.5	60.0	[36.5]
3. Minimum diameter at base	19.0	18.0	21.3	30.5	35.5	31.0	[26.5]
4. Length of front edge		100.0	110.0	245.0			[235.0]
5. Total length			80.0			200.0	
6. Sex						♂	♀

	D743 L. III	A38 L.III+IV	A361 L. IV	B1507 L. IV	BD625 L. IV	BE558 L. IV	D787a L. IV	D787b L. IV	Dcut12 B21 L.IV+V	DE496 L. V
1.	144.0	140.0	90.0	90.0	88.0	76.0	82.0	80.0	85.0	84.0
2.	54.0		34.0	35.5	35.0	29.0	31.3	31.0	33.0	30.0
3.	37.0	31.5	22.0	20.5	21.0	18.5	21.0	20.3	20.0	21.0
4.				142.0		87.0				160.0
5.				140.0						
6.	♂	♂	♀	♀	♀	♀	♀	♀	♀	♀

Capra hircus

	DE532 L. V	DE543 L. V	B1536a L. VI	B1536b L. VI	B1536c L. VI	B1536d L. VI	B1536e L. VI	B1536f L. VI	B1536g L. VI	B1536h L. VI
1.	92.0	83.0	82.0	73.0	73.0	70.0	76.0	86.0	81.0	115.0
2.	34.0	31.0	33.0	29.0	28.0	26.0	28.5	32.5	30.0	41.5
3.	23.3	20.6	20.0	18.0	16.5	15.0	17.1	21.0	21.0	31.0
4.										
5.										
6.	♀	♀	♀	♀	♀	♀	♀	♀	♀	♀

MEASUREMENT TABLE 29

MAXILLA

	Ovis aries	
	AF1a L. V	AF1b L. V
Length of premolar row	35.0	35.0

MEASUREMENT TABLE 30

MANDIBULA

	Ovis aries	
	B1507 L. IV	DE497 L. V
Length of tooth row (P_2–M_3)	77.0	72.0
Length of molar row	51.0	47.5
Length of premolar row	27.0	23.4
Length of M_3	22.5	24.0
Breadth of M_3	7.4	8.9
Length of diastema	42.0	
Height of corpus behind M_3	37.0	32.0
Height of corpus before M_1	22.3	
Minimum breadth of corpus	9.1	8.6
Breadth of corpus at minimum height	9.2	8.6
Breadth of corpus at P_2	10.5	
Minimum height of corpus	13.5	12.6
Height of corpus before P_2	15.2	14.0
Breadth of processus articularis		21.0

Measurement Table 31

Atlas

	Ovis aries AF1 L. V
Maximal length from cranial to caudal articular surfaces	41.0

Measurement Table 32

Scapula

	Ovis aries	
	A159 L. V	AF1 L. V
Length of articular processus	30.0	30.0
Length of articular surface	25.0	
Minimum breadth of 'neck'	17.0	19.0
Diameter at minimum breadth of 'neck'	11.2	10.0

Measurement Table 33

Humerus

	Ovis aries			
	A477a L. III	A477b L. III	A159 L. V	DE533 L. V
Maximal length				135.0
Maximal distal breadth	35.0	36.0	27.0	29.5
Breadth of trochlea	33.0	34.0	26.5	28.0
Minimum breadth of diaphysis				14.5
Maximal proximal diameter				38.7

Measurement Table 34

Radius

	Ovis aries						
	BD577 L.II+III	A159 L. V	AF1a L. V	AF1b L. V	DE497 L. V	B1536a L. VI	B1536b L. VI
Maximal length	160.0	148.0			147.0	144.0	
Maximal proximal breadth	31.4	30.5	30.0	30.0	34.0	30.6	33.0
Maximal breadth of proximal articular surface	29.0		27.0	27.0	30.0	28.0	31.0
Maximal distal breadth	28.2	28.0			31.6	27.0	
Minimum breadth of diaphysis	15.0	21.0			17.3	15.5	19.0
Maximal proximal diameter	16.0	14.8	15.0	15.1	16.2	14.0	17.0
Diameter at minimum breadth of diaphysis	8.2	9.0			10.0	8.0	10.6
Maximal distal diameter	20.1	18.3			20.0	17.7	

Measurement Table 35

Ulna

	Ovis aries		
	A159 L. V	AF1 L. V	B733 L. VI
Length of olecranon	36.5	37.0	
Maximal breadth of articular surface	17.0	17.0	18.0
Diameter of processus anconaeus	25.0	26.0	29.0
Minimum diameter of olecranon	20.5	21.0	24.4

MEASUREMENT TABLE 36

METACARPUS

Ovis aries

	B1507 L. IV	BD308 L. IV	A159 L. V	AF1a L. V	AF1b L. V	DE496 L. V	B733 L. VI	B1536a L. VI	B1536b L. VI	B1536c L. VI
1. Maximal length	149.0	129.0	117.0			127.0	113.2	121.0	114.0	115.0
2. Maximal length without epiphysis						114.0				
3. Maximal proximal breadth	25.0	25.2	21.6	23.0	22.5	22.0	22.0	24.0	20.5	22.0
4. Maximal distal breadth	28.0	29.0	25.8			25.5	25.0	27.0	24.0	25.0
5. Minimum breadth of diaphysis	15.1	15.0	13.0	14.0	12.6	14.0	12.3	13.5	12.0	12.0
6. Minimum diameter of diaphysis	9.3	10.1	8.6	9.9	9.0	9.6	9.0	9.1	8.2	8.5

Capra hircus

	A445 L.III+IV	A447 L.IV	D607 L. IV	B1481 L. V	DE441a L. V	DE441b L. V	B1536 L. VI
1.		120.0	106.0	127.0	114.0	114.0	105.0
2.							
3.	28.6		24.0	27.0	23.2	23.1	23.1
4.		23.2	27.5	32.1	26.0	26.0	25.8
5.	20.0	13.5	16.1	21.0	16.5	17.0	14.5
6.	13.0	10.0	9.7	11.1	9.6	9.4	9.3

MEASUREMENT TABLE 37

PELVIS

Capra hircus

	A479a L. IV	A479b L. IV
Length of acetabulum	24.5	23.0

Measurement Table 38

Femur

	Ovis aries			
	A159 L. V	AF1a L. V	AF1b L. V	AF1c L. V
Breadth (diameter) of caput		19.0	19.0	19.0
Minimum breadth of diaphysis	14.0	15.0	15.0	15.0
Maximal proximal diameter		23.0	23.0	23.0

Measurement Table 39

Tibia

	Ovis or Capra G43 L. III	*Ovis aries*					*Capra hircus* BE147 L. V
		A462 L. I	BD577 L.II+III	A159 L. V	AF1a L. V	AF1b L. V	
Maximal length							208.0
Maximal proximal breadth							38.3
Maximal distal breadth		22.0	26.2	25.0	25.2	25.3	23.3
Minimum breadth of diaphysis	13.1	11.2	15.0		13.0	13.0	14.5
Diameter at minimum breadth of diaphysis	11.3	10.4	11.5		11.5	11.6	12.0
Maximal proximal diameter							38.0
Maximal distal diameter		18.0	21.4	19.0	20.0	20.1	19.3
Breadth of articular surface							37.0

Measurement Table 40

Astragalus

	Ovis aries		
	A462 L. I	A159 L. V	AF1 L. V
Maximal lateral length	25.0	26.0	27.0
Maximal medial length	23.5	24.2	25.0
Length of articular surface for calcaneus		7.0	10.0
Maximal breadth	16.1	18.5	19.2
Breadth of trochlea		19.0	19.8
Breadth of caput		17.2	18.0
Lateral part of caput		9.0	8.4
Maximal medial diameter		15.0	16.0
Maximal lateral diameter		15.4	15.2
Height of articular surface for calcaneus		3.8	4.0

Measurement Table 41

Calcaneus

	Ovis aries			
	A462 L. I	A159 L. V	AF1a L. V	AF1b L. V
Maximal length	51.5	52.0	53.6	54.0
Length of tuber calcanei	35.0	34.0	36.5	37.0

MEASUREMENT TABLE 42

METATARSUS

	Ovis aries					Capra hircus		
	A159 L. V	AF1 L. V	B1536a L. VI	B1536b L. VI	D784 L. IV	B1472 L. V	B1481a L. V	B1481b L. V
Maximal length	123.0		148.0				138.0	136.0
Maximal proximal breadth	19.5	19.4	20.5	20.0	19.0	21.0	22.0	21.5
Maximal distal breadth	22.5		24.2				29.0	30.0
Minimum breadth of diaphysis	11.0	11.5	12.1	11.0	11.6		15.0	14.9
Maximal proximal diameter	18.5	18.6	20.1	19.0	17.0	21.0	19.3	19.5
Diameter at minimum breadth of diaphysis		11.0	10.2	9.9			14.3	14.5
Maximal distal diameter	14.0		16.8				17.0	17.0

MEASUREMENT TABLE 43

PHALANX I

	Ovis aries		Capra hircus	
	A159a L. V	A159b L. V	B329 L. V	B1481 L. V
Maximal length of outer surface	33.0	31.8	36.0	44.0
Maximal proximal breadth	12.0	11.4	11.4	15.0
Maximal distal breadth	11.9	10.1	11.1	15.6
Minimum breadth of diaphysis	9.4	8.1	10.0	

MEASUREMENT TABLE 44

PHALANX II

	Ovis aries	
	A159a L. V	A159b L. V
Diagonal proximal	13.2	12.0
Maximal length of outer surface	17.0	17.0
Maximal proximal breadth	11.8	10.5
Minimum breadth of diaphysis	9.0	7.2

MEASUREMENT TABLE 45

PHALANX III

	Ovis aries A159 L. V
Length of dorsal articular surface	8.6
Length of dorsal wall	19.2
Diagonal length of sole	26.1
Medial breadth of articular surface	7.0
Medial breadth of sole	6.0
Diameter (height)	14.0

BOS PRIMIGENIUS AND BOS TAURUS

Measurement Table 46

Horn-core

	Bos primigenius?		*Transitional and Bos taurus*			
	BA219 L. III	A353 L. IV	A479 L. IV	BE558 L. IV	D787a L. IV	D787b L. IV
1. Circumference of base		210.0	128.0	138.0	195.0	158.0
2. Maximal diameter at base	80.0	72.0	45.0	47.0	69.5	55.0
3. Minimum diameter at base	57.0	61.0	34.0	38.5	51.5	44.5
4. Length of exterior curvature			160.0			
5. Total length	260.0		130.0			
6. Length of interior curvature			115.0			
7. Sex	♀?	♀	♀	♀	♂	♂

	Transitional and Bos taurus										
	G158 L. IV	B1467a L. V	B1467b L. V	D568 L. V	DE537 L. V	DE543 L. V	DB1(9) L.V+VI	B733 L. VI	B1536a L. VI	B1536b L. VI	J831 S&M
1.	126.0	134.0	119.0			173.0		136.0		118.0	180.0
2.	45.0	45.0	42.5		65.0	57.0	64.0	46.5	40.0	41.0	65.0
3.	35.0	37.0	34.0	30.0	48.0	48.0	50.0	36.0	31.0	33.5	43.0
4.	140.0	185.0								110.0	
5.		161.0							73.0	92.0	
6.		150.0								85.0	
7.	♀	♀	♀	♀	♂	♂	♂	♀	♀	♀	♂

Measurement Table 47

Mandibula (distal part)

	Transitional and Bos taurus			
	A479 L. IV	BE559 L. IV	G110 L.IV+V	B1536 L. VI
Length of premolar row	48.0	54.5		
Length of diastema			91.0	86.0
Minimum breadth of corpus	18.6	14.0	15.3	14.0
Breadth of corpus at minimum height			16.0	14.5
Breadth of corpus at P_2	20.0	17.0	19.0	15.5
Height of corpus before M_1		47.0		
Minimum height of corpus	29.7	26.0	25.5	23.3
Height of corpus before P_2		35.0	32.0	31.0

Measurement Table 47
Mandibula (proximal part) and Single Teeth

	Bos primigenius M₂₋₃ BE 564 L. III	Bos primigenius M₃ BD423 L. IV+V	Ma B1472 L. V	Transitional and Bos taurus M₃ J624 L. II	M₃ J741 L. II	M₃ J595 L. II+III	M₃ A414 L. III	M₃ G86 L. IV	M₃ G148 L. IV	M³ B1536a L. VI	M³ B1536b L. VI
Length of molar row			83.0								
Maximal length of P4			19.8								
Maximal breadth of P4			11.2								
Maximal length of M1			21.0								
Maximal breadth of M1			15.1								
Maximal length of M2	32.3		24.5								
Maximal breadth of M2	17.0		17.1								
Height of crown of M2	53.0										
Maximal length of M3	43.0	47.5	38.2	40.0	42.0	40.0	39.5	40.0	40.0	29.0	30.5
Maximal breadth of M3	17.0	20.2	17.0				15.0			21.0	23.3
Height of crown of M3	64.0	50.0								35.0	33.0

Measurement Table 48
Scapula

	Bos primigenius J667 L. II
Length of articular processus	81.5
Length of articular surface	70.5
Breadth of articular surface	64.0
Minimum breadth of 'neck'	72.5
Diameter at minimum breadth of 'neck'	30.0

Measurement Table 49
Humerus

	Transitional and Bos taurus BE575 L. II
Maximal distal breadth	84.0
Breadth of trochlea	80.0

MEASUREMENTS

MEASUREMENT TABLE 50

RADIUS

	Bos primigenius	
	J893	G302
	L. I + II	L. V
Maximal proximal breadth	107.0	
Maximal breadth of proximal articular surface	94.0	
Maximal proximal diameter	52.0	
Maximal distal diameter		45.0

MEASUREMENT TABLE 51

METACARPUS

	Bos prim.	*Transitional and Bos taurus*						
	A438	BE332	C27	D799	A347a	A347b	B1474	B1536
	L. III	L. IV	L. IV	L. IV	L. V	L. V	L. V	L. VI
Maximal length	231.0	203.0		204.0			195.0	
Maximal length without epiphysis	210.0							
Maximal proximal breadth	73.0		59.2	56.0			61.2	52.7
Maximal distal breadth	80.0	63.0		56.0	59.5	67.3	66.0	
Minimum breadth of diaphysis	44.0	33.0		29.0			32.8	
5. × 100 : 1.	19.0	16.3		14.2			16.8	
Minimum diameter of diaphysis	27.0	22.0		20.2			21.9	
Sex		♂?		♀			♂?	♀

MEASUREMENT TABLE 52

SACRUM

	Transitional and Bos taurus
	A35
	L. III + IV
Maximal breadth	200.0
Maximal breadth of cranial articular surface	69.0

MEASUREMENT TABLE 53

FEMUR

	Bos primigenius
	J894
	L. I
Diameter of caput	53.0

Measurement Table 54

Tibia

	Transitional and Bos taurus D563 L. IV
Maximal proximal breadth	98.0

Measurement Table 55

Astragalus

	Bos primigenius J889 L. I	Bos primigenius A321 L. V	Transitional and Bos taurus A469 L.II+III	Transitional and Bos taurus A470 L.II+III
Maximal lateral length	77.0	80.0	65.5	57.0
Maximal medial length		73.0	59.5	53.0
Length of articular surface for calcaneus	25.5	25.0	19.0	21.0
Maximal breadth	56.0	54.0	43.0	39.0
Breadth of trochlea	52.0	51.0	40.5	38.0
Breadth of caput		52.0	39.5	38.0
Lateral part of caput		25.0	18.0	20.0
Maximal medial diameter	43.0		35.0	32.0
Maximal lateral diameter	42.0		33.0	30.0
Height of articular surface for calcaneus	12.5	15.0	10.0	9.0

Measurement Table 56

Centrotarsale

	Transitional and Bos taurus A479 L. IV
Maximal breadth	50.0

Measurement Table 57

Calcaneus

	Bos primigenius BD602 L. II	Transitional and Bos taurus A479 L. IV	Transitional and Bos taurus A347 L. V	Transitional and Bos taurus B1536 L. VI
Maximal length	154.0	117.0	138.0	114.0
Length of tuber calcanei	99.0	71.0	89.0	73.0
Sex			♂?	

MEASUREMENT TABLE 58

METATARSUS

	Bos primigenius					Transitional and Bos taurus						
	BE594 L. I	A438 L. III	A207 L. V	A479 L. IV	A347 L. V	B1467 L. V	B733 L. VI	B1536a L. VI	B1536b L. VI	D245 L. VII+V
Maximal length							196.0			
Maximal proximal breadth		55.0	53.2	44.6		42.0	40.3			
Maximal distal breadth	66.0				48.0		44.0	49.0	47.0	41.3
Minimum breadth of diaphysis							21.1		22.3	20.0
Maximal proximal diameter		53.0	51.0	41.0		38.0				
Diameter at minimum breadth of diaphysis							18.5		21.0	17.0
Maximal distal diameter								28.0	28.0	

MEASUREMENT TABLE 59

PHALANX I

	Bos primigenius				Transitional and Bos taurus						
	BD615 L. I	J894 L. I	BD423 L.IV+V	D602 L. V	BD591 L. II	BD577 L. II+III	A475 L. III	A479 L. IV	BE559 L. IV	BE560 L. IV	DE537 L. V	B1536 L. VI
Maximal length of outer surface	71.0	65.0	60.0	64.0	58.0	59.0	56.0	62.0	60.0	62.0		55.5
Maximal proximal breadth	(38.0)	34.5	36.4	38.0	27.2		30.0	31.0	33.3	29.0	28.6	30.0
Maximal distal breadth	34.0	33.0	31.0	34.4	26.4	25.0	25.5	27.0	30.0	27.2		29.0
Minimum breadth of diaphysis	33.5	30.0	30.0	29.0	23.1	23.0	25.0	24.0	25.0	23.5	25.0	25.0
2. × 100 : 1.	53.5	53.08	60.67	59.38								
Front or hind leg	fr	fr	hi	hi								

Measurement Table 60

Phalanx II

	Bos primigenius BD423 L.IV+V	BD577 L.II+III	A479a L. IV	A479b L. IV	BE559 L. IV	B1536 L. VI
Maximal length of outer surface	46.0	38.0	35.0		35.0	33.0
Maximal proximal breadth	34.0	28.6	26.0		27.0	27.0
Diagonal proximal	39.5	34.0	33.0	35.0	30.5	31.5
Minimum breadth of diaphysis	28.2	22.0	22.0		22.0	22.0
2. × 100 : 1.	72.91					
Front or hind leg	hi					

Columns headed "Transitional and Bos taurus": BD577, A479a, A479b, BE559, B1536.

Measurement Table 61

Phalanx III

	Bos primigenius BE567 L. II	A474 L. III	DE533 L. V
Length of dorsal articular surface	39.0		31.5
Length of dorsal wall	70.0		63.0
Diagonal length of sole	93.0	76.0	86.0
Medial breadth of articular surface	25.3	26.0	23.3
Medial breadth of sole	31.8	29.0	27.5
Diameter (height)	38.0	40.0	

Columns headed "Transitional and Bos taurus": A474, DE533.

ASINUS ASINUS AND EQUUS CABALLUS

Measurement Table 62

Maxilla

	Asinus asinus G74 L. IV	J470 L. IV	J833 L. IV	G82 L. IV	G288 L. IV	Equus caballus D244 L.V+VII	D565 L.V+VII	F15 L.VII	D237 L.VII+V
Maximal length of I^3			16.0						
Maximal breadth of I^3			11.3						
Maximal length of P^2	32.0								
Maximal breadth of P^2	21.2								
Maximal length of P^3					25.0			27.5	
Maximal breadth of P^3					25.0			27.1	
Maximal length of P^4								25.0	
Maximal breadth of P^4								27.0	
Maximal length of M^1								22.0	
Maximal breadth of M^1								26.0	
Maximal length of M^2				22.0		25.6	31.0	23.0	
Maximal breadth of M^2				23.4		25.0	27.0	25.0	
Maximal length of M^3			23.2						20.6
Maximal breadth of M^3			21.0						

Measurement Table 63
Mandibula

	Asinus asinus D264 L.VII+V	J75 S&M	*Equus caballus* F15 L. VII	BE14a S&M	BE14b S&M	BE14c S&M
Maximal length of P_3				29.3		
Maximal breadth of P_3				20.0		
Maximal length of P_4					28.0	
Maximal breadth of P^4					19.0	
Maximal length of M_1			23.5			27.0
Maximal breadth of M_1			18.0			18.0
Maximal length of M_2	29.0		22.5			
Maximal breadth of M_2	14.2		17.2			
Maximal length of M_3	27.0	26.3				
Maximal breadth of M_3	12.3	14.6				

Measurement Table 64
Humerus

	Asinus asinus J485 L. III
Minimum breadth of diaphysis	27.5

Measurement Table 65
Radius

	Asinus asinus D707 L. IV	B733 L. VI	BA224 Arc + Class	*Equus caballus* D241 L. V
Maximal proximal breadth				77.5
Maximal breadth of proximal articular surface				67.0
Maximal distal breadth	61.2		57.0	
Maximal breadth of distal articular surface	51.5		46.5	
Minimum breadth of diaphysis	35.0	31.0		
Maximal proximal diameter				42.0
Diameter at minimum breadth of diaphysis	24.2			
Maximal distal diameter	39.0		30.0	

Measurement Table 66
Ulna

	Equus caballus F15 L. VII
Maximal breadth of articular surface	39.0
Length of olecranon	82.0
Minimum diameter of olecranon	48.5
Diameter of processus anconaeus	62.4

Measurement Table 67

Metacarpus

	Asinus asinus A363 L. IV	*Asinus asinus* BA224 Arc + Class	*Equus caballus* F15 L. VII
Maximal length			226.0
Maximal proximal breadth	39.0	37.5	48.0
Maximal distal breadth			47.5
Minimum breadth of diaphysis		25.0	32.6
Minimum diameter of diaphysis		18.7	22.8

Measurement Table 68

Tibia

	Asinus asinus B1536 L. VI	*Asinus asinus* WellA1 Class
Maximal distal breadth	58.5	55.1
Minimum breadth of diaphysis		33.5
Diameter at minimum breadth of diaphysis		22.3
Maximal distal diameter	40.0	37.0

Measurement Table 69

Metatarsus

	Equus caballus DE456 L. VI
Maximal proximal breadth	50.5
Maximal proximal diameter	41.0

Measurement Table 70

Phalanx I

	Asinus asinus HTS73 L. III	*Asinus asinus* D240 L.VII+V	*Asinus asinus* BA224 Arc + Class
Maximal length of outer surface	73.0	65.0	70.0
Maximal proximal breadth	38.5	33.0	36.0
Maximal distal breadth	35.0	27.1	32.0
Minimum breadth of diaphysis	23.2	21.0	23.0

Measurement Table 71

Phalanx II

	Asinus asinus BA224 Arc + Class
Maximal length of outer surface	36.0
Maximal proximal breadth	36.0
Minimum breadth of diaphysis	32.5

Measurement Table 72

Phalanx III

	Asinus asinus J470 L. IV
Maximal length	38.0
Length of dorsal articular surface	19.0
Length of dorsal wall	35.0
Maximal breadth of sole	43.0
Diameter (height)	28.5

ERINACEUS EUROPAEUS

Measurement Table 73

Mandibula

Erinaceus eur.	GQ57 L. IV	DE483 L. V
Length from middle of condylus to proximal edge of C-alveole	39.4	
Length from incisura between condylus and processus angularis to proximal edge of C-alveole	34.1	
Height of corpus before M_2	7.9	7.6
Length from P_1 to M_3	18.2	
Length of molar row	13.4	13.6
Length from proximal edge of M_3-alveole to proximal edge of C-alveole	21.0	
Breadth of processus articularis	6.0	
Maximal breadth of corpus	3.4	

Measurement Table 74

Ulna

Erinaceus eur.	G32 L. III
Maximal breadth of articular surface	6.4
Diameter of processus anconaeus	8.0
Minimum diameter of olecranon	7.4

MEASUREMENTS

VULPES VULPES
Measurement Table 75
Mandibula

Vulpes vulpes	J598 L. II	J666 L. II	G47 L. II+III	B1497 L. IV	HTN104 L. IV	BA202 L. V	DE510 L. V	B733 L. VI	B1536 L. VI	D240 L. VII+V
Length from middle of condylus to distal point of mandible						98.0				
Length from incisura between condylus and processus angularis to distal point of mandible						92.0				
Length from middle of condylus to proximal edge of C-alveole						90.0				
Length from incisura between condylus and processus angularis to proximal edge of C-alveole						83.4				
Height of corpus behind M_3		15.1			16.3	14.7	14.9	14.9	14.1	15.1
Height of corpus between P_2–P_3		12.2		13.5		12.0		11.1	11.3	11.8
Height of corpus before M_2		15.0	16.0		14.8	14.0	14.0	15.0	13.2	14.8
Maximal breadth of corpus	6.9	6.5	6.9	7.1	6.5	6.5	7.0	7.2	7.0	6.5
Length from proximal edge of M_2-alveole to distal point of C-alveole		70.5				66.0		69.0		70.1
Length from proximal edge of M_3-alveole to proximal edge of C-alveole		66.0				59.0		63.6	60.0	64.5
Length from P_1–M_3		61.7				55.0		58.0	56.0	61.0
Length of premolar row		35.0						33.0		35.0
Length from P_2–P_4		30.0		29.0				28.5		30.5
Length from P_2–M_3		56.2				50.5		54.0	52.5	56.5
Length of molar row	15.5	26.5	26.3		27.0		24.6	25.0		26.5
Length of carnassial		14.6	15.4				14.0	14.1		
Breadth of carnassial	6.8	5.6	6.0				5.6	6.0		

Measurement Table 76
Ulna

	B733 L. VI
Vulpes vulpes	
Maximal breadth of articular surface	9.0

Measurement Table 77
Pelvis

	J651 L. II
Vulpes vulpes	
Length of acetabulum	11.4

Measurement Table 78
Femur

	B1536 L. VI
Vulpes vulpes	
Minimum breadth of diaphysis	8.4

Measurement Table 79
Metapodials

Vulpes vulpes	Mc2 A404 L. III	DE505 L. V	Mc3 A401 L. III	Mt2 B1536 L. VI
Maximal length	55.0	51.8	51.3	53.0
Maximal proximal breadth	5.0	5.3	5.0	5.3
Maximal distal breadth	6.1	6.5	5.1	5.9
Minimum breadth of diaphysis	4.1	4.2	3.3	4.4
Maximal proximal diameter				8.7
Minimum diameter of diaphysis	3.5	3.8	3.3	
Diameter at minimum breadth of diaphysis				3.5
Maximal distal diameter				4.8

URSUS ARCTOS

Measurement Table 80
Mt 2

	DE536 L. V
Maximal proximal breadth	14.5
Minimum breadth of diaphysis	10.4
Maximal proximal diameter	24.0

MELES MELES

Measurement Table 81
Mandibula

Meles meles	TrBcut8 L. IV	G81 L. IV
Length from middle of condylus to distal point of I_1-alveole		90.0
Length from processus angularis to distal point of I_1-alveole		93.5
Length from incisura between condylus and processus angularis to distal point of I_1-alveole		89.5
Length from middle of condylus to proximal edge of C-alveole		78.3
Length from processus angularis to proximal edge of C-alveole		81.2
Length from incisura between condylus and processus angularis to proximal edge of C-alveole		77.6
Height of ramus from lower edge of processus angularis to highest point of processus coronoideus		37.8
Height of corpus behind M_2 medially	19.0	19.5
Height of corpus between P_4 and M_1	14.0	15.0
Breadth of corpus at P_3	8.0	
Breadth of processus articularis		20.7
Length from proximal edge of M_2-alveole to distal point of C-alveole		51.5
Length from proximal edge of M_2-alveole to proximal edge of C-alveole	44.0	43.0
Length of tooth row (P_1–M_2)	41.8	41.2
Length of premolar row (P_1–P_4)	18.5	18.3
Length of molar row (M_1–M_2)		23.0
Length of carnassial (M_1)	17.0	17.3
Breadth of carnassial	8.0	7.6

Measurement Table 82
Vertebra

Meles meles	J457 S & M
Maximal length	11.2
Maximal diameter at corpus	14.0

Measurement Table 83
Scapula

Meles meles	D785 L. IV
Length of articular processus	19.5
Length of articular surface	16.0
Breadth of articular surface	11.3
Minimum breadth of 'neck'	15.8
Diameter at minumim breadth of 'neck'	7.4

Measurement Table 84
Humerus

Meles meles	BE559 L. IV
Minimum breadth of diaphysis	8.9

Measurement Table 85
Radius

Meles meles	A362 L. IV	J457 S & M
Maximal length	82.0	79.5
Maximal proximal breadth	12.1	11.2
Maximal distal breadth	17.0	15.2
Minimum breadth of diaphysis	5.8	6.1
Maximal proximal diameter	8.8	7.3
Diameter at minimum breadth of diaphysis	4.6	5.0
Maximal distal diameter	12.1	10.2

Measurement Table 86
Ulna

Meles meles	J457 S & M
Maximal length	100.0
Length of olecranon	17.5
Diameter of processus anconaeus	15.0
Maximal breadth of articular surface	9.1
Minimum diameter of olecranon	13.1

LUTRA LUTRA

Measurement Table 87

Scapula

Lutra lutra	C33 L. IV
Maximal length	70.5
Length of articular processus	18.0
Length of articular surface	15.2
Breadth of articular surface	10.2
Minimum breadth of 'neck'	16.0
Diameter at minimum breadth of 'neck'	6.9

Measurement Table 88

Ulna

Lutra lutra	BE419 L. V
Maximal breadth of articular surface	8.1

MARTES FOINA

Measurement Table 89

Mandibula

Martes foina	BD432 L. IV
Height of corpus behind M_2 medially	11.0
Height of corpus between P_4 and M_1	9.2
Breadth of corpus between P_4 and M_1	4.4
Length of tooth row (P_1–M_2)	29.0
Length of carnassial (M_1)	10.0
Breadth of carnassial	4.2

Measurement Table 90

Humerus

Martes foina	BE355 L. IV
Maximal length	60.0
Maximal proximal diameter	11.8
Minimum breadth of diaphysis	4.5
Maximal distal breadth	13.7
Breadth of trochlea	9.6

Measurement Table 91

Femur

Martes foina	BC122 L. IV
Minimum breadth of diaphysis	6.0

LYNX LYNX

Measurement Table 92

Radius

	DE496 L. V	NRM 33	NRM 34	NRM 35	NRM 43
Maximal proximal breadth	15.2	15.2	16.3	17.6	15.1
Maximal breadth of proximal articular surface	13.8	13.8	13.9	15.4	13.3
Maximal proximal diameter	11.5	11.6	11.9	12.8	11.0

MEASUREMENTS

LEPUS EUROPAEUS

Measurement Table 93
Mandibula

Lepus eur.	DE497 L. V
Length of tooth row (P_1–M_2)	19.7
Length of diastema	22.0
Maximal breadth of corpus	6.0
Minimum breadth of corpus	5.0

Measurement Table 94
Scapula

Lepus eur.	A320 L. V	DE497 L. V
Length of articular processus	13.5	14.2
Length of articular surface	12.0	12.0
Breadth of articular surface	11.3	9.8
Minimum breadth of 'neck'	7.5	8.2
Diameter at minimum breadth of 'neck'	4.0	4.0

Measurement Table 95
Humerus

Lepus eur.	A320 L. V	DE513 L. V	DE531 L. V
Maximal length	104.0		100.0
Maximal proximal breadth	17.2	15.9	16.3
Maximal proximal diameter	19.3	19.0	18.6
Minimum breadth of diaphysis	6.1	5.8	6.0
Maximal distal breadth	13.0		12.0
Breadth of trochlea	6.0		5.8

Measurement Table 96
Radius

Lepus eur.	A320 L. V	DE483 L. V	B1536 L. VI
Maximal length	110.0		
Maximal proximal breadth	9.1		9.1
Maximal distal breadth	10.0	10.0	
Minimum breadth of diaphysis	6.0	6.6	6.0
Maximal proximal diameter	6.1		5.9
Diameter at minimum breadth of diaphysis	4.1	4.0	4.0
Maximal distal diameter	6.2	6.4	

Measurement Table 97
Ulna

Lepus eur.	G81 L. IV	A320 L. V
Length of olecranon		12.3
Diameter of processus anconaeus		12.1
Maximal breadth of articular surface	8.6	8.8
Minimum diameter of olecranon		11.5

Measurement Table 98
Pelvis

Lepus eur.	B733 L. VI	B1536a L. VI	B1536b L. VI	B1536c L. VI	D554 L.VII+V
Length of acetabulum	10.7	11.5	11.0	12.0	11.0

Measurement Table 99
Femur

Lepus eur.	B733 L. VI
Maximal distal breadth	19.7

Measurement Table 100

Tibia

Lepus eur.	A456 L. I	A446 L. III+IV	D798 L. IV	G278 L. IV	B1536 L. VI
Maximal length			152.0	143.5	
Maximal proximal breadth			19.9	19.7	
Minimum breadth of diaphysis	7.2		7.3	7.0	6.1
Maximal distal breadth	15.5	14.0	15.5	14.5	15.0
Breadth of articular surface				19.0	
Maximal proximal diameter			21.9	20.4	
Diameter at minimum breadth of diaphysis			7.5	6.6	6.2
Maximal distal diameter	10.0	9.2	10.0	9.1	10.0

CERVUS ELAPHUS

Measurement Table 101

Antler

Cervus el.	BD575 L. II	D563 L. IV	B1472 L. V	BE398 L. V	DO33 L. V	B735 L. V+VI
Circumference of pedicle under burr	134.0	79.0	147.0	75.0	144.0	145.0
Circumference of burr		100.0	230.0		224.0	
Circumference above burr			195.0	98.0	177.0	

Measurement Table 102

Cranium

Cervus el.	B1536 L. VI
Maximal breadth at processus mastoidei	123.0
Maximal breadth over condyli occipitales	68.0

Measurement Table 103

Maxilla

Cervus el.	B1484 L. V	DE538a L. V	DE538b L. V	DE545 L. V
Length of molar row		66.5		
Maximal length of P^2			15.5	
Maximal breadth of P^2			15.0	
Maximal length of P^3	20.5		15.0	
Maximal breadth of P^3	15.0		17.0	
Maximal length of P^4	19.5		15.0	15.2
Maximal breadth of P^4	16.2		18.0	18.2
Maximal length of M^1	22.0	20.0		21.8
Maximal breadth of M^1	18.4	20.0		20.0
Maximal length of M^2		23.0		25.0
Maximal breadth of M^2		23.5		23.5
Maximal length of M^3		25.0		
Maximal breadth of M^3		23.5		

Measurement Table 104
Mandibula

Cervus el.	A31 L. IV	D562 L.IV+V	A345 L. V	B1536a L. VI	B1536b L. VI
Length of molar row			73.0		
Length of premolar row	43.0				46.7
Height of corpus before M_1	30.0				30.0
Height of corpus before P_2	27.0				27.5
Minimum height of corpus	19.0				
Maximal breadth of corpus				18.0	
Breadth of corpus at minimum height					9.0
Breadth of corpus at P_2	12.0				
Length of M_3		31.8	31.0		
Breadth of M_3		14.5	13.0		

Measurement Table 105
Scapula

Cervus el.	BD626 L. III	BE434 L. V
Length of articular processus		53.0
Length of articular surface	42.0	42.3
Breadth of articular surface	38.0	40.0
Minimum breadth of 'neck'	35.0	34.7
Diameter at minimum breadth of 'neck'	17.2	17.8

Measurement Table 106
Humerus

Cervus el.	BE568 L. III	DE548 L. V
Maximal distal breadth	50.6	53.0
Breadth of trochlea	49.0	49.0

Measurement Table 107
Radius

Cervus el.	A37 L. III	D605 L. IV	BE424 L. V	DE548 L. V
Maximal proximal breadth	61.0	54.5	50.2	53.0
Maximal breadth of proximal articular surface	57.0	48.5	48.0	50.0
Minimum breadth of diaphysis	37.0			
Maximal proximal diameter	32.0	27.0	27.8	28.0
Diameter at minimum breadth of diaphysis	20.0			

Measurement Table 108
Ulna

Cervus el.	BC207 L. III + IV
Diameter of processus anconaeus	55.0
Maximal breadth of articular surface	40.0
Minimum diameter of olecranon	45.0

Measurement Table 109

Metacarpus

Cervus el.	J839 L. II+III	A335 L. V	BE395 L. V	D200 L. V	B1536a L. VI	B1536b L. VI
Maximal length				268.0		
Maximal length without epiphysis				242.0		
Maximal proximal breadth	40.0	41.2	42.5	42.2	41.1	
Maximal distal breadth				44.0		41.0
Minimum breadth of diaphysis		21.0		23.5		26.0
Minimum diameter of diaphysis				20.6		21.0

Measurement Table 110

Tibia

Cervus el.	J872 L. II	J105 L.II+III	A167 L. V	B733 L. VI
Maximal proximal breadth	72.0			
Maximal distal breadth		48.0	46.0	43.0
Minimum breadth of diaphysis		27.0	27.0	
Maximal proximal diameter	75.0			
Diameter at minimum breadth of diaphysis		22.0	21.5	
Maximal distal diameter		37.0	33.0	30.5

Measurement Table 111

Astragalus

Cervus el.	J105 L. II + III
Maximal lateral length	53.5
Maximal medial length	50.0
Maximal lateral diameter	29.5
Breadth of caput	33.5
Maximal breadth	35.2
Breadth of trochlea	34.5
Lateral part of caput	18.0
Maximal medial diameter	30.5
Height of articular surface for calcaneus	11.0

Measurement Table 112

Metatarsus

Cervus el.	D605 L. IV	DE528 L. V
Maximal proximal breadth	35.0	
Minimum breadth of diaphysis		22.0
Diameter at minimum breadth of diaphysis		22.5

Measurement Table 113

Phalanx I

Cervus el.	C14 L. V	B1536a L. VI	B1536b L. VI
Maximal length of outer surface	56.0	51.0	50.5
Maximal proximal breadth	22.0	22.0	21.0
Maximal distal breadth	19.5	20.2	19.9
Minimum breadth of diaphysis	16.2	17.0	16.0

MEASUREMENTS

CAPREOLUS CAPREOLUS

Measurement Table 114
Antler

	BE284 L. V	DE465 L. V
Circumference of pedicle under burr	79.0	
Circumference of burr	155.0	
Circumference above burr	85.0	73.0

Measurement Table 115
Mandibula

	A18 L. V
Length of premolar row	29.0
Length of diastema	35.0
Minimum height of corpus	10.6
Breadth of corpus at minimum height	5.1
Breadth of corpus at P_2	7.0

AVES

Measurement Table 116
Coracoid

	Whooper swan G73 L. IV
Maximal diagonal length	105.0

Humerus

	Mallard		Garganey		Wigeon	
	A359 L. IV	J833 L. IV	BD600 L. II	BC201x L.III + IV	BABB218a L. III	BABB218b L. III
Maximal length						
Minimum breadth of diaphysis	7.7	7.6	4.8	4.9		
Proximal breadth		20.9			17.2	
Distal breadth						13.2

	Duck sp		Tufted duck	Peregrine	Domestic fowl	Hooded crow
	BD324 L. IV	J826 S & M	DE521 L. V	A325 L. V	BE14 S & M	A447 L. IV
Maximal length			78.0			
Minimum breadth of diaphysis	5.9		5.0		5.8	
Proximal breadth			16.5			
Distal breadth		12.0	10.2	17.5	13.1	15.8

Radius

	Mallard			Gray lag goose		Goshawk	Domestic fowl
	BABB218 L. III	BC122 L. IV	G245 L. IV	D799 L. IV	G124 L. IV	G299 L. V	BE14 S & M
Maximal length		74.5	77.7				
Minimum diameter of diaphysis	2.8	3.3	3.4	4.5	4.3	3.5	3.6
Proximal breadth		5.1	5.1				5.3
Distal breadth		6.8	7.1	11.2	10.5	7.8	
Proximal diameter		6.1	5.9				5.9

Ulna

	Cormorant BE570 L. II	J887 L. I	Mallard BD580 L.II+III	BD380 S&M	Gray lag goose G125a L.III+IV	G125b L.III+IV	D799 L. IV
1. Maximal length							
2. Proximal diagonal							
3. Distal diagonal			10.6	10.2	16.0	16.0	16.3
4. Minimum breadth of diaphysis			6.2	5.7	8.4	8.2	8.4
5. Proximal breadth	11.3	8.4					

	Goshawk A401 L. III	G133 L.III+IV	D801 L.III+IV	B1536 L. VI	Peregrine A325 L. V	Pigeon G182 L. IV	Raven A363 L. IV	Hooded crow DE543 L. V
1.	98.5	121.0		112.5		51.0		
2.	12.1	13.6		14.7		7.6		
3.	9.6	10.0	10.6	11.4		6.7		
4.	5.8	6.0	6.1	6.1	5.8	4.0		5.2
5.	8.0	9.2		9.2		6.4	10.2	

Carpometacarpus

	Mallard BD613 L. I	HTN130 L. II	Goshawk J853 L. II	G133 L.III+IV
Maximal length	57.2		60.8	
Proximal breadth	13.4	12.0	15.3	15.0
Maximal breadth of fissura			5.2	
Distal diagonal	6.8		10.0	
Breadth of both shafts			10.0	

Femur

	Mallard J317 L. III	D357 L. V	Peregrine DE546 L. V	Domestic fowl D357 L. V	Hooded crow B1512 L. IV	Eagle owl BE419 L. V
Minimum breadth of diaphysis	4.6	4.3		6.8	4.3	
Proximal breadth			8.9	10.7	5.7	10.0
Proximal diameter			14.7	15.5	10.1	20.1
Distal breadth	10.0	9.9				
Distal diameter	11.2	11.1				

Tibiotarsus

	Mallard BC122a L. IV	Mallard BC122b L. IV	Mallard J179 L. IV	Whooper swan G206 L. IV	Crane BA214 L. IV	Rock partridge A479 L. IV	Rock partridge D240 L. VII + V	Domestic fowl BD883 S&M	Domestic fowl BE14 S&M	Great bustard A332 L. V
Proximal breadth					22.0					
Distal breadth			9.2	9.1		7.9	9.6	11.6	12.1	22.0
Minimum breadth of diaphysis	3.4		3.5			3.4		5.5	5.2	10.4
Proximal breadth (with processus lateralis)				11.9	34.0		13.8			
Minimum diameter of diaphysis	4.7	5.0	4.4			4.0			7.0	

Tarsometatarsus

	Cormorant G302 L. V	Heron G65 L. IV	Crane J801 L. I	Crane A470 L.II+III	Goshawk J239 S&M
Maximal length	65.0				75.0
Maximal proximal breadth	14.0		25.8	25.1	12.6
Maximal distal breadth		12.7			
Minimum breadth of diaphysis	7.6	6.4	10.1		6.0

APPENDIX

THE PROGRAMMING

by

Ulf Bjälkefors

For the handling of the Lerna animal bone material we have used a computer of the IBM type 1401 with punch cards. The work has been carried out as three different programs: a listing of measurements with the calculation of means (list no. 1); the typing of registered characteristics such as side, dental status, traces of gnawing etc. (two lists). We are giving here a short account of how the three programs work; this will also be clear in the flow schedules which are given in addition.

The material was punched on standard punch cards using a special series of codes. On the cards were registered the datings, identification characteristics and number, class-species-bone (in the flow schedule called species), number of fragments and information concerning each fragment such as part, side, dental status, traces of gnawing etc. The measurements which occur have been punched in some of 11 fields. Ten fields of the card were reserved for the commonest measurements while the more unusual were placed in an eleventh field together with their measurement number according to the code. In such cases where unusual measurements occur one single measurement was punched on each card. The rest of the data on each card of this kind were copied over and a mark was made, O for "others" in column 30. On the measurement cards column 80 was punched with C, M or A for Cranium, Mandibula and Al.

List number 1 includes all information on the bone fragments except the measurements. The cards were sorted according to bone, species, class and date. The O-marked cards were sorted out. During the listing the program has at the top of each page two headings: first the main headings such as dental status, age etc.; then the code numbers which could occur within these main headings. Next a new heading was written with class, species and bone. Below this follow all the data for each card. Guided by the code numbers on the cards the figure representing "number of" has been moved to the correct column in the list. For example the figure 15 in the columns for dental status has caused "number of" to be moved to the columns of the list which have dental status as main heading and 15 as sub-heading. This "number of" is also added to a corresponding additional area in the computer. On each line date and identification number also are written.

When the program has read the next card of data, it makes a test to see whether this card has the same date and bone code number as the preceding card. If it has not, the numbers in each column are added and written out. (The computer has, of course, as many addition areas as there are columns in the list.) Two types of total occur: totals within each subperiod, and totals for the bone within each main period of dating.

List number 2 differs from number 1 as follows: the cards are sorted first according to date and then according to bone, species and class. When writing out, the program does only one

APPENDIX

test to check whether the bone is the same, and then writes the totals in each column of the list when the bone is not the same. In this way we get the totals for any given bone through all datings.

The programs for list 1 and list 2 are the same. When we run list 2 the computer is switched over on its control panel and the testing of the dating group is off function (cf. flow schedule).

In running the list of measurements the cards are sorted as for list 2. In this case, however, only the O-marked cards are included. Except for this the cards are sorted according to C, M, and A in column 80.

On each card is punched the number of measurements made on the registered bone fragment. The program will have to write all these measurements on one line. If there are many unusual measurements for the fragment being considered the program has to read many cards to find all the measurements. The measurements of the next bone fragment must be written on the next line with the same measurements, according to the code, in the correct order in columns. For the measurements in each column we also want the mean within each bone, group and date.

To arrange this we need two programs. The first punches the cards with the data that will be written out in the list. All data are placed in their correct positions for the final form of the list. When the program is testing and finds that bone and date are not the same as on the preceding card, it punches a heading card containing the code numbers of the various measurements. This card is given a number immediately before that of the first measurement card. Before the cards that have been made in this way are listed, they are sorted according to their numbers. Thus the heading will come first for each kind of bone and for each dating group.

The listing program writes out the cards as they have been punched. The measurements are added in additional areas for the calculation of means. Maximum and minimum measurement values within each measurement column are stored in the computer. As soon as the program discovers a heading card, the mean for the earlier measurements in each column is calculated, and these means are written out with the maximum and minimum values. After that, the additional areas are adjusted to zero, and the program continues with the next group of cards.

The reason for making two programs for list 3 is the low storage capacity of the computer used. Tape stations and disc memories are completely lacking, and therefore it is impossible to make sortings with the 1401 computer.

LIST OF PLATES

Plate I

Fig.			Dating L
1	A456	Humerus of domestic dog	I
2	J855	Mandible of domestic dog	II
3	J862	Mandible of domestic dog	II
4	BD573,574	Mandible of domestic dog	II+III
5	J98	Mt 4 of domestic dog	III
6	A438	Mandible of domestic dog	III
7	HTS61	Mandible of domestic dog	III
8	J250	Humerus of domestic dog	IV
9	J250	Ulna of domestic dog	IV
10	J475	Mandible of domestic dog	III+IV
11	D786	Maxilla of domestic dog	IV
12	D781	Mandible of domestic dog	IV
13	G206	Mandible of domestic dog	IV
14	B1515	Mandible of domestic dog	IV
15	B362	Mandible of domestic dog	IV
16	BD617	Humerus of domestic dog	IV
17	Deut13 B22	Mandible of domestic dog	IV+V
18	B324	Mandible of domestic dog	IV+V
19	D607	Mandible of domestic dog	IV

Scale 1:2

Plate II

Fig.			Dating L
1	D565	Mandible of domestic dog	V+VII
2	B1472	Maxilla of domestic dog	V
3	B1472	Mandible of domestic dog	V
4	G323	Mandible of domestic dog	V
5	DE483	Mandible of domestic dog	V
6	D253	Mandible of domestic dog	V
7	BE198	Mandible of domestic dog	V
8	B1469	Mt 4 of domestic dog	V
9	B735	Mandible of domestic dog	V+VI
10	B733	Mandible of domestic dog	VI
11	DE456	Mandible of domestic dog	VI
12	B733	Mandible of domestic dog	VI
13	B1536	Mandible of domestic dog	VI
14	B334	Mandible of domestic dog	Class
15	B334	Mandible of domestic dog	Class
16	B334	Mandible of domestic dog	Class
17	BE37	Mandible of domestic dog	S&M

Scale 1:2

LIST OF PLATES

Plate III

Fig.			Dating L
1	A345	Cut marks in dog mandible	V
2	G323	Cut marks in dog mandible	V
3	BD343	Erosion marks in dog mandible	IV

Scale 3:1

Plate IV

Fig.			Dating L
1	BD312	Mc 3 of wild boar	IV
2	BE559	Upper tusk of wild boar	IV
3	D563	Humerus of wild boar	IV
4	DE221	Upper tusk of wild boar	V
5	B1472	Lower tusk of wild boar	V
6	G276	Third lower molar of wild boar	IV
7	B1466	Ulna of wild boar	IV
8	J229	Mt 4 of wild boar	IV
9	J855	Maxilla of domestic pig	II
10	A445	Tibia of domestic pig (path)	III+IV
11	B1461	Tibia of domestic pig (path)	V
12	B1536b	Mt 3 of domestic pig	VI
13	B1536a	Mc 2 of domestic pig	VI
14	D652	Lacrymal and zygomatic bone of wild boar	IV
15	D591	Lacrymal bone of domestic pig	V

Scale ca. 1:2

Plate V

Fig.			Dating L
1	A462	Tibia of sheep ⎫	I
2	A462	Talus of sheep ⎬ same individual	I
3	A462	Calcaneus of sheep ⎭	I
4	G43	Tibia of sheep or goat; path	III
5	J268	Horn-core of young sheep (?)	III+IV
6	G65	Horn-core of young sheep (?)	IV
7	J465	Mandible of sheep or goat; path	IV
8	BD577	Radius of sheep	II+III
9	BD577	Tibia of sheep	II+III
10	A477a	Humerus of sheep	III
11	A477b	Humerus of sheep	III
12	Dcut12B21	Horn-core of young sheep	IV+V
13	DE496	Horn-core of ram	V
14	J455	Horn-core of sheep ♂	S&M

Scale ca. 1:2

Plate VI

Fig.			Dating L
1	BD581	Horn-core of goat ♂	II+III
2	A476	Horn-core of goat ♀?	III
3	D743	Horn-core of goat ♂	III
4	A38	Horn-core of goat ♂	III+IV
5	A361	Horn-core of goat ♀	IV

102 THE FAUNA

Fig.			Dating L
6	B1507	Horn-core of goat ♀	IV
7	BD625	Horn-core of goat ♀	IV
8	BE558	Horn-core of goat; young	IV
9	D787a	Horn-core of goat ♀	IV
10	Dcut12B21	Horn-core of goat ♀	IV+V
		Scale 1:2	

Plate VII

Fig.			Dating L
1	B1471	Skull fragment of young sheep	V
2	DE497	Mandible of sheep	V
3	DE533	Humerus of sheep	V
4	DE497	Radius of sheep	V
5	DE496	Mc of sheep	V
6	B733	Ulna of sheep	VI
7	B1536	Radius of sheep	VI
8	B733	Mc of sheep	VI
9	B1536	Mc of sheep	VI
10	A445	Mc of goat	III+IV
11	D607	Mc of goat	IV
12	A447	Mc of goat; path	IV
13	D784:II	Mt of goat; path	IV
14	B329	Phalanx I of goat; path	IV
15	B1481	Mc of goat	V
16	B1481	Mt of goat	V
17	B1481	Mt of goat	V
18	B1481	Phalanx I of goat; path	V
19	B1481	Fused phalanx II+III of goat; path } same individual	V
20	B1472	Mt of goat; path	V
		Scale 1:2	

Plate VIII

Fig.			Dating L
1	J894	Supraorbital fragment from skull of wild ox	I
2	J894	Phalanx I of wild ox	I
3	J894	Caput femoris of young wild ox	I
4	J893	Proximal part of radius of wild ox; note cut marks around metaphysis	I+II
5	J889	Talus of wild ox	I
6	BD615	Phalanx I of wild ox	I
7	BE567	Phalanx III of wild ox	II
8	J667	Scapula of wild ox	II
9	BD602	Calcaneus of wild ox	II
10	A479	Calcaneus of young domestic cattle	IV
		Scale 1:2	

Plate IX

Showing cut marks connecting the talus J889 (L. I) with calcaneus BD602 (L. II), both of wild ox
Scale 4:1

LIST OF PLATES

Plate X

Fig.			Dating L
1	A438	Mc of wild ox	III
2	BE594	Mt of wild ox	I
3	A438	Mt of wild ox	III
4	A207	Mt of wild ox; used as tool	V
5	D799	Mc of domestic cattle ♀	IV
6	BE332	Mc of domestic cattle ♂?; subadult	IV
7	B1474	Mc of domestic cattle	V
8	A479	Mt of domestic cattle ♀	IV
9	A347	Mt of domestic cattle ♀	V
10	B1467	Mt of slender built domestic cattle ♀	V
11	B733	Mt of domestic cattle ♀	VI
12	D245	Mt of domestic cattle ♀	VII+V

Scale 1:2.5

Plate XI

Fig.			Dating L
1	BD591	Phalanx I of domestic cattle	II
2	A469	Talus of domestic cattle	II+III
3	A470	Talus of domestic cattle	II+III
4	BD577	Phalanx I of domestic cattle	II+III
5	BD577	Phalanx II of domestic cattle	II+III
6	A475	Phalanx I of domestic cattle	III
7	A479	Phalanx I of domestic cattle	IV
8	A479	Phalanx II of domestic cattle	IV
9	DE537	Phalanx I of domestic cattle; path	V
10	BE564	Third lower molar of wild ox	III
11	A414	Third lower molar of transitional or domestic cattle	III
12	A474	Phalanx III of transitional or domestic cattle	III
13	BD423	Third lower molar of wild ox	IV+V
14	BD423	Phalanx I of wild ox	IV+V
15	BD423	Phalanx II of wild ox	IV+V
16	D602	Phalanx I of wild ox	V
17	A321	Talus of wild ox	V
18	G302	Radius of wild ox	V

Scale 1:2

Plate XII

Fig.			Dating L
1	BA-BB219	Horn-core of wild ox or transitional?	III
2	A353	Horn-core of wild ox or transitional?	IV
3	A479	Horn-core of domestic cattle ♀	IV
4	BE558	Horn-core of domestic cattle ♀	IV
5	D787a	Horn-core of domestic cattle ♂	IV
6	D787b	Horn-core of domestic cattle ♂	IV
7	G158	Horn-core of domestic cattle ♀	IV

Scale *ca.* 1:2.2

Plate XIII

Fig.			Dating L
1	B1467a	Horn-core of domestic cattle ♀	V
2	B1467b	Horn-core of domestic cattle ♀	V

104   THE FAUNA

Fig.			Dating L
3	D568	Horn-core of domestic cattle ♀	V
4	DE543	Horn-core of domestic cattle ♂	V
5	DE537	Horn-core of domestic cattle ♂	V
6	DB1(9)	Horn-core of domestic cattle ♂	V+VI
7	B733	Horn-core of domestic cattle ♀	VI
8	B1536a	Horn-core of domestic cattle ♀; young	VI
9	B1536b	Horn-core of domestic cattle ♀	VI

Scale *ca.* 1:2.2

Plate XIV

Fig.			Dating L
1	BE284	Antler of roe buck	V
2	A18	Mandible of roe deer	V
3	J485	Medial humerus of ass	III
4	HT873	Phalanx I of ass	III
5	A445	Maxilla fragment of (?)ass	III+IV
6	B348	Mandible fragment of ass	IV
7	J833	Upper incisor of (?) ass	IV
8	G74	Second upper premolar of ass	IV
9	G82	Molar (?M²) of ass	IV
10	J470	Third upper molar of ass	IV
11	D707	Radius of ass; path	IV
12	A363	Mc of ass	IV
13	J470	Phalanx III of ass	IV

Scale *ca.* 1:2

Plate XV

Fig.			Dating L
1	G288	(?)Third upper premolar of ass	IV
2	B733	Radius of ass	VI
3	B1536	Tibia of ass	VI
4	D264	Mandible fragment of young ass	VII+V
5	D240	Phalanx I of young ass	VII+V
6	BA224	Radius of ass	Arc+Class
7	BA224	Mc of ass	Arc+Class
8	BA224	Phalanx I of ass	Arc+Class
9	BA224	Phalanx II of ass	Arc+Class
10	Well A1	Tibia of ass	Class
11	J75	Third lower molar of ass	S&M

Scale 1:2

Plate XVI

Fig.			Dating L
1	D241	Radius of horse	V
2	DE456	Mt of horse	VI
3	F7.15.20	Mc of horse	VII
4	D565	(?)Second upper molar of horse	V+VII
5	D244	(?)Second upper molar of horse	V+VII
6	D237	Third upper molar of horse	VII+V
7	F7.15.20	Third upper molar of horse	VII
8	F7.15.20	Mandible fragment of horse	VII
9	F7.15.20	Femur fragment of horse	VII
10	F7.15.20	Ulnar fragment of horse	VII

LIST OF PLATES

Fig.				Dating L
11	BE14a	P_3 of horse		S&M
12	BE14b	P_4 of horse		S&M
13	BE14c	M_1 of horse		S&M
		Scale 1:2		

Plate XVII

Fig.			Dating L
1	GQ57	Mandible of hedgehog	IV
2	A456	Tibia of european hare	I
3	D798	Tibia of european hare	IV
4	G278	Tibia of european hare	IV
5	DE497	Mandible of european hare	V
6	DE497	Scapula of european hare	V
7	A320	Ulna of european hare	V
8	A320	Radius of european hare	V
9	A320	Humerus of european hare	V
10	DE531	Humerus of european hare	V
11	D554	Pelvis of european hare	VII+V
12	B329	Ulna of common otter	IV
13	C33	Scapula of common otter	IV
14	BD432	Mandible of beach marten	IV
15	BE355	Humerus of beach marten	IV
16	DE36	Parts of a whole skeleton of a weasel	V
		Scale 1:2	

Plate XVIII

Fig.			Dating L
1	HTJ14	Mc 5 of wolf	III
2	D595	Ulna of wolf	V
3	B766	Skull fragment of wolf	V
4	J666	Mandible of red fox	II
5	B733	Mandible of red fox	VI
6	D240	Mandible of red fox	VII+V
7	B733	Ulna of red fox	VI
8	DE536	Mt 2 of brown bear	V
9	TrBcut8	Mandible of badger	IV
10	G81	Mandible of badger	IV
11	D785	Scapula of badger	IV
12	BE559	Humerus of badger	IV
13	A362	Radius of badger	IV
14	DE496	Radius of lynx	V
		Scale 1:2	

Plate XIX

Fig.			Dating L
1	BD575	Antler of red deer	II
2	D563	Antler of red deer; young	IV
3	DWallO33	Antler of red deer	V
4	BE398	Antler of red deer; young	V
5	B1472	Antler of red deer	V
6	B735	Antler of red deer	V+VI
7	BE168	Tibia of red deer; path	V
8	BE395	Mc of red deer; path	V
		Scale 1:2	

Plate XX

Fig.			Dating L
1	G302	Tarsometatarsus of cormorant	V
2	G65	Tarsometatarsus of heron	IV
3	BD613	Carpometacarpus of mallard	I
4	J317	Femur of mallard	III
5	J833	Humerus of mallard	IV
6	BC122	Radius of mallard	IV
7	BD600	Humerus of garganey	II
8	BA-BB218a	Humerus of wigeon	III
9	DE521	Humerus of tufted duck	V
10	A325	Humerus of peregrine	V
11	A479	Tibiotarsus of rock partridge	IV
12	D240	Tibiotarsus of rock partridge	VII+V
13	D357	Femur of domestic fowl	V
14	BD383	Tibiotarsus of domestic fowl	S&M
15	A332	Tibiotarsus of great bustard	V
16	G182	Ulna of pigeon	IV
17	A363	Ulna of raven	IV
18	A447	Humerus of hooded crow	IV
19	B1512	Femur of hooded crow	IV

Scale 1:1.5

Plate XXI

Fig.			Dating L
1	J894	Coracoid of gray lag goose	I
2	G125	Ulna of gray lag goose	III+IV
3	D799	Ulna of gray lag goose	IV
4	D799	Radius of gray lag goose	IV
5	G73	Coracoid of whooper swan	IV
6	J801	Tarsometatarsus of crane	I
7	BA214	Tibiotarsus of crane	IV
8	J853	Carpometacarpus of goshawk	II
9	G133	Ulna of goshawk	III+IV
10	J239	Tarsometatarsus of goshawk	S&M
11	BE331	Humerus of eagle owl	IV

Scale 1:1.1

Plate XXII

Fig.			Dating L
1	J886	Left premaxillary bone of Johnius hololepidotus Lac.	I+II
2	HTN130	Vertebra of Johnius hololepidotus Lac.	II
3	HTN141	Basioccipitale + parasphenoideum of Johnius hololepidotus Lac.	II
		(Figs. 1–3, fishes of the Croaker family)	
4	J480	Vertebral center of the Great blue shark, Carcharinus glaucus L.	III
5	A360	Vertebral center of the Gray shark, Galeorhinus galeus L.	IV
6	DE497	Left dentale of the Gold brass, Sparus auratus L.	V
7	DE483	Carapax of the Greek turtle, Testudo hermanni Gm.	V

Scale 1:1

LIST OF PLATES

Plate XXIII

Fig.			Dating L
1	B1536	Glyphis italica Defrance	VI
2	B733	Patella coerulea L.	VI
3	BE593	Patella ferruginea Gmelin	I
4	BC18	Monodonta fragarioides Lamarck	V+VII
5	B1536	Cerithium vulgatum L.	VI
6	BE568	Talparia lurida L.	III
7	B796	Dolium galea L.	Class
8	B1536	Murex trunculus L.	VI
9	B1536	Murex brandaris L.	VI
10	A401	Triton tritonis L.	III
11	A470	Thais haemostoma L. (Purpura)	II+III
12	B1536	Eutria cornea L.	VI
13	A16	Conus mediterraneus Hwass.	IV+V
14	BE172	Rumina decollata L.	V
15	B1515	Helix mazulli Jan.	IV

Scale 9:10

Plate XXIV

16	B733	Arca noae L.	VI
17	BD575	Arca barbata L.	II
18	A401	Glycemeris glycemeris L.	III
19	BD579	Mytilus edulis L.	II+III
20	B733	Pinna nobilis L.	VI
21	B733	Spondylus gaederopus L.	VI
22	BE588	Cardium edule L.	I+II
23	B733	Venus rugosa L.	VI
24	BE578	Tapes decussatus L.	II
25	BF53	Mactra stultorum L.	S&M
26	BE578	Pholas dactylus L.	II

Scale 9:10

Plate XXV

X-ray photographs

			Dating L
1	A445	Tibia of domestic pig with path. changes	III+IV
2	B1461	Tibia of domestic pig with path. changes (healed fracture)	V
3	G43	Tibia of sheep or goat with arthrosis deformans	III
4	B1472	Mt of goat with sequelae of healed fracture	V
5	B1481	Phalanx I of goat with arthrosis deformans	V
6	B1481	Fused Phalanx II and Phalanx III of same individual with heavy arthritic sequelae	V
7	DE537	Phalanx I of domestic cattle with arthrosis deformans	V
8	D707	Radius of ass, path.	IV
9	BE168	Tibia of red deer with arthrosis deformans	V
10	BE395	Mc of red deer with arthrosis deformans	V

Fig. 1 Coding List and Punch Card arranged for the Lerna Bone Material

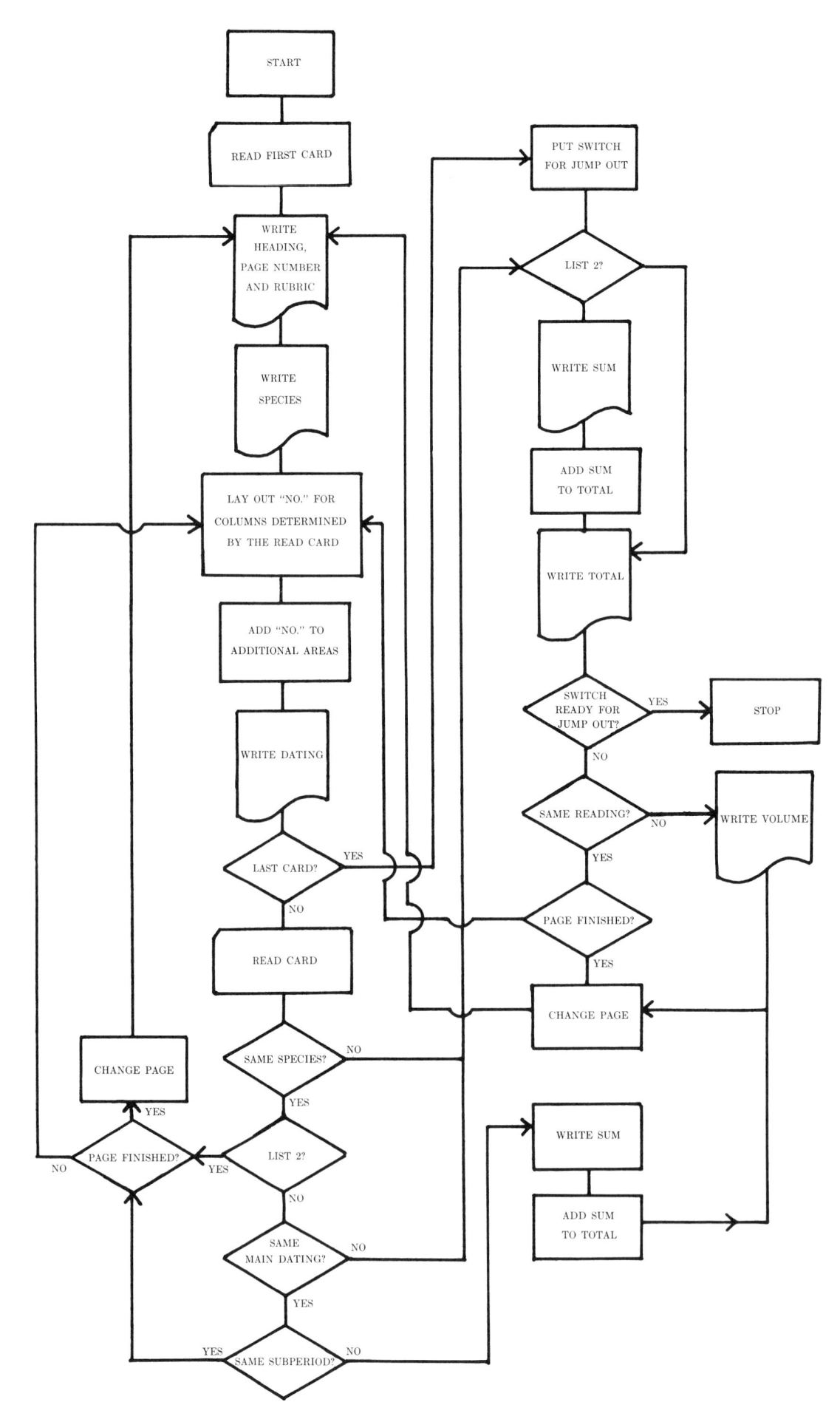

Flow Schedule for Program No. 1

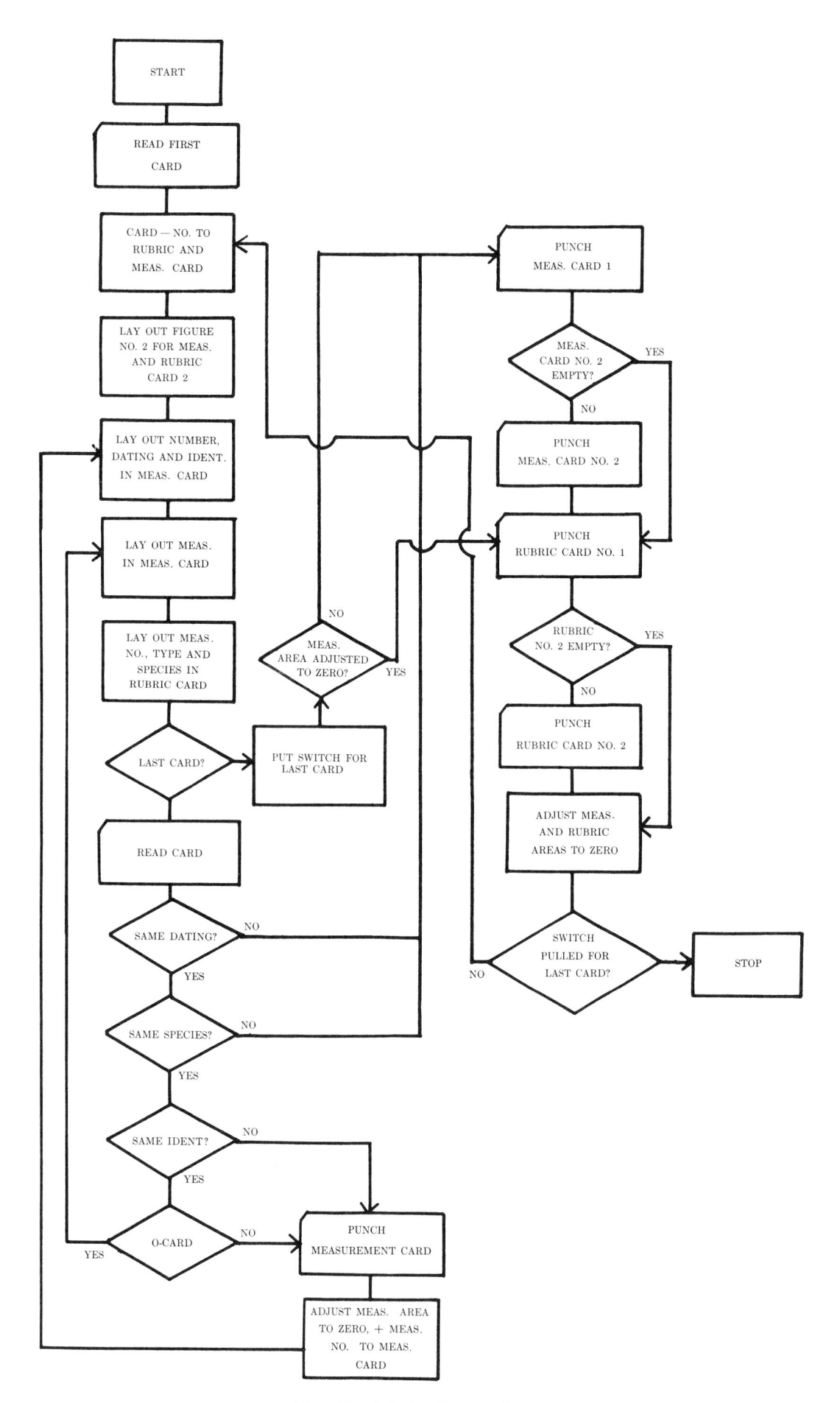

Flow Schedule for Program No. 2

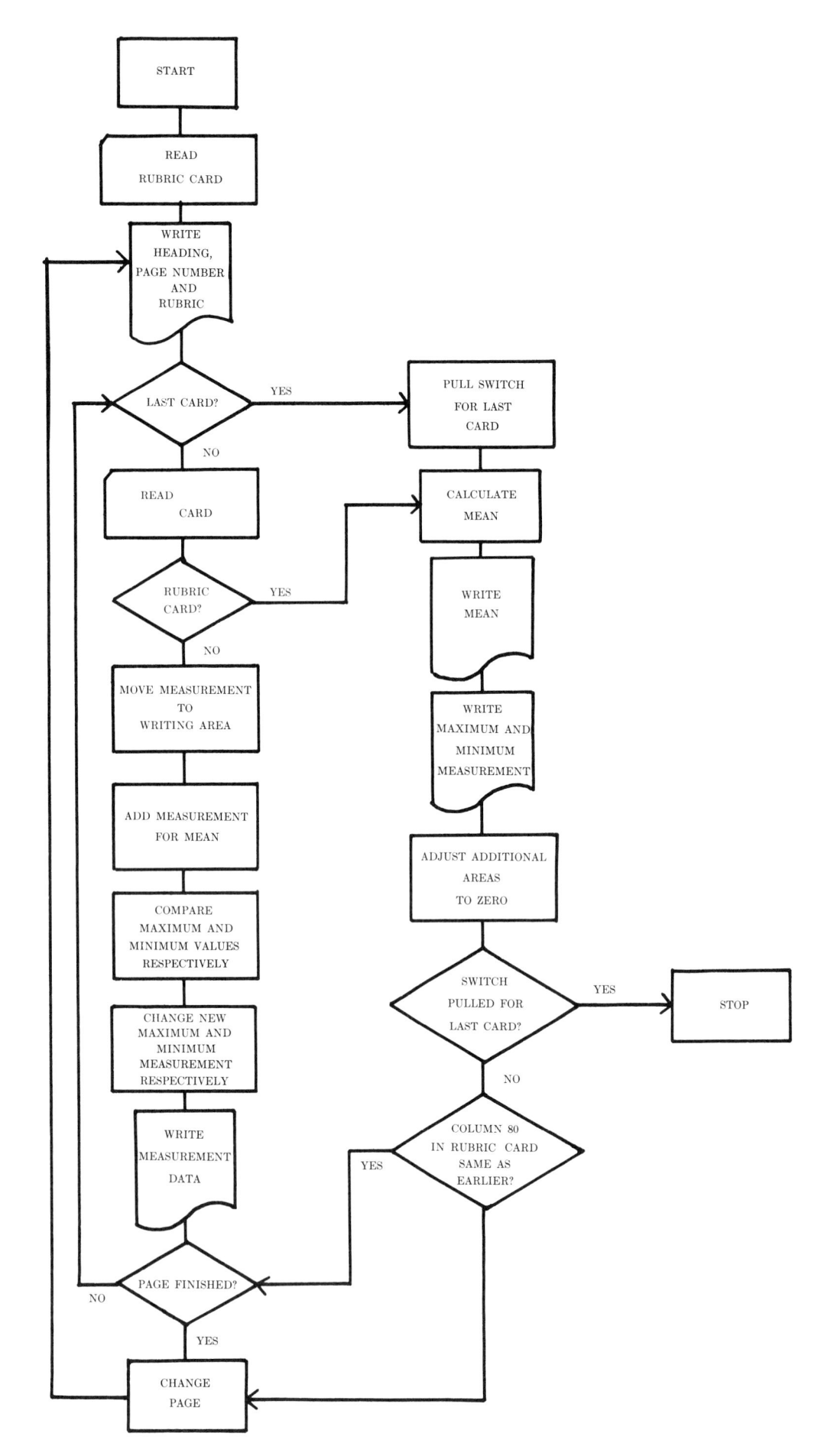

```
                    ┌─────────┐
                    │  START  │
                    └────┬────┘
                         │
                    ┌────┴────┐
                    │  READ   │
                    │ RUBRIC  │
                    │  CARD   │
                    └────┬────┘
                         │
                    ┌────┴────┐
                    │  WRITE  │
                    │ HEADING,│
                    │PAGE NUM.│
                    │   AND   │
                    │ RUBRIC  │
                    └─────────┘
```

Flow Schedule for Program No. 3

Diagram 1. Minimum Calculated Number of Individuals (MIND) of Domestic Pig (—·—), Sheep/Goat (—+—), and Cattle (———) versus Number of Identified Fragments

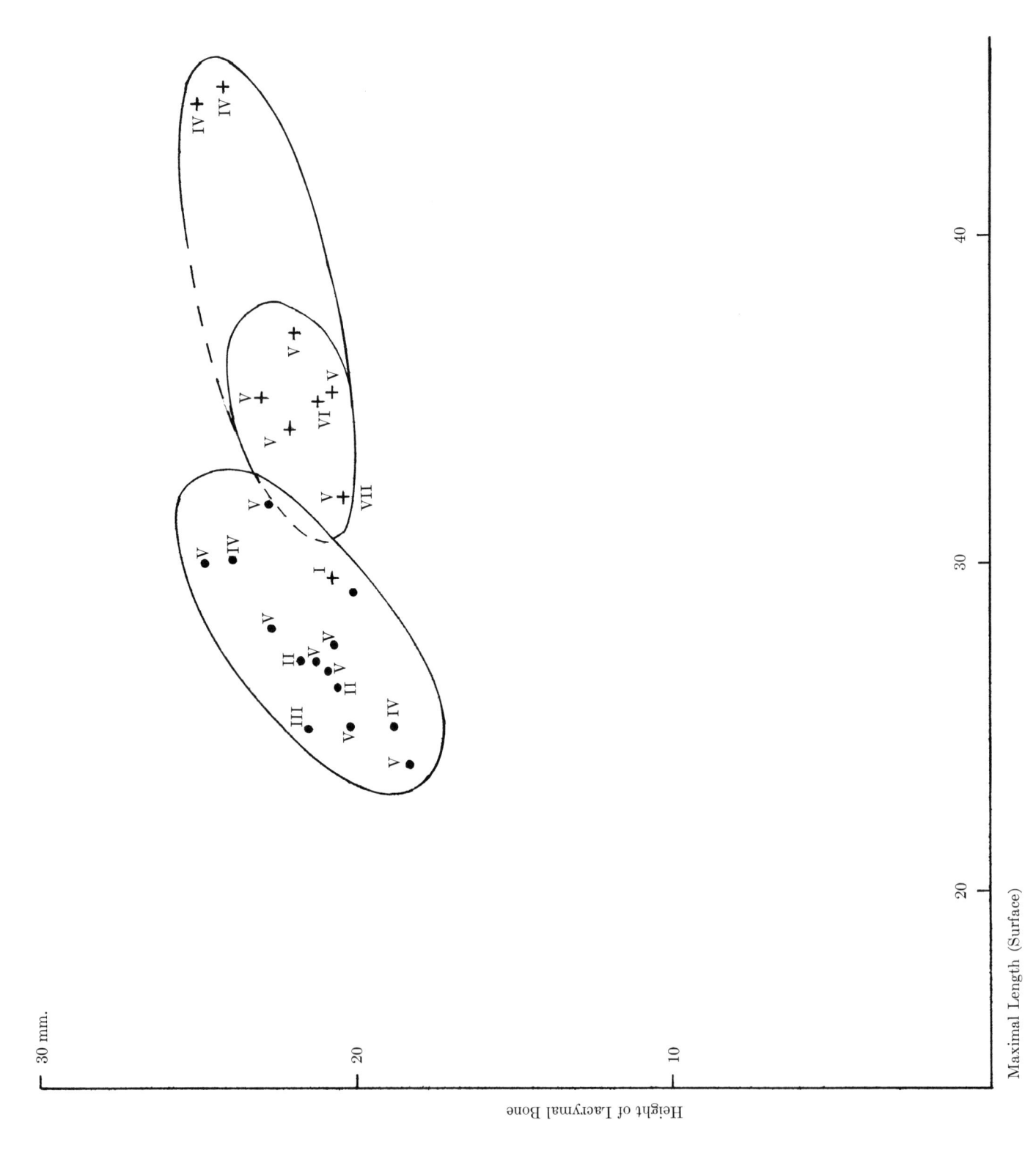

Diagram 2. Ossa Lacrymalia in the Adult Individuals of Wild Boar (+) and Domestic

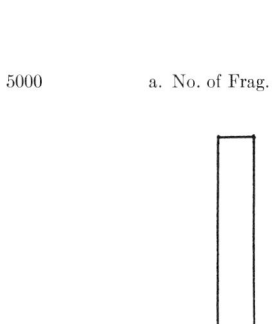

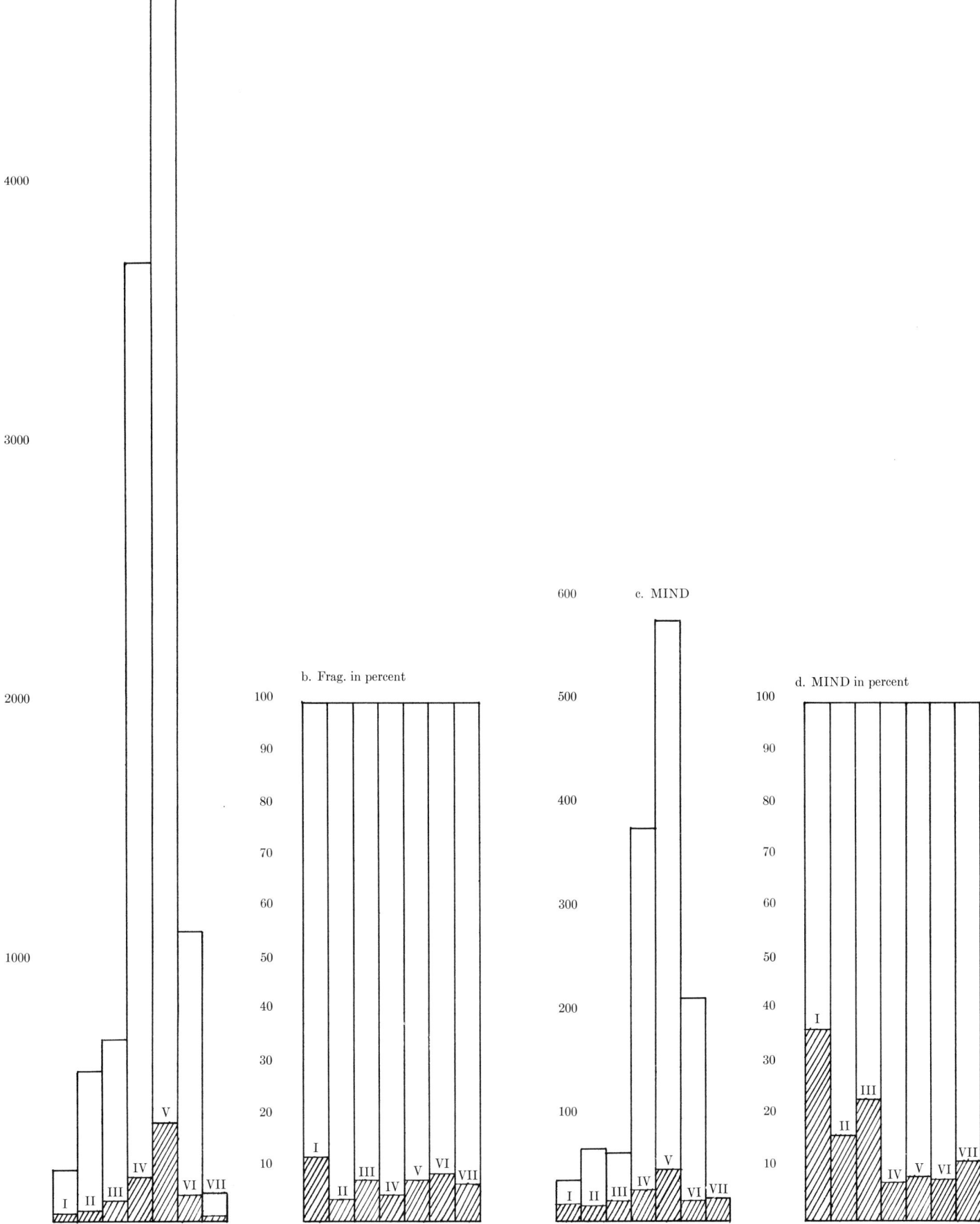

Diagram 3. Wild versus Domestic Animals in Lerna I through Lerna VII

Wild

Domestic

Diagram 4.

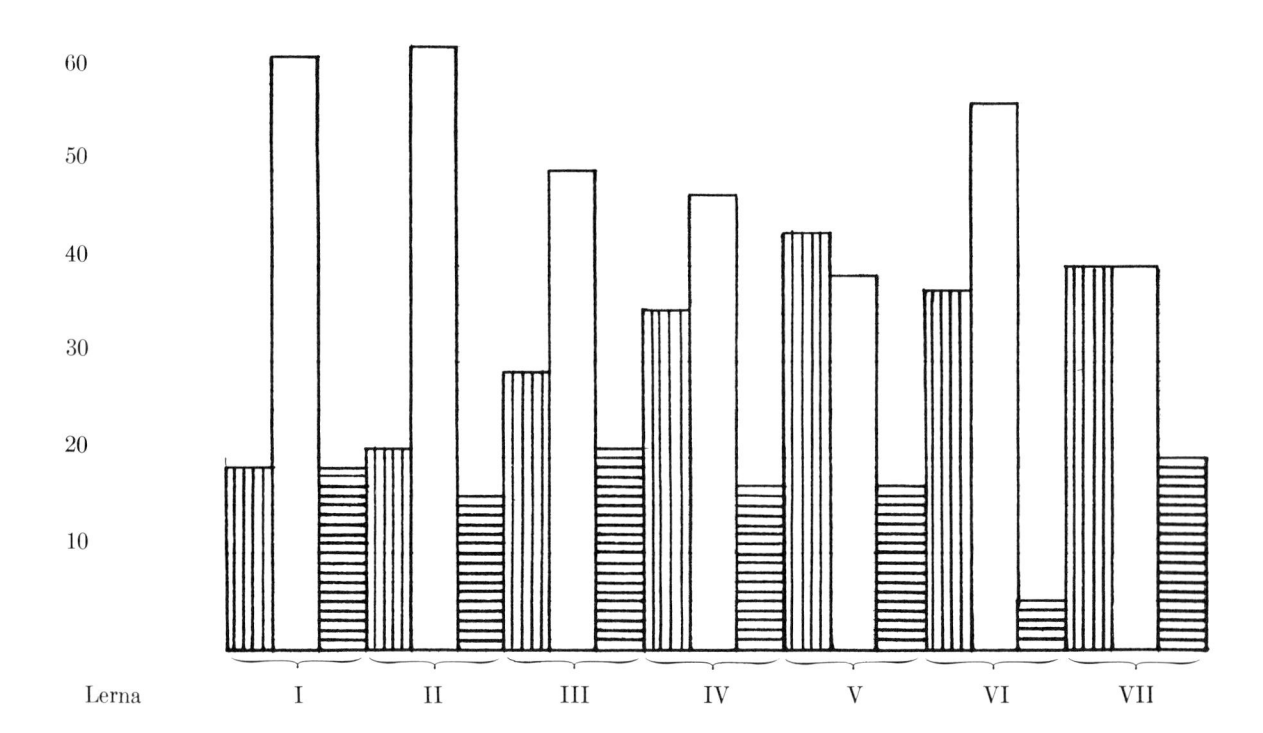

Diagram 4. Minimum Number of Individuals (MIND) of Pig ▦ , Sheep/Goat ☐ , Cattle ☰ , in Lerna I through VII

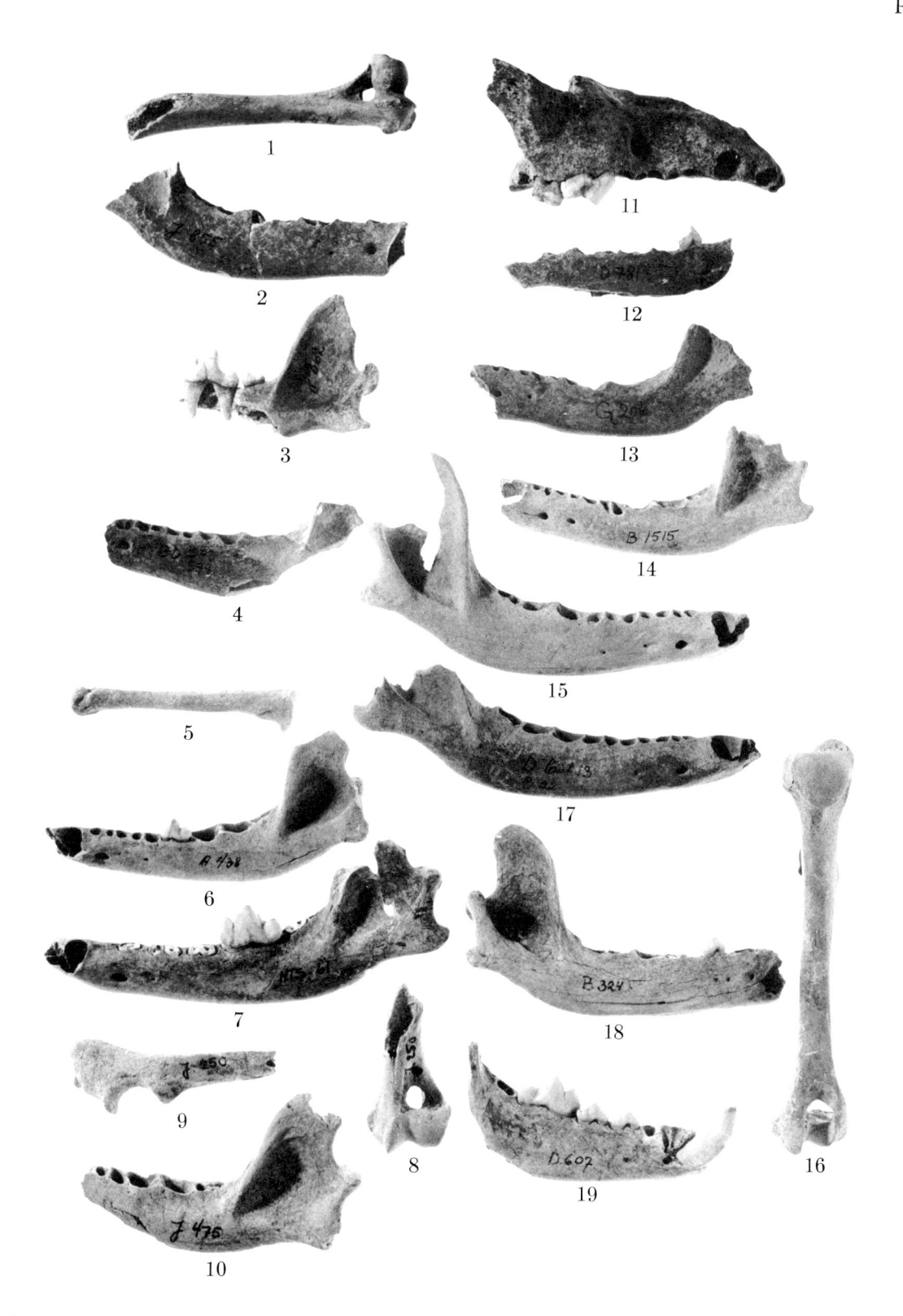

PLATE I

Scale 1:2
1 Humerus of domestic dog.   2 Mandible of domestic dog.   3 Mandible of domestic dog.   4 Mandible of domestic dog.
5 Mt 4 of domestic dog.   6 Mandible of domestic dog.   7 Mandible of domestic dog.   8 Humerus of domestic dog.
9 Ulna of domestic dog.   10 Mandible of domestic dog.   11 Maxilla of domestic dog.   12 Mandible of domestic dog.
13 Mandible of domestic dog.   14 Mandible of domestic dog.   15 Mandible of domestic dog.   16 Humerus of domestic dog.   17 Mandible of domestic dog.   18 Mandible of domestic dog.   19 Mandible of domestic dog.

PLATE II

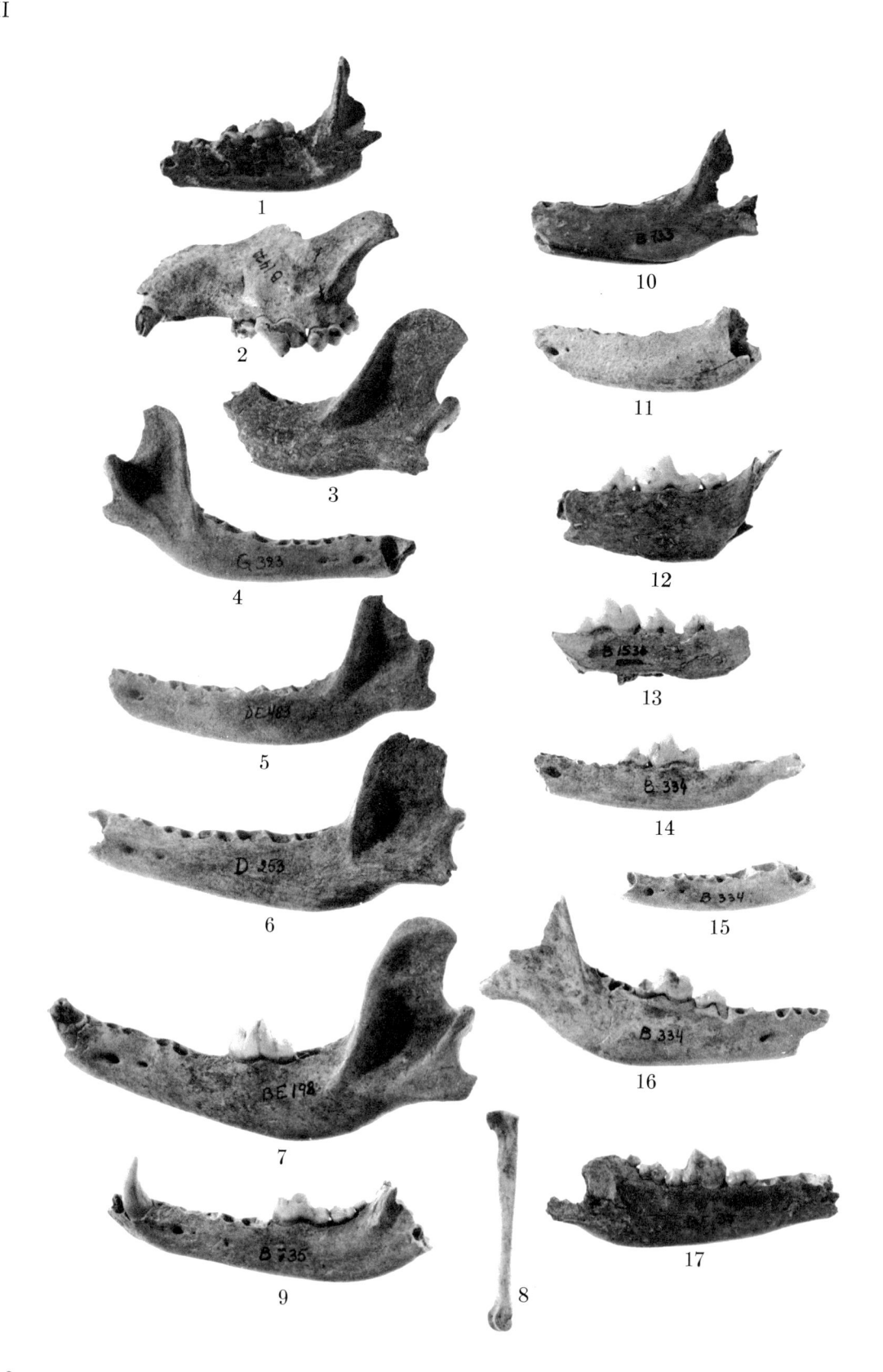

Scale 1:2
1 Mandible of domestic dog. **2** Maxilla of domestic dog. **3** Mandible of domestic dog. **4** Mandible of domestic dog. **5** Mandible of domestic dog. **6** Mandible of domestic dog. **7** Mandible of domestic dog. **8** Mt 4 of domestic dog. **9** Mandible of domestic dog. **10** Mandible of domestic dog. **11** Mandible of domestic dog. **12** Mandible of domestic dog. **13** Mandible of domestic dog. **14** Mandible of domestic dog. **15** Mandible of domestic dog. **16** Mandible of domestic dog. **17** Mandible of domestic dog.

PLATE III

Scale 3:1
1 Cut marks in dog mandible. **2** Cut marks in dog mandible. **3** Erosion marks in dog mandible.

PLATE IV

Scale *ca.* 1:2
1 Mc 3 of wild boar.   **2** Upper tusk of wild boar.   **3** Humerus of wild boar.   **4** Upper tusk of wild boar.
5 Lower tusk of wild boar.   **6** Third lower molar of wild boar.   **7** Ulna of wild boar.   **8** Mt 4 of wild boar.   **9** Maxilla of domestic pig.   **10** Tibia of domestic pig (path).   **11** Tibia of domestic pig (path).   **12** Mt 3 of domestic pig.
13 Mc 2 of domestic pig.   **14** Lacrymal and zygomatic bone of wild boar.   **15** Lacrymal bone of domestic pig.

PLATE V

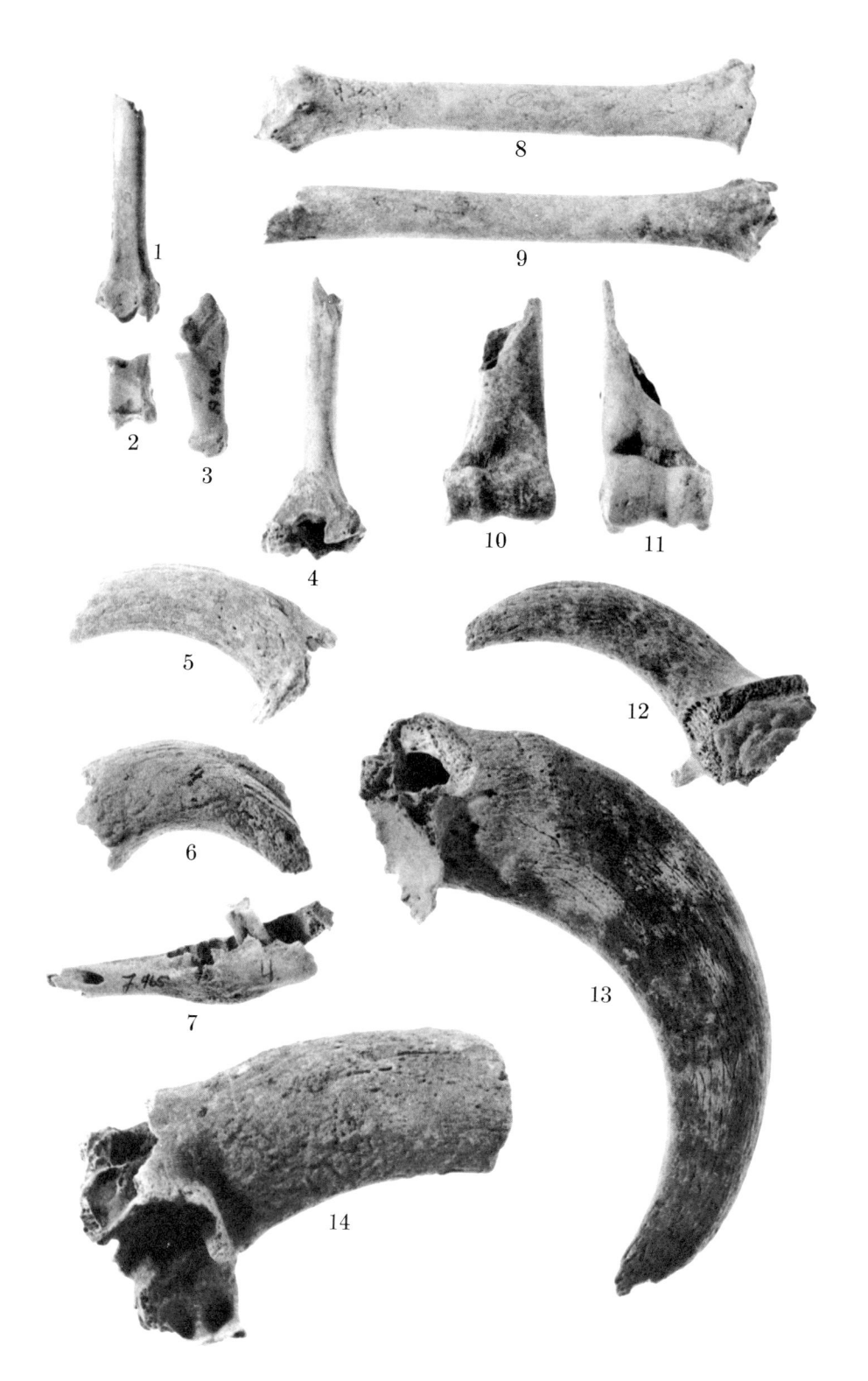

Scale *ca.* 1:2
1 Tibia of sheep. **2** Talus of sheep. **3** Calcaneus of sheep. **4** Tibia of sheep or goat; path. **5** Horn-core of young sheep(?). **6** Horn-core of young sheep (?). **7** Mandible of sheep or goat; path. **8** Radius of sheep. **9** Tibia of sheep. **10** Humerus of sheep. **11** Humerus of sheep. **12** Horn-core of young sheep. **13** Horn-core of ram. **14** Horn-core of sheep ♂.

PLATE VI

Scale 1:2
1 Horn-core of goat ♂.   **2** Horn-core of goat ♀(?).   **3** Horn-core of goat ♂.   **4** Horn-core of goat ♂.   **5** Horn-core of goat ♀.   **6** Horn-core of goat ♀.   **7** Horn-core of goat ♀.   **8** Horn-core of goat; young.   **9** Horn-core of goat ♀.   **10** Horn-core of goat ♀.

PLATE VII

Scale 1:2
1 Skull fragment of young sheep.   **2** Mandible of sheep.   **3** Humerus of sheep.   **4** Radius of sheep.   **5** Mc of sheep.
6 Ulna of sheep.   **7** Radius of sheep.   **8** Mc of sheep.   **9** Mc of sheep.   **10** Mc of goat.   **11** Mc of goat.
12 Mc of goat; path.   **13** Mt of goat; path.   **14** Phalanx I of goat; path.   **15** Mc of goat.   **16** Mt of goat.
17 Mt of goat.   **18** Phalanx I of goat; path.   **19** Fused phalanx II + III of goat; path.   **20** Mt of goat; path.

PLATE VIII

Scale 1:2
1 Supraorbital fragment from skull of wild ox. **2** Phalanx I of wild ox. **3** Caput femoris of young wild ox. **4** Proximal part of radius of wild ox; note cut marks around metaphysis. **5** Talus of wild ox. **6** Phalanx I of wild ox. **7** Phalanx III of wild ox. **8** Scapula of wild ox. **9** Calcaneus of wild ox. **10** Calcaneus of young domestic cattle.

PLATE IX

Scale 4:1
Showing cut marks connecting the talus J889 (L. I) with calcaneus BD602 (L. II), both of wild ox.

PLATE X

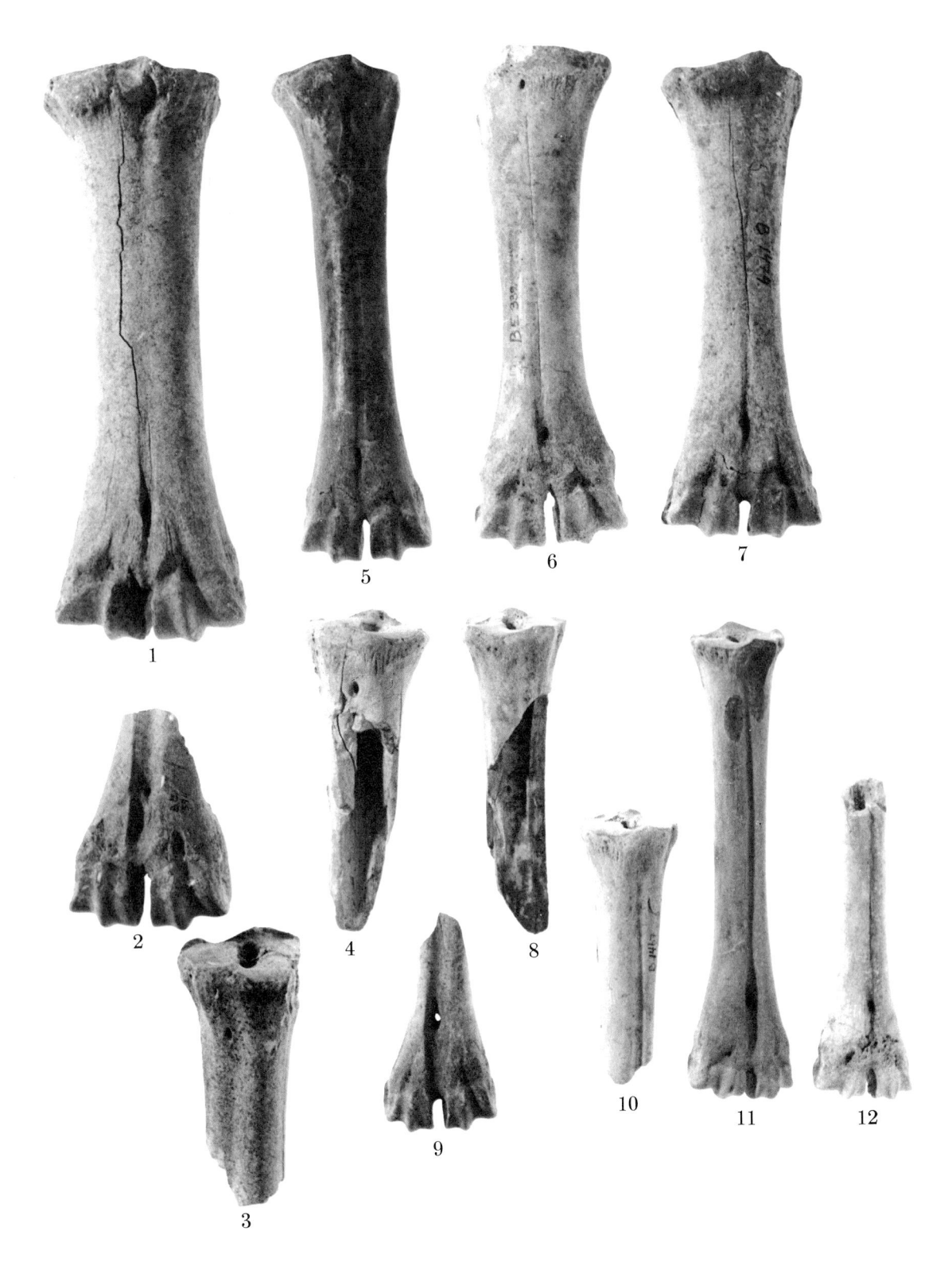

Scale 1:2.5
1 Mc of wild ox. **2** Mt of wild ox. **3** Mt of wild ox. **4** Mt of wild ox; used as tool. **5** Mc of domestic cattle ♀.
6 Mc of domestic cattle ♂(?); subadult. **7** Mc of domestic cattle. **8** Mt of domestic cattle ♀. **9** Mt of domestic cattle ♀.
10 Mt of slender built domestic cattle ♀. **11** Mt of domestic cattle ♀. **12** Mt of domestic cattle ♀.

PLATE XI

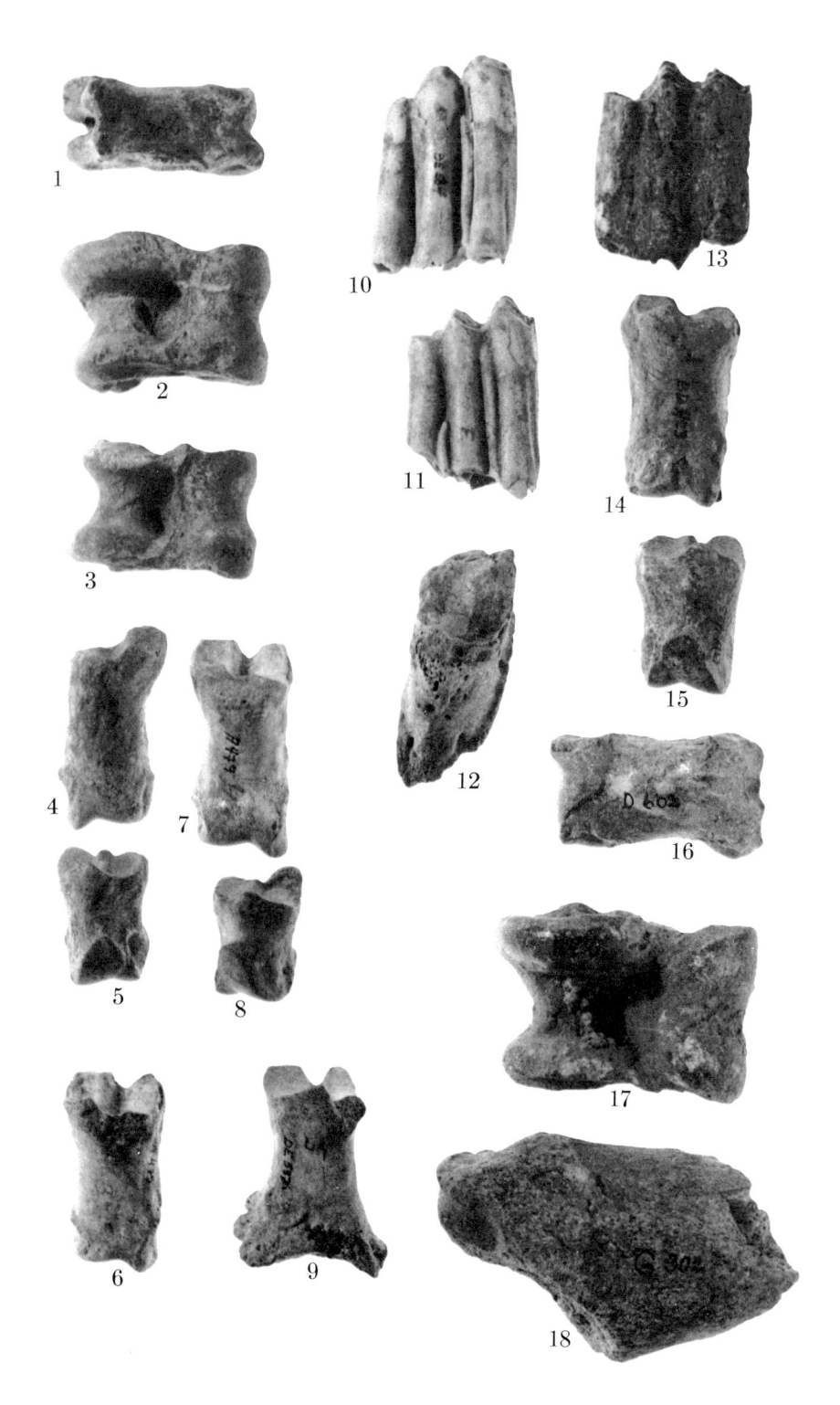

Scale 1:2
1 Phalanx I of domestic cattle. **2** Talus of domestic cattle. **3** Talus of domestic cattle. **4** Phalanx I of domestic cattle. **5** Phalanx II of domestic cattle. **6** Phalanx I of domestic cattle. **7** Phalanx I of domestic cattle. **8** Phalanx II of domestic cattle. **9** Phalanx I of domestic cattle; path. **10** Third lower molar of wild ox. **11** Third lower molar of transitional or domestic cattle. **12** Phalanx III of transitional or domestic cattle. **13** Third lower molar of wild ox. **14** Phalanx I of wild ox. **15** Phalanx II of wild ox. **16** Phalanx I of wild ox. **17** Talus of wild ox. **18** Radius of wild ox.

PLATE XII

Scale *ca.* 1:2.2
1 Horn-core of wild ox or transitional (?). **2** Horn-core of wild ox or transitional (?). **3** Horn-core of domestic cattle ♀. **4** Horn-core of domestic cattle ♀. **5** Horn-core of domestic cattle ♂. **6** Horn-core of domestic cattle ♂. **7** Horn-core of domestic cattle ♀.

PLATE XIII

Scale *ca.* 1:2.2
1 Horn-core of domestic cattle ♀.   **2** Horn-core of domestic cattle ♀.   **3** Horn-core of domestic cattle ♀.   **4** Horn-core of domestic cattle ♂.   **5** Horn-core of domestic cattle ♂.   **6** Horn-core of domestic cattle ♂.   **7** Horn-core of domestic cattle ♀.   **8** Horn-core of domestic cattle ♀; young.   **9** Horn-core of domestic cattle ♀.

PLATE XIV

Scale *ca.* 1:2
1 Antler of roe buck. **2** Mandible of roe deer. **3** Medial humerus of ass. **4** Phalanx I of ass. **5** Maxilla fragment of (?) ass. **6** Mandible fragment of ass. **7** Upper incisor of (?) ass. **8** Second upper premolar of ass. **9** Molar (?M^2) of ass. **10** Third upper molar of ass. **11** Radius of ass; path. **12** Mc of ass. **13** Phalanx III of ass.

PLATE XV

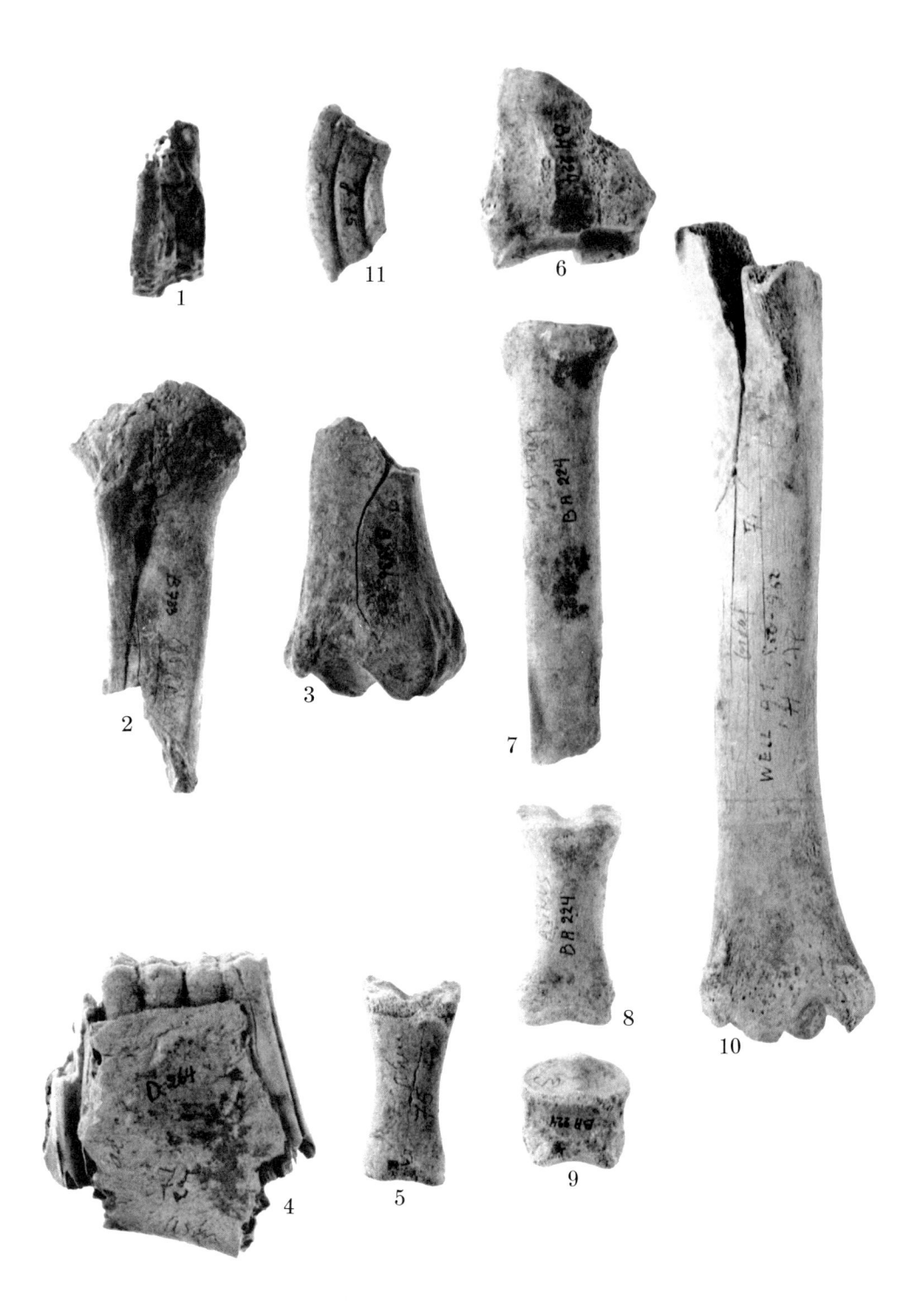

Scale 1:2
1 (?)Third upper premolar of ass.   **2** Radius of ass.   **3** Tibia of ass.   **4** Mandible fragment of young ass.   **5** Phalanx I of young ass.   **6** Radius of ass.   **7** Mc of ass.   **8** Phalanx I of ass.   **9** Phalanx II of ass.   **10** Tibia of ass.
11 Third lower molar of ass.

PLATE XVI

Scale 1:2
1 Radius of horse.   **2** Mt of horse.   **3** Mc of horse.   **4** (?)Second upper molar of horse.   **5** (?)Second upper molar of horse.   **6** Third upper molar of horse.   **7** Third upper molar of horse.   **8** Mandible fragment of horse.   **9** Femur fragment of horse.   **10** Ulnar fragment of horse.   **11** P_3 of horse.   **12** P_4 of horse.   **13** M_1 of horse.

PLATE XVII

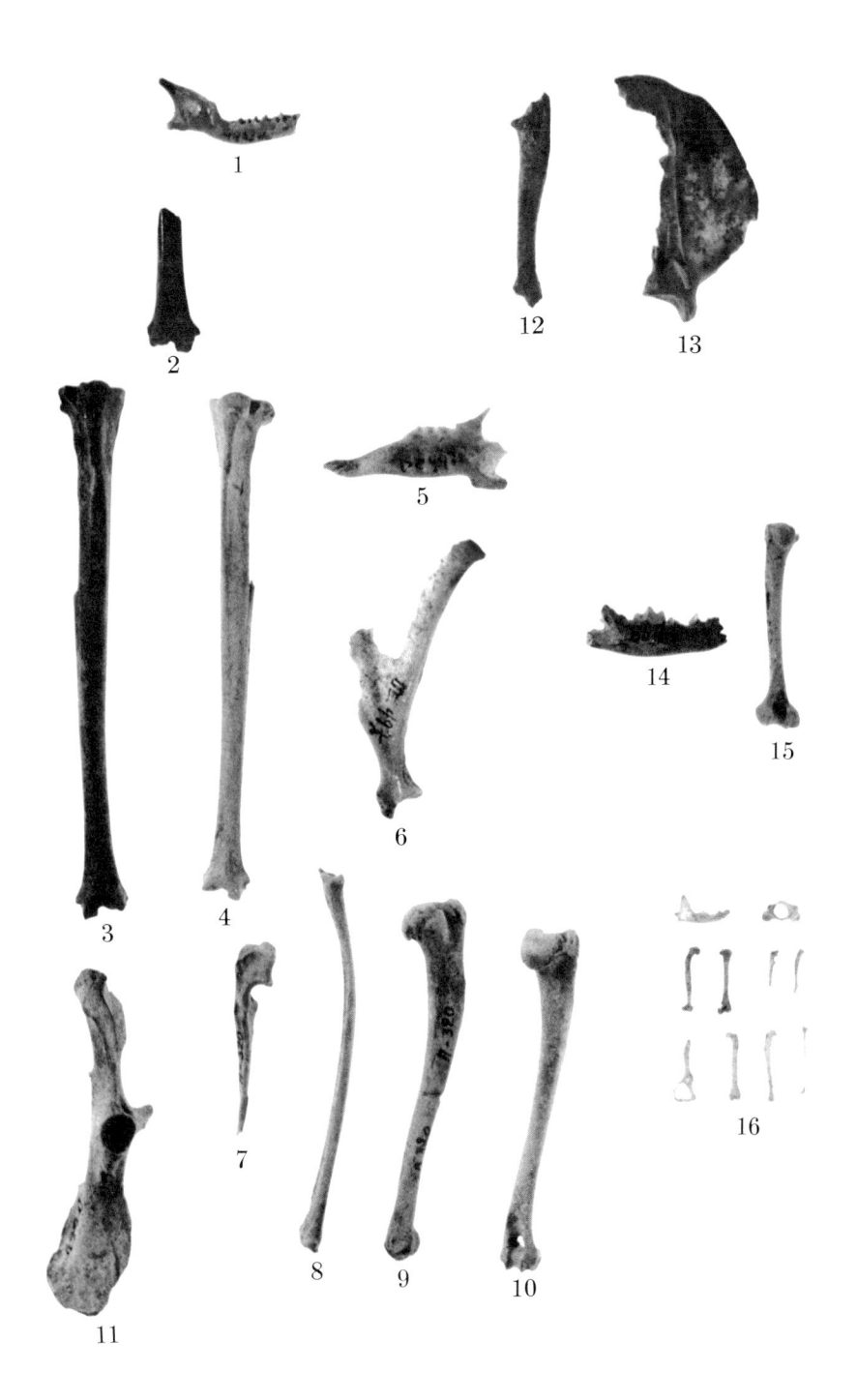

Scale 1:2
1 Mandible of hedgehog. 2 Tibia of european hare. 3 Tibia of european hare. 4 Tibia of european hare.
5 Mandible of european hare. 6 Scapula of european hare. 7 Ulna of european hare. 8 Radius of european hare.
9 Humerus of european hare. 10 Humerus of european hare. 11 Pelvis of european hare. 12 Ulna of common otter.
13 Scapula of common otter. 14 Mandible of beach marten. 15 Humerus of beach marten. 16 Parts of a whole skeleton of a weasel.

PLATE XVIII

Scale 1:2
1 Mc 5 of wolf.   **2** Ulna of wolf.   **3** Skull fragment of wolf.   **4** Mandible of red fox.   **5** Mandible of red fox.
6 Mandible of red fox.   **7** Ulna of red fox.   **8** Mt 2 of brown bear.   **9** Mandible of badger.   **10** Mandible of badger.
11 Scapula of badger.   **12** Humerus of badger.   **13** Radius of badger.   **14** Radius of lynx.

PLATE XIX

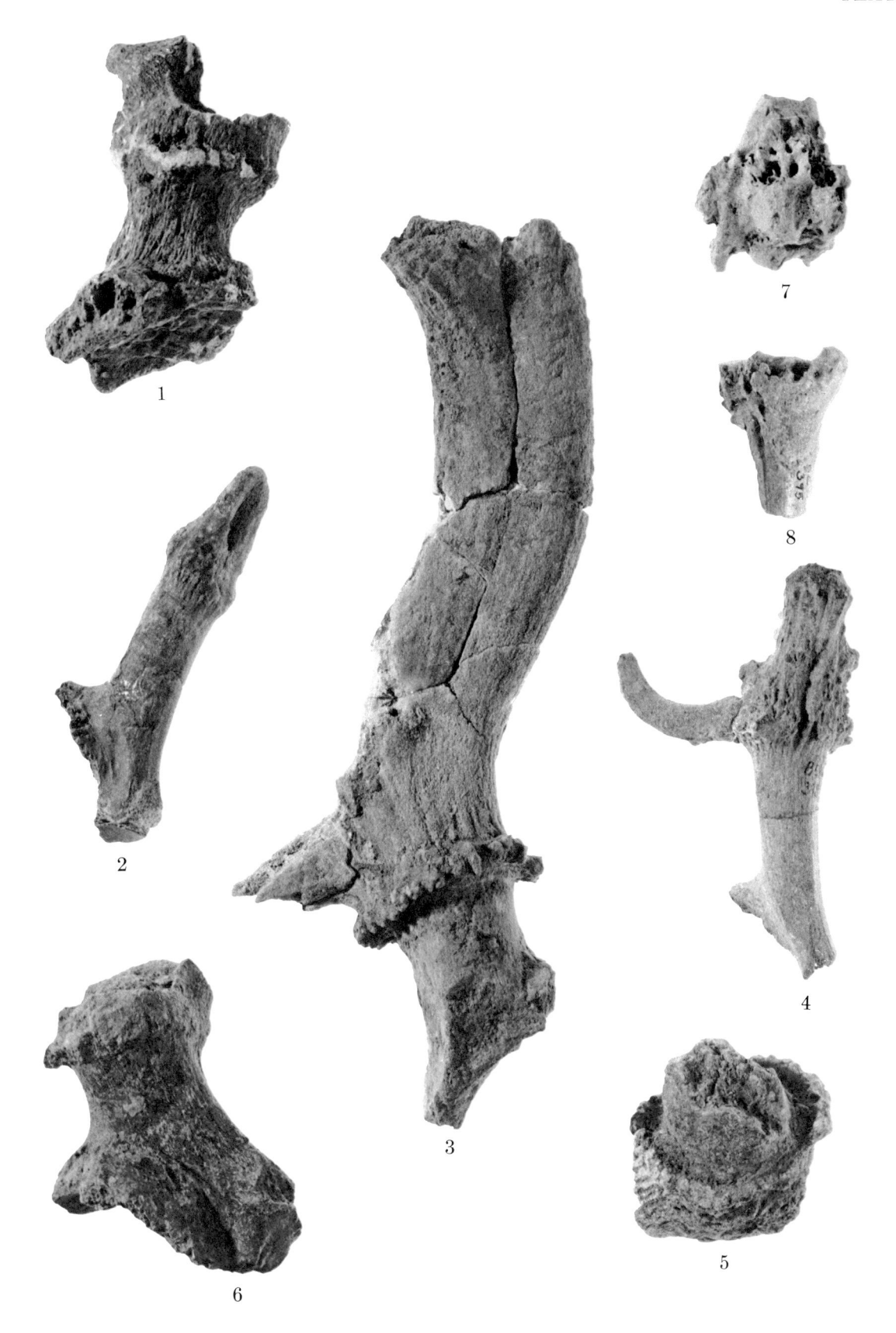

Scale 1:2
1 Antler of red deer.   2 Antler of red deer; young.   3 Antler of red deer.   4 Antler of red deer; young.   5 Antler of red deer.   6 Antler of red deer.   7 Tibia of red deer; path.   8 Mc of red deer; path.

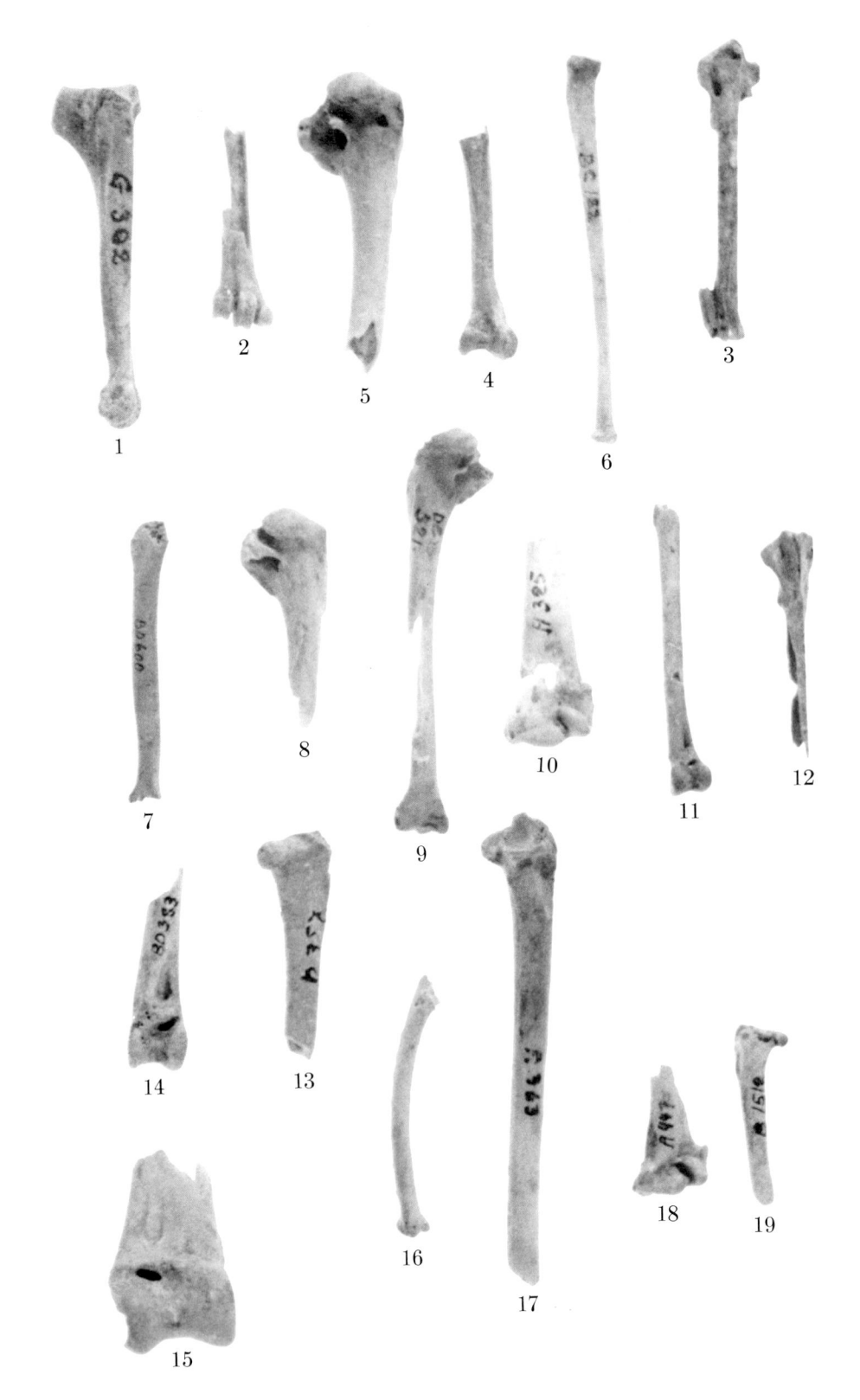

PLATE XX

Scale 1:1.5
1 Tarsometatarsus of cormorant.   **2** Tarsometatarsus of heron.   **3** Carpometacarpus of mallard.   **4** Femur of mallard.
5 Humerus of mallard.   **6** Radius of mallard.   **7** Humerus of garganey.   **8** Humerus of wigeon.   **9** Humerus of tufted duck.   **10** Humerus of peregrine.   **11** Tibiotarsus of rock partridge.   **12** Tibiotarsus of rock partridge.
13 Femur of domestic fowl.   **14** Tibiotarsus of domestic fowl.   **15** Tibiotarsus of great bustard.   **16** Ulna of pigeon.
17 Ulna of raven.   **18** Humerus of hooded crow.   **19** Femur of hooded crow.

PLATE XXI

Scale 1:1.1
1 Coracoid of gray lag goose.　　2 Ulna of gray lag goose.　　3 Ulna of gray lag goose.　　4 Radius of gray lag goose.
5 Coracoid of whooper swan.　　6 Tarsometatarsus of crane.　　7 Tibiotarsus of crane.　　8 Carpometacarpus of goshawk.
9 Ulna of goshawk.　　10 Tarsometatarsus of goshawk.　　11 Humerus of eagle owl.

PLATE XXII

Scale 1:1
1 Left premaxillary bone of Johnius hololepidotus Lac.   **2** Vertebra of Johnius hololepidotus Lac.   **3** Basioccipitale + parasphenoideum of Johnius hololepidotus Lac. (Figs. 1–3, fishes of the Croaker family).   **4** Vertebral center of the great blue shark, Carcharinus glaucus L.   **5** Vertebral center of the gray shark, Galeorhinus galeus L.   **6** Left dentale of the gold brass, Sparus auratus L.   **7** Carapax of the Greek turtle, Testudo hermanni Gm.

PLATE XXIII

Scale 9:10
1 Glyphis italica Defrance.   **2** Patella coerulea L.   **3** Patella ferruginea Gmelin.   **4** Monodonta fragarioides Lamarck.
5 Cerithium vulgatum L.   **6** Talparia Lurida L.   **7** Dolium galea L.   **8** Murex trunculus L.   **9** Murex brandaris L.
10 Triton tritonis L.   **11** Thais haemostoma L. (Purpura).   **12** Eutria cornea L.   **13** Conus mediterraneus Hwass.
14 Rumina decollata L.   **15** Helix mazulli Jan.

PLATE XXIV

Scale 9:10
16 Arca noae L.   **17** Arca barbata L.   **18** Glycemeris glycemeris L.   **19** Mytilus edulis L.   **20** Pinna nobilis L.
21 Spondylus gaederopus L.   **22** Cardium edule L.   **23** Venus rugosa L.   **24** Tapes decussatus L.   **25** Mactra stultorum L.   **26** Pholas dactylus L.

PLATE XXV

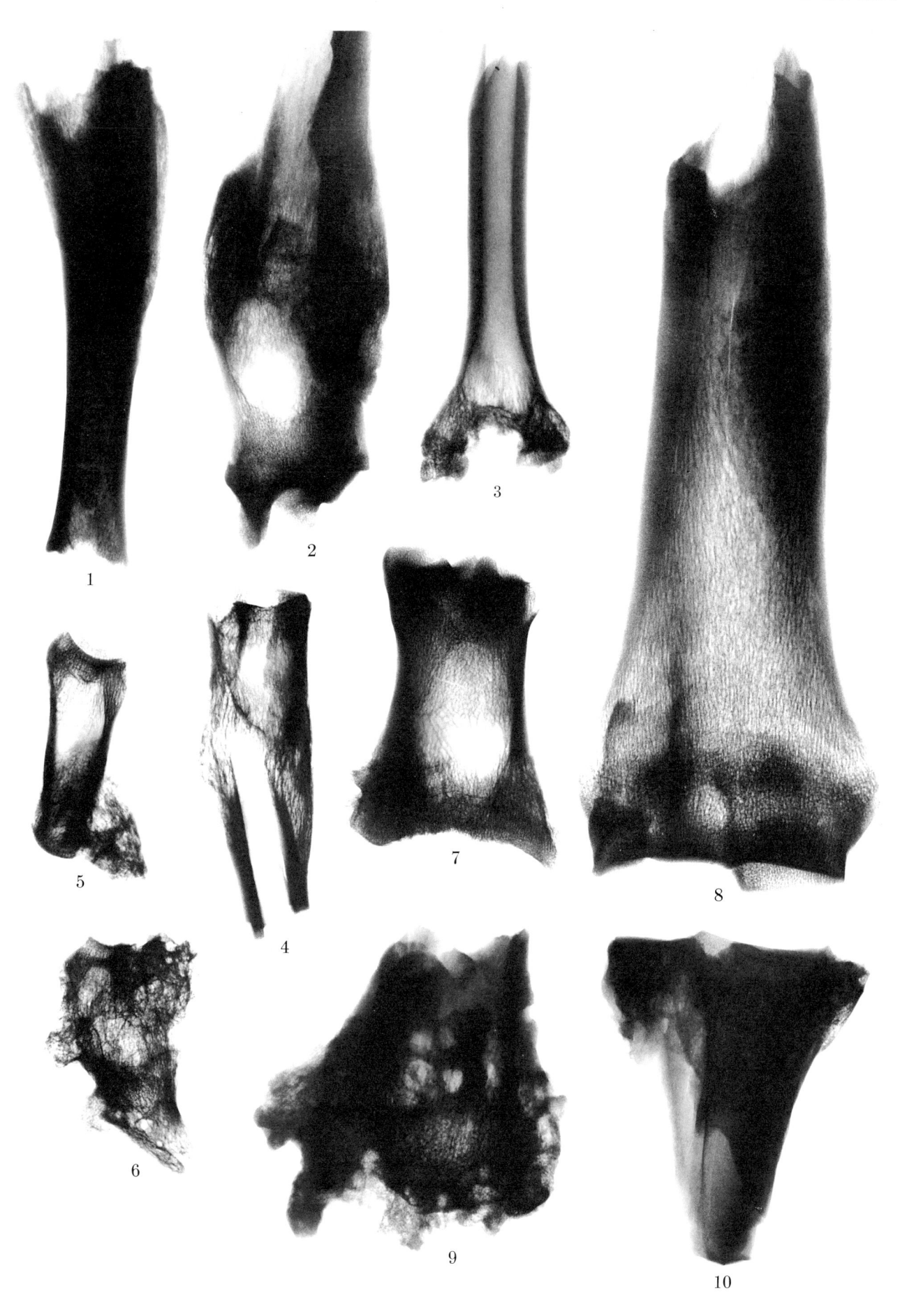

X-ray Photographs.

2 (E)